Samuel S. Randall

History of the State of New York

For the Use of Common Schools, Academies, Normal and High Schools

Samuel S. Randall

History of the State of New York
For the Use of Common Schools, Academies, Normal and High Schools

ISBN/EAN: 9783337158705

Printed in Europe, USA, Canada, Australia, Japan

Cover: Foto ©Paul-Georg Meister /pixelio.de

More available books at **www.hansebooks.com**

HISTORY

OF THE

STATE OF NEW YORK.

FOR THE USE OF

COMMON SCHOOLS, ACADEMIES, NORMAL AND HIGH SCHOOLS,

AND OTHER SEMINARIES OF INSTRUCTION.

BY

S. S. RANDALL,

SUPERINTENDENT OF PUBLIC SCHOOLS OF THE CITY OF NEW YORK.

PREFACE.

So far as I am aware, the compilation now presented to the public is the first attempt at providing for our elementary and higher institutions of learning a separate History of the State of New York. Many of the most important events in that history are, it is true, contained in the current school histories of the United States; necessarily, however, greatly abridged and condensed. It has seemed to me, and to others interested in the work of popular education, that some attempt should be made to supply this deficiency by presenting within a convenient compass the prominent outlines of those interesting details which have rendered our own "Empire State" so conspicuous in the history of the great American Republic.

In the execution of the work it has, of course, been found necessary to draw very largely upon the materials furnished by the earlier and later annalists of the State and nation; and I take especial pleasure in acknowledging the obligations I have been under to my esteemed friend, MARY L. BOOTH, whose "History of the City of New York," as condensed from the most reliable sources, embodies the principal events of that of the State up to the period of the Revolutionary War. I have also been greatly indebted to Judge HAMMOND's "Political History" of the State for a clear and lucid detail of the successive administrations of the government from its origin to the termination of that of Governor WRIGHT. From that period to the close of the present year I have carefully consulted the various Public Documents of the State, and the contemporary annals of the public press. To my respected friend, HENRY B. DAWSON, the well-known author of the "Battles of the American Republic," I am under special obligations for the accurate details of the military and naval contests which have shed so brilliant a lustre upon our history as a State.

The Appendix will be found to contain the Constitution of the State as amended by the Convention of 1867 – 68; a statistical account of the population according to the census of 1835, and the several subsequent enumerations down to 1870; lists of the respective Governors from 1624 to the present time, and Lieutenant-Governors and Speakers of the Assembly from the period of the adoption of the first State Constitution; and lists of Railroads and Canals in the State, their extent, and the cost of their construction and maintenance.

In the confident hope that the work may be found worthy of adoption in our common schools, academies, and other seminaries of learning throughout the State, I respectfully commend it to the favorable regard of the great body of teachers, school officers, and other friends of education, within its borders.

S. S. RANDALL.

NEW YORK, January, 1870.

TABLE OF CONTENTS.

INTRODUCTION.

PAGE

PHYSICAL FEATURES OF THE STATE. — PUBLIC WORKS. — GEOLOGY. — CLIMATE, ETC. 7–9

FIRST PERIOD.
INDIAN OCCUPANCY.

The Algonquins or Delawares. — Mohegans. — Manhattans. — The Five Nations. — Character and Objects of the Confederacy. — Chiefs, Sachems, and Orators. — The Tortoise, Bear, and Wolf Tribes. — Founders of the Confederacy. — Traditions. — Strawberry of the Great Spirit. — Conquests of the Iroquois. — Accession of the Tuscaroras. — Fidelity to the English. — Comparative Numbers . . 10–13

SECOND PERIOD.

DISCOVERIES AND SETTLEMENTS. — THE DUTCH GOVERNMENTS.

CHAPTER I.

John de Verrazzano. — Samuel Champlain. — Henry Hudson. — His Employment by the Dutch East India Company. — Entrance into New York Bay. — Intercourse with the Indians. — Discovery of the River. — Voyage up the Hudson to Albany. — Return to Europe. — His Death. — Fur-Trade Expeditions from Holland. — Adrien Block. — Foundation of New York City. — Explorations and Discoveries. — New Charter. — Association of Merchants. — United New Netherlands Company. — Indian Council at Tawasentha. — Treaty of Alliance. — Progress of the Fur-Trade. — English Claims. — Charter to Ferdinando Gorges and his Associates. — West India Company. — Colonization of New Netherlands. — Cornelissen Jacobsen May. — Settlements on Manhattan and Long Island and Fort Orange. — William Verhulst 14–19

CHAPTER II. — ADMINISTRATION OF PETER MINUIT.

Purchase and Settlement of Manhattan Island. — Friendly Relations with English Colonists. — Church Organization. — Murder of a Westchester Indian. — Grants of Territory to Patroons and other Settlers. — Introduction of Slavery. — The Rensselaerwyck Patroons. — Progress of Manhattan Colony. — Controversy with Patroons. — English Claims. — Recall of Minuit. — Swedish Settlement on the Delaware. — Death of Minuit 19–22

CHAPTER III. — Administration of Wouter Van Twiller.

His Character. — Controversy with Dominie Bogardus. — Adam Roelandsen, the First Teacher. — Rebuilding of the Fort. — Erection of a Church. — Jacob Eelkins's Visit to Manhattan. — Defiance of the Governor's Authority. — Proceedings of Van Twiller. — Difficulties with the English Colonies on the Connecticut. — Invasion and Reconquest of Fort Nassau. — Rapacity and Wealth of Van Twiller. — Controversy with Van Dincklagen. — Recall of Van Twiller. — Purchase of Pavonia 22

CHAPTER IV. — Administration of Wilhelm Kieft.

Difficulties with the Swedish Colonies. — New Charter of Privileges. — Settlements on Long Island. — Indian Hostilities. — Attack upon the Raritan, Westchester, and Mohawk Indians. — Indian Massacre at Pavonia. — Terrible Retaliation. — Murder of Anne Hutchinson. — Massacre of Long Island and Connecticut Indians. — Treaty of Peace. 25

CHAPTER V. — Administration of Peter Stuyvesant.

Representative Council. — Treatment of the Indians. — Adjustment of Boundaries between the Dutch and English Governments. — Manhattan and Brooklyn Governments. — English Intrigues. — Reconquest of Swedish Forts on the Delaware. — Renewal of Indian Hostilities. — Patent to the Duke of York. — Surrender of the Colony to the English. — Death of Governor Stuyvesant 32

THIRD PERIOD.
ENGLISH GOVERNMENT.

CHAPTER I. — Administrations of Governors Nicolls, Lovelace, and Andros.

New City Charter. — Arbitrary Measures of Lovelace. — Reconquest by the Dutch. — Restoration to the English. — Proceedings against Lovelace and Manning. — Arbitrary Conduct of Andros. — His recall 37

CHAPTER II. — Administration of Thomas Dongan.

Representative Assembly. — Charter of Liberties. — Arbitrary Measures of James II. — Alliance and Conquests of the Iroquois. — Council at Albany. — Invasion of the French. — De la Barre. — Denonville. — Lambert. — Retreat of the French. — Recall of Governor Dongan. — Abdication of James II. — Organization of Parties. — Jacob Leisler 41

CHAPTER III. — Administrations of Jacob Leisler and Governors Sloughter and Fletcher.

Committee of Safety. — The Battery. — Burning of Schenectady. — Naval Expedition against Quebec and Montreal. — Arrival of Ingoldsby and Governor Sloughter. — Refusal of Leisler to surrender the Government. — Arrest and Execution of Leisler and Milborne. — Treaties with the Iroquois. — Governor Fletcher. — Bradford's Printing-Press. — Church Controversy. — Trinity Church. — Invasion of Frontenac. — Piratical Depredations 45–49

CHAPTER IV. — ADMINISTRATIONS OF THE EARL OF BELLAMONT, LORDS CORNBURY AND LOVELACE, AND LIEUTENANT-GOVERNOR INGOLDSBY.

Captain William Kidd. — Honors to Leisler and Milborne. — Trial and Conviction of Bayard. — Lord Cornbury. — Establishment of a Grammar-School. — Lord Lovelace. — Queen Anne's War. — Expeditions against Canada 49–52

CHAPTER V. — ADMINISTRATIONS OF ROBERT HUNTER, WILLIAM BURNET, AND JOHN MONTGOMERIE.

German Immigrants. — Lewis Morris. — Failure of the Canadian Expeditions. — Governor Hunter and the Assembly. — Court of Chancery. — Chief-Justice Morris. — Peter Schuyler. — Governor Burnet. — His Counsellors. — French Missionaries and Traders. — Convention at Albany. — Opposition of the Assembly. — New York Gazette. — Governor Montgomerie 52–55

CHAPTER VI. — ADMINISTRATION OF GOVERNOR COSBY.

Contest with Rip Van Dam. — Arbitrary Measures of Cosby. — Trial and Acquittal of John Peter Zenger on an Indictment for Libel. — Popular Triumph. — Andrew Hamilton. — Sons of Liberty . . 55–59

CHAPTER VII. — ADMINISTRATIONS OF GEORGE CLARKE, ADMIRAL CLINTON, SIR DANVERS OSBORNE, AND SIR CHARLES HARDY.

Dissolution of the Assembly. — Disfranchisement of Jews. — Slavery in New York. — The Negro Plot. — Reign of Terror. — Number of Victims. — Dissensions with the Assembly. — Popular Discontent. — Suicide of Governor Osborne. — Lieutenant-Governor De Lancey. — Changed Position of Parties. — Sir Charles Hardy 59–63

FOURTH PERIOD.

FRENCH AND INDIAN WAR.

CHAPTER I. — ADMINISTRATION OF LIEUTENANT-GOVERNOR DE LANCEY.

French Incursions. — Washington's Mission to St. Pierre. — Fort du Quesne. — Surrender of Fort Necessity. — Treaties with the Iroquois. — Convention at Albany. — Franklin's Plan of Confederation. — Events of 1755. — General Johnson's Campaign. — Fort Edward. — Lake George. — Repulse of Dieskau. — Fort William Henry. — Shirley's Expedition against Niagara. — Campaign of 1756. — Attack upon Oswego. — Death of Colonel Mercer. — Quartering of Troops in New York 64–69

CHAPTER II.

Campaign of 1757. — Siege of Fort William Henry. — Treachery of Webb. — Surrender of the Fort and Massacre of the Garrison by the Indians. — Campaign of 1758. — Attack upon Fort Ticonderoga. — Death of Lord Howe. — Retreat of the English. — Fort Frontenac. — Capture of Forts Du Quesne, Ticonderoga, Crown Point, and Niagara. — Siege and Capture of Quebec. — Death of Wolfe and Montcalm. — Capture of Montreal. — Naval Warfare. — Treaty of Peace. — Death of Lieutenant-Governor De Lancey. — Administration of Cadwallader Colden and Robert Monckton. — Independence of the Judiciary . . . . 70 – 75

FIFTH PERIOD.
THE REVOLUTIONARY WAR.
CHAPTER I.

Relation between the Colonies and England. — Restrictions upon Commerce and Navigation. — Sacrifices of the Colonies. — Demands of the Crown. — Passage of the Stamp Act. — Its reception in the Colonies. — Proceedings at New York. — First Colonial Congress. — Declaration of Rights. — Arrival of the Stamps. — Proceedings of the Sons of Liberty. — Attack on the Fort. — Non-Intercourse Agreement. — Articles of Confederation proposed. — Arrival of Sir Henry Moore as Governor. — Proceedings of the Assembly. — Repeal of the Stamp Act. — Patriotic Celebrations. — Erection of the Liberty Pole . 76 – 82

CHAPTER II.

Controversies between the Governor and Assembly. — Disturbances between the Soldiers and Citizens. — The Liberty Pole. — Legislative Powers of the Assembly suspended. — Tax on Tea. — Indignation of the Colonies. — The Sons of Liberty. — Proceedings of the Assembly. — Renewal of Non-Importation Agreement. — Death of Governor Moore. — Lieutenant-Governor Colden. — Public Meetings. — Issue of Colonial Bills of Credit. — Arrest of John Lamb and Imprisonment of McDougall . . . . 82 – 86

CHAPTER III.

Attacks upon the Liberty Pole. — Riotous Proceedings of the Soldiers. — Excitement of the Citizens — Public Meeting. — Sons of Liberty. — Battle of Golden Hill. — Governor Colden's Despatches. — Hampden Hall. — Successful defence of the Liberty Pole. — Violation of Non-Importation Agreement. — Proceedings of the Sons of Liberty. — Lord Dunmore. — Proceedings against McDougall . 86 – 91

CHAPTER IV. — ADMINISTRATIONS OF GOVERNORS TRYON AND COLDEN.

Shipments of Tea — Spirited Proceedings of the Sons of Liberty. — New York " Tea Party." — Vigilance Committee. — Public Meeting

of Citizens. — Non-Importation League. — Second Colonial Congress.
— Proceedings of the Assembly. — First and Second Provincial
Congress. — First Continental Congress. — Arrival of the Asia —
Disturbances in the City. — Sons of Liberty. — Provisional Government. — Patriotic Demonstrations. — Capture of Ammunition at
Turtle Bay — General Wooster encamps at Harlem. — Embarkation
of Royal Troops. — Recapture of Arms by the Citizens . . . 91–97

CHAPTER V. — Events of 1775.

Capture of Ticonderoga and Crown Point. — Organization of New York
Regiments. — Removal of the Guns on the Battery. — Cannonade of
the City by the Asia. — Demand for Satisfaction. — Abdication of
Governor Tryon. — Demolition of Rivington's Press. — Invasion of
Canada. — Siege and Capture of St. John's. — Disastrous Expedition
of Allen. — Siege of Quebec. — Death of Montgomery and Defeat of
Morgan and Arnold. — Retreat of American Troops . . 97–102

CHAPTER VI. — Events of 1776.

Investment of New York by Howe and Clinton. — Preparations for Defence. — Declaration of Independence. — Proceedings of Provincial
Congress at White Plains. — Battle of Long Island. — Retreat of
Washington to New York and Harlem Heights. — Arrest and Execution of Nathan Hale as a Spy. — Landing of Howe at Kip's Bay. —
Evacuation of the City. — Skirmish at Harlem. — Retreat to White
Plains. — Battle of White Plains. — Captures of Forts Washington
and Lee. — Retreat through New Jersey. — Naval Combat on Lake
Champlain 103–110

CHAPTER VII. — Administration of Governor George Clinton. — Events of 1777. — First State Constitution.

Occupation of the City of New York by the British. — The Neutral
Ground. — Cow-Boys and Skinners. — The Provincial Congress. —
Committee of Safety. — Destruction of Military Stores at Peekskill.
— Attack on Sag Harbor. — Constitutional Convention. — Election of
Governor and Staff Officers. — Congressional Delegates. — Barbarous
Treatment of Prisoners. — The Sugar-House. — Provost Jail and
Jersey Prison-Ships. — Attack on Ticonderoga. — Retreat of Schuyler and St. Clair. — Murder of Jane McCrea. — Kosciusko. — Attack upon Fort Schuyler. — Battle of Oriskany. — Indian Ambuscade 110–116

CHAPTER VIII. — Events of 1777. — Burgoyne's Campaign.

First and Second Battles of Stillwater. — Battle at Bemis's Heights.
— Dissension between Gates and Arnold. — Retreat of Burgoyne to
Saratoga. — His Surrender. — Its Effects. — Capture of Forts Clinton,
Montgomery, and Constitution by the British. — Burning of Kingston 116–121

CHAPTER IX. — Events of 1778 and 1779.

Indian and Tory Atrocities. — Destruction of Cobleskill. — Massacre at

Cherry Valley. — Capture and Recapture of Stony Point and Verplanck's Point. — Surprise of British at Paulus Hook. — Attack upon Minisink by Brant. — Sullivan and Clinton's Expedition against the Indians. — Destruction of their Villages and Crops . . . 122-128

CHAPTER X. — EVENTS OF 1780, 1781. — TREASON OF BENEDICT ARNOLD.

His Occupation of West Point. — Correspondence with André. — Arrangements for an Interview. — Arrival of Washington and Lafayette. — Interview between Arnold and André. — Retreat and Capture of André at Tarrytown. — Washington's Discovery of the Treason. — Flight of Arnold. — Conduct of André. — His Trial, Conviction, and Sentence. — Efforts for the Capture of Arnold. — His Subsequent Career. — Execution of Major André. — General Sympathy for his Fate. — Close of the War. — General Rejoicings. — Treaty of Peace. — Disbandment of the Army. — Evacuation of New York. — Parting of Washington with his Officers. — His Resignation and Retirement to Mount Vernon 128-136

SIXTH PERIOD.
THE STATE GOVERNMENT.

CHAPTER I. — ADMINISTRATION OF GOVERNOR GEORGE CLINTON.

Position of Affairs at the Close of the War. — Articles of Confederation. — Propositions for their Modification. — State Jealousies. — Position of New York. — Proceedings of the Legislature. — Congress. — National Convention at Philadelphia. — Delegates from New York. — Their Instructions. — State of Parties in the Convention. — Formation of the Constitution. — Its Submission to the States. — Organization of Parties. — "The Federalist." — Views and Arguments of the Respective Parties. — State Convention at Poughkeepsie. — Ratification of the Constitution. — Choice of Presidential Electors and Representatives in Congress 137-144

CHAPTER II. — ADMINISTRATION OF GOVERNOR GEORGE CLINTON.

First Meeting of Congress at New York. — Organization of the National Government. — Arrival of the President and Vice-President. — Triumphal Progress of Washington. — The Inauguration. — Re-election of Governor Clinton. — Hamilton's Plan for the Assumption of the Public Debt. — Appointment of United States Senators. — Removal of the Capital to Philadelphia. — Meeting of the Legislature. — Population of the State. — Internal Improvements. — Public Lands. — Western and Northern Inland Lock Navigation Companies. — Presidential Electors. — Third Election of Governor Clinton. — Citizen Genet 144-150

CHAPTER III. — ADMINISTRATIONS OF GOVERNORS GEORGE CLINTON AND JOHN JAY.

Meeting of the Legislature. — Governor's Message. — Foundation of the Common-School System. — United States Senators. — John Jay elected Governor. — Bill for the Abolition of Slavery. — Presidential Electors. — Congressional Elections. — Comptroller. — Location of the Capital at Albany. — Election of Adams and Jefferson as President and Vice-President. — State Elections. — Re-election of Governor Jay and Lieutenant-Governor Stephen Van Rensselaer. — State of Parties. — Legislative Proceedings. — Apprehension of War with France. — Internal Improvements. — Origin of the Canal System. — General Washington's Exploration and Views. — Christopher Colles. — Legislative Encouragement. — Philip Schuyler and Elkanah Watson. — Manhattan Bank Charter. — Alien and Sedition Laws. — Death of Washington. — Funeral Honors. — Legislature of 1800. — State Elections. — Triumph of the Democratic Party. — Presidential Electors. — United States Senators. — Nominations of National and State Candidates . . . . 150 – 158

CHAPTER IV. — ADMINISTRATION OF GOVERNOR GEORGE CLINTON.

Organization of the Common-School System. — Contest between Jefferson and Burr for the Presidency. — Re-election of Governor George Clinton and Lieutenant-Governor Jeremiah Van Rensselaer. — State Constitutional Convention. — Appointment of Chancellor Lansing. — Meeting of the Legislature. — Attorney-General. — United States Senators. — De Witt Clinton and Aaron Burr. — Duel between Clinton and Swartwout. — Parties in the Legislature. — Appointments and Removals. — Proceedings of the Legislature. — Election of Governor Lewis and Lieutenant-Governor Broome. — Duel between Hamilton and Burr. — Death of Hamilton. — His Character and Services. — Funeral Obsequies. — Governor Clinton elected Vice-President . . . . 158 – 163

CHAPTER V. — ADMINISTRATIONS OF GOVERNORS MORGAN LEWIS AND DANIEL D. TOMPKINS.

Meeting of the Legislature. — Special Message of the Governor relative to Common-School Education. — Common-School Fund. — Free-School Society in New York. — Stephen Arnold. — Coalition of Federalists and Republicans. — Election of Governor Tompkins. — Trial and Acquittal of Burr for Treason. — First Steamboat on the Hudson. — History of the Enterprise. — Livingston and Fulton. — British Orders in Council. — Berlin and Milan Decrees. — The Embargo. — State of Parties. — Proposed Erie Canal. — Survey of the Route. — Appointment of Commissioners. — Departure of Burr for Europe. — Election of President Madison and Vice-President Clinton. — Proceedings of the Legislature. — Spring Elections. — Re-election of Governor Tompkins and Lieutenant-Governor Broome. — Preparations for War with England . . . . 163 – 168

CHAPTER VI. — ADMINISTRATION OF GOVERNOR TOMPKINS. — SECOND WAR WITH GREAT BRITAIN.

Condition of National Affairs. — Nomination of De Witt Clinton for the Presidency. — Proceedings of the Legislature. — Appointment of Commissioners for the Establishment of Common Schools. — Bill for the Construction of the Erie Canal. — Application to Congress and State Legislatures. — Death of Lieutenant-Governor Broome and Election of Nicholas Fish. — Organization of the Common-School System. — Bank of America. — Prorogation of the Legislature. — Death of Vice-President George Clinton. — Return of Colonel Burr. — Death of Theodosia Burr Alston. — Subsequent Career and Death of Burr. — West Point Military Academy. — Trial and Acquittal of David Thomas and Solomon Southwick for Bribery. — Progress of the War. — Campaign of 1812. — Surrender of Detroit by Hull. — Naval Victories. — Fleets on Lakes Erie and Ontario. — Attack on Sackett's Harbor and Ogdensburg. — Battle of Queenstown Heights. — Capture of British Troops at St. Regis. —Presidential Electors in favor of Mr. Clinton chosen. — Re-election of President Madison 169–178

CHAPTER VII. — ADMINISTRATION OF GOVERNOR TOMPKINS. — SECOND WAR WITH GREAT BRITAIN.

Election of United States Senator. — Superintendent of Common Schools. — Death of Chancellor Livingston. — Re-election of Governor Tompkins. — Progress of the War. — Campaign of 1813. — Naval Victories and Defeats. — Death of Captain Lawrence. — Rescue of American Prisoners in Canada. — Capture of Ogdensburg. — Capture of York and Death of Zebulon Montgomery Pike. — Capture of Fort George. — Attempted Capture of Sackett's Harbor. — Attack upon Black Rock. — Capture of the Argus by the Pelican. — The Boxer. — The Enterprise. — Perry's Victory on Lake Erie. — Battle of the Thames. — Recovery of Michigan Territory. — Abortive Expeditions against Canada. — Action at Chateaugay. — Battle of Chrystler's Farm. — Evacuation of Fort George. — Burning of Newark and Queenstown. — Retaliatory Descent upon Fort Niagara, Lewiston, Youngstown, and other Places. — Destruction of Buffalo and Black Rock 178–186

CHAPTER VIII. — ADMINISTRATION OF GOVERNOR TOMPKINS. — SECOND WAR WITH GREAT BRITAIN.

Legislative Proceedings. — Appointments and Removals. — Appropriations to Colleges. — Revision of Common-School Law. — State Elections. — Progress of the War. — Campaign of 1814. — Movements of General Wilkinson and General Brown. — Attack upon Rouse's Point. — Removal of Wilkinson. — General Izard. — Repulse of the British at Oswego. — Transportation of Military Stores to Sackett's Harbor. — Action at Sandy Creek. — Capture of Fort Erie. — Battles of Chippewa and Lundy's Lane 186–192

CHAPTER IX. — ADMINISTRATION OF GOVERNOR TOMPKINS. — SECOND WAR WITH GREAT BRITAIN. — CAMPAIGN OF 1814.

Siege of Fort Erie. — Defeat of the British. — Capture and Burning of Washington. — Preparations for Defence of the City of New York. — Patriotic Conduct of Governor Tompkins. — Invasion of New York. — Attack upon Plattsburg. — McDonough's Victory on Lake Champlain. — Special Meeting of the Legislature. — Spirited Proceedings for the Public Defence. — Their Reception at Washington. — Governor Tompkins declines the State Department . . . 192–199

CHAPTER X. — ADMINISTRATIONS OF GOVERNORS TOMPKINS AND DE WITT CLINTON. — CLOSE OF THE WAR.

Treaty of Peace with Great Britain. — Battle of New Orleans. — United States Senator. — Attorney-General. — Erie and Champlain Canals. — Great Meetings in New York and Albany. — Energetic Efforts of De Witt Clinton. — Canal Commissioners. — Survey of Route. — Election of President Monroe and Vice-President Tompkins. — Abolition of Slavery. — Resignation of Governor Tompkins. — Election of Governor De Witt Clinton and Lieutenant-Governor Tayler. — Act for the Construction of the Canal. — Commencement of the Work. — New Organization of Parties. — Common Schools. — The Lancasterian System of Instruction. — Domestic Manufactures. — Spring Elections. — Clintonian Triumph. — Meeting of the Legislature. — Governor Clinton's Message. — Accounts of Vice-President Tompkins. — Controversy with the Comptroller. — First Boat on the Erie Canal. — United States Senator. — Exciting Political Campaign. — Re-election of Governor Clinton and Lieutenant-Governor Tayler. — Canal Policy . 199-206

CHAPTER XI. — ADMINISTRATION OF GOVERNOR DE WITT CLINTON.

Legislature of 1821. — Special Message of the Governor. — Act for Constitutional Convention. — United States Senator. — Canal Commissioner. — Removal of Gideon Hawley as Superintendent of Common Schools. — Appointment of his Successor. — Abolition of the Office, and its Annexation to the State Department. — Meeting, Organization, and Proceedings of the State Constitutional Convention. — Outlines of the New Constitution. — Its Adoption by the People . 207-210

SEVENTH PERIOD.

FROM THE CONSTITUTION OF 1821 TO THE CONSTITUTION OF 1846.

CHAPTER I. — ADMINISTRATIONS OF GOVERNORS JOSEPH C. YATES AND DE WITT CLINTON.

Abolition of Lotteries. — Literature Lottery. — Election of Governor Yates and Lieutenant-Governor Erastus Root. — Democratic Majority in the Legislature. — Appointment of Chancellor, Judges of Supreme Court, and Circuit Judges. — Election of State Officers. — Fall Elections. — The "People's Party." — Legislative Proceedings. — The Electoral Law. — Removal of Governor Clinton as Canal Commissioner. — Public Indignation. — Extra Session of the Legislature. — Election of Governor Clinton and Lieutenant-Governor Tallmadge. — Triumph of the "People's Party." — Candidates for the Presidency. — State of Parties. — Visit of General Lafayette, and his Public Reception in New York. — Election of President John Quincy Adams and Vice-President Calhoun. — State Road through Southern Tier of Counties. — Minister to England. — Tour of Governor Clinton through Pennsylvania, Ohio, and Kentucky. — Completion of the Erie and Champlain Canal. — Grand Celebration. — Imposing Ceremonies at New York. — Illuminations, Processions, and Fireworks 211-218

CHAPTER II. — THIRD ADMINISTRATION OF GOVERNOR DE WITT CLINTON.

Common Schools. — Education of Teachers. — State Road. — United States Senator. — Chancellor, Secretary of State, and Superintendent of Common Schools. — Report of John C. Spencer on the Common-School System. — Abduction of William Morgan. — Re-election of Governor Clinton. — Lieutenant-Governor Pitcher. — Proceedings of the Legislature. — The Canals and State Road. — Chenango Canal. — Literature Fund. — Revision of the Laws. — Death of Thomas Addis Emmett. — Anti-Masonic Excitement. — Public Meetings. — Arrests, Trials, and Convictions. — Public Indignation against Masons. — Political Organization 218–223

CHAPTER III. — ADMINISTRATIONS OF LIEUTENANT-GOVERNOR PITCHER, GOVERNOR VAN BUREN, AND LIEUTENANT-GOVERNOR THROOP.

Legislature of 1828. — Last Message of Governor Clinton. — His Death and Character. — Proceedings of Public Bodies. — Succession of Lieutenant-Governor Pitcher. — Public Prosecutor of the Morgan Outrage. — Defeat of the Chenango and Chemung Canal Bills. — Presidential Campaign. — Election of Governor Van Buren and Lieutenant-Governor Throop. — Election of President Jackson and Vice-President Calhoun. — Progress of the Anti-Masonic Excitement. — Legislature of 1829. — Governor's Message. — Internal Improvements. — Safety-Fund Law and Renewal of Bank Charters. — State Officers. — Choice of Presidential Electors by General Ticket. — Governor Van Buren appointed United States Secretary of State. — His Resignation as Governor, and Succession of Lieutenant-Governor Throop. — Passage of the Chemung Canal Bill. — Chenango Canal. — Death of Ex-Governor John Jay 223–227

CHAPTER IV. — ADMINISTRATION OF GOVERNOR ENOS E. THROOP.

Legislature of 1830. — Governor's Message. — Report of Canal Commissioners on the Chenango Canal. — Defeat of the Bill. — Election of Governor Enos T. Throop and Lieutenant-Governor E. P. Livingston. — Proceedings of the Public Prosecutor. — Legislature of 1831. — Election of William L. Marcy as United States Senator, and Samuel Nelson Judge of Supreme Court. — Appointment of Governor Van Buren as Minister to England. — Death of Ex-President Monroe. — Legislature of 1832. — Election of Governor Marcy and Lieutenant-Governor Tracy. — Termination of Political Anti-Masonry. — Its Results. — Revival of Masonry 228–232

CHAPTER V. — ADMINISTRATION OF GOVERNOR WILLIAM L. MARCY.

Internal Improvements. — Common Schools. — Election of Silas Wright, Jr., and Nathaniel P. Tallmadge as United States Senators. — State Officers. — Passage of the Chenango Canal Bill. — Re-election of Governor Marcy and Lieutenant-Governor Tracy. — Proposed Enlargement of the Erie Canal. — Loan of State Credit to Banks. — Commercial Revulsion. — Increase of Bank Charters. — General

Spirit of Speculation. — Academical Departments for Preparation of Teachers. — Common-School Libraries. — Death of Surveyor-General De Witt. — Construction of the Croton Aqueduct and High Bridge. — Great Fire in New York. — Black River and Genesee Valley Canals. — New York and Erie Railroad Loan. — Proceedings against Senators Kemble and Bishop. — Third Election of Governor Marcy and Lieutenant-Governor Tracy. — Election of President Van Buren and Vice-President R. M. Johnson. — United States Deposit Fund. — Its Investment. — General Suspension of State Banks. — Proceedings of the Legislature. — Death of Ex-Governor Yates and Abraham Van Vechten — Canadian Insurrection. — Occupation of Navy Island. — Burning of the Caroline. — Proclamation of Neutrality. — General Scott despatched to the Frontier. — Diplomatic Negotiations between the English and American Governments. — Legislature of 1838. — Mr. Ruggles's Report on Internal Improvements. — Passage of General Banking Law. — November Elections. — Triumph of the Whigs. — Election of Governor Seward and Lieutenant-Governor Bradish 233-241

CHAPTER VI. — ADMINISTRATION OF GOVERNOR WILLIAM H. SEWARD.

Legislature of 1839. — Governor's Message. — Repeal of Act prohibiting Small Bills. — State Officers. — Death of Stephen Van Rensselaer. — Visit and Reception of President Van Buren. — Legislature of 1840. — Governor's Message. — Canal Enlargement. — Common Schools. — Instruction of Children of Foreigners. — Controversy with Virginia. — Abolition of Imprisonment for Debt. — Political Campaign. — Election of President Harrison and Vice-President Tyler. — Death of the President. — Succession of Vice-President. — Re-election of Governor Seward and Lieutenant-Governor Bradish. — Legislature of 1841. — Governor's Message. — Revenues of the Canals. — State Indebtedness. — Education of the Children of Foreigners. — Teachers' Departments in Academies. — State Normal School. — Virginia Correspondence. — Report of Secretary Spencer on the Public-School System of the City of New York. — Revision of the Common-School Law. — County Superintendents. 242-248

CHAPTER VII. — ADMINISTRATION OF GOVERNOR WILLIAM H. SEWARD.

Arrest of Alexander McLeod for the Burning of the Caroline. — Demand of the British Government for his Release. — Reply of Secretary Webster. — Decision of the Supreme Court. — Trial and Acquittal of McLeod. — Legislature of 1842. — Governor's Message. — The Virginia Controversy. — Appropriation of School Money in New York. — Colleges, Academies, and Common Schools. — Revenue of the Canals. — State Debt. — Internal Improvements. — Financial Condition of the State. — Suspension of Public Works. — State Tax. — The Virginia Controversy. — Joint Resolution of the Legislature. — Refusal of the Governor to transmit the Resolution. — Election of Governor Bouck and Lieutenant-Governor Dickinson. — Democratic Triumph . 248-253

CHAPTER VIII. — ADMINISTRATION OF GOVERNOR WILLIAM C. BOUCK.

Legislature of 1843. — Governor's Message. — Re-election of Silas Wright as United States Senator. — Geological Survey of the State. — Communication of Secretary Young. — Controversy between Lieutenant-Governor Dickinson and the Secretary. — Mr. Hulburd's Report on Common Schools. — Death of Smith Thompson and Appointment of Chief-Justice Nelson to the Bench of the United States Supreme Court. — Legislature of 1844. — Governor's Message. — Public Debt. — Canal Revenues. — Common Schools. — State Normal School. — Executive Committee. — Enlargement of the Erie Canal. — Proposed Constitutional Amendment. — Anti-Rent Disturbances. — Anti-Rent and Native-American Parties. — Election of President Polk and Vice-President Dallas. — Appointment of United States Senators. — Election of Governor Silas Wright and Lieutenant-Governor Addison Gardiner 253–258

CHAPTER IX. — ADMINISTRATION OF GOVERNOR SILAS WRIGHT.

Legislature of 1845. — Governor's Message. — Prosecution of the Public Works. — Common Schools. — School Funds. — Anti-Rent Outrages. — State Officers. — Election of John A. Dix and Daniel S. Dickinson United States Senators. — Rejection of Constitutional Amendments. — State Constitutional Convention. — Act in Relation to the Canals. — Governor's Veto. — Continued Anti-Rent Outrages. — Imprisonment of Dr. Boughton. — Murder of Deputy-Sheriff Steel. — Insurrection in Delaware County. — Martial Law proclaimed. — Trial and Conviction of Anti-Rent Rioters. — Suppression of the Insurrection. — November Elections. — State Constitutional Convention approved. — Railroads. — Magnetic Telegraph. — Professor Morse and Henry O'Reilly 258–263

CHAPTER X. — ADMINISTRATION OF GOVERNOR SILAS WRIGHT.

Legislature of 1846. — Governor's Message. — Anti-Rent Excitement. — State Debt. — Canal Revenues. — Report of Superintendent of Common Schools. — District Librarian. — Distress for Rent abolished. — Constitutional Convention. — Organization of the Executive, Legislative, and Judicial Departments of the State. — Qualification of Voters. — Provision for Payment of Canal Debts, and Prosecution of the Public Works. — Loans of State Credit prohibited. — Limitation of Power to contract Debts. — Banking Associations and Registry of Notes. — Corporations to be formed under General Laws. — Common-School, Literature, and United States Deposit Funds. — Failure of Efforts to establish Free Schools throughout the State. — Incorporation of Cities and Villages. — Adoption of the Constitution. — Election of Governor Young and Lieutenant-Governor Gardiner. — Death of General Root 263–269

EIGHTH PERIOD.

FROM 1846 TO 1870.

CHAPTER I. — ADMINISTRATION OF GOVERNOR JOHN YOUNG.

The Mexican War. — Successful Campaigns of Generals Taylor and Scott. — Brilliant Services of Generals Wool, Worth, and Kearney. — Conquest of Mexico. — Negotiations for Peace. — The Wilmot Proviso. — Proceedings of the Legislature. — Pardon of the Anti-Rent Convicts. — Grounds of Executive Clemency. — New York Free Academy. — Indian and Colored Schools. — Resumption of the Public Works. — Termination of the Mexican War. — Cession of California. — Death of Silas Wright. — His Character. — Public Honors to his Memory. — State Officers. — Abolition of the Office of County Superintendent of Common Schools. — Its Effects. — Legislature of 1848. — Governor's Message. — Manorial Titles. — Common Schools. — Appropriations for Resumption of the Public Works. — Corporate Associations. — Free Schools. — State Normal School. — Death of Principal Page. — Election of President Taylor and Vice-President Fillmore. — Election of Governor Fish and Lieutenant-Governor Patterson 270–275

CHAPTER II. — ADMINISTRATION OF GOVERNOR HAMILTON FISH. — FREE-SCHOOL CONTROVERSY.

Legislature of 1849. — Governor's Message. — Act for Establishment of Free Schools throughout the State. — Teachers' Departments in Academies. — Ex-Governor Seward appointed United States Senator. — State Elections. — Approval of Free-School Bill. — Obstacles to its Execution. — Causes of its Unpopularity. — Demand for Repeal. — Efforts of its Friends. — Legislature of 1850. — Governor's Message. — State Asylum for Idiots. — Railroad Restrictions. — Slavery in the Territories. — Bill for Repeal of Free-School Law. — Death of President Taylor. — Accession of Vice-President Fillmore. — Admission of California. — Mr. Clay's Compromise Bill. — Free-School Canvass. — Majority against Repeal. — Election of Governor Hunt and Lieutenant-Governor Church 276–280

CHAPTER III. — ADMINISTRATION OF GOVERNOR WASHINGTON HUNT.

Legislature of 1851. — Governor's Message. — Free Schools. — Erie Canal Enlargement. — Proposed Amendment to Constitution. — Agricultural College. — Propositions for Modifications of the Free-School Law. — Passage of the Act. — Election of Ex-Governor Fish as United States Senator. — Commission for Revision of School Laws. — State Officers. — Visit of Kossuth. — Legislature of 1852. — Governor's Message. — State Debt. — Canal Revenues — Taxable Property. — Free-School Controversy. — Election of Governor Seymour and Lieutenant-Governor Church. — President Pierce and Vice-President King 280–283

CHAPTER IV. — First Administration of Governor Horatio Seymour.

Legislature of 1853. — Governor's Message. — Canal Enlargement. — State Agricultural and Scientific College. — Manorial Titles. — Railroad Companies. — Financial Embarrassments. — Special Session of the Legislature. — Proposed Amendment to the Constitution. — Public Schools of the City of New York. — Consolidation of the System. — State Officers. — Legislature of 1854. — Governor's Message. — Review of the History and Condition of the State. — Prosecution of the Public Works. — Reorganization of the Militia. — Criminal Code. — Department of Public Instruction. — Constitutional Amendment. — Appointment of Superintendent of Public Instruction. — Free and Union Schools. — Teachers' Departments. — Teachers' Institutes. — State Normal School. — Election of Governor Clark and Lieutenant-Governor Raymond 283–287

CHAPTER V. — Administrations of Governors Myron H. Clark and John A. King.

Legislature of 1855. — Free Schools. — County Supervision. — Excise Laws. — Prohibitory Restriction of the Sale of Liquor. — Controversy with Virginia. — The Lemmon Case. — Destruction of Property by Mobs. — State Elections. — Triumph of the Native-American Party. — Legislature of 1856. — Railroads. — Free Schools and Academies. — State Tax for Support of Schools. — District Commissioners. — Election of Governor King and Lieutenant-Governor Selden. — President Buchanan and Vice-President Breckenridge. — Legislature of 1857. — Governor King's Message. — Canals. — Modification of the Excise Law. — Colored Voters. — Slavery in the Territories. — Election of Preston King as United States Senator. — License Law. — Tax for Completion of Public Works. — Death and Character of Ex-Governor Marcy. — State Officers. — Legislature of 1858. — Election of Governor Morgan and Lieutenant-Governor Campbell 287–290

CHAPTER VI. — Administration of Governor Edwin D. Morgan. — The Southern Rebellion.

Legislature of 1859. — Excise Laws. — Colored Suffrage. — National Affairs. — John Brown's Invasion of Virginia. — State Officers. — Rejection of Colored-Suffrage Amendment. — Legislature of 1860. — Capital Punishment. — Rights of Married Women. — Visit of the Prince of Wales. — Election of Abraham Lincoln and Hannibal Hamlin as President and Vice-President. — Re-election of Governor Morgan and Lieutenant-Governor Campbell. — The Kansas and Nebraska Struggle. — Freedom in the Territories. — Efforts at Compromise between the North and South. — Their Failure. — Secession of the Southern States. — Formation of a Southern Provisional Government. — Legislature of 1861. — Temperate and Conciliatory Message of the Governor. — Joint Resolution. — Patriotic Attitude of the Legislature. — Renewed Efforts for Conciliation. — Meeting of Merchants and Others. — Proposition of Virginia for a Peace Congress at Washington. — Appointment of Delegates from New York. — Failure of the Effort. — Election of Ira Harris as United States Senator. — Bombardment and Fall of Fort Sumter. — Proclamation of President Lincoln. — Response of New York. — Appointment of Major-Generals Dix and Wadsworth. — March of the Seventh Regiment. — General Enthusiasm. — Great Public Meeting in New York. — Party Distinctions merged. — Battle of Bull Run. — Defeat of the Union Army. — Additional Troops forwarded to Washington. — One Hundred Regiments sent to the Field . . . . 291 – 298

CHAPTER VII. — ADMINISTRATION OF GOVERNOR EDWIN D. MORGAN. — SECOND ADMINISTRATION OF GOVERNOR HORATIO SEYMOUR. — THE SOUTHERN REBELLION.

Legislature of 1862. — Governor's Message. — Prosecution of the War. — Continued Support of the Government. — Completion of the Erie Canal Enlargement. — Election of Governor Seymour and Lieutenant-Governor Jones. — Legislature of 1863. — Governor Seymour's Message. — Election of Governor Morgan as United States Senator. — Condition of Public Affairs. — National Reverses. — Factious Opposition to the War. — Governor Seymour's Fourth-of-July Oration at New York. — The Draft Riots. — Interposition of the Governor. — Property and Lives destroyed. — United States Troops ordered to New York. — The Riots suppressed and the Drafts resumed and enforced. — Enlistments and Volunteers. — Legislature of 1864. — Governor's Message. — National Affairs. — Revenue of the Canals. — State Tax. — Payment of Foreign Creditors in Gold. — Continued Enlistments of Troops. — Presidential Election. — General Butler in Command of the City of New York. — Re-election of President Lincoln and Election of Andrew Johnson Vice-President. — Election of Governor Fenton and Lieutenant-Governor Alvord. — Conspiracy to burn the City of New York. — Execution of Robert Kennedy. — Grant's Campaign of 1864. — Brilliant Succession of Victories. — Defeat of the Confederate Army at Petersburg. — Capture of Richmond. — Surrender of General Lee's Army at Appomattox Court House. — Surrender of Johnston. — Termination of the War. — Assassination of President Lincoln. — Funeral Honors. — Succession of Vice-President Johnson . . . . 298 – 305

CHAPTER VIII. — ADMINISTRATION OF GOVERNOR REUBEN E. FENTON.

Legislature of 1866. — Governor's Message. — Visit of President Johnson and Cabinet, General Grant, and Admiral Farragut to the State. — Re-election of Governor Fenton and Election of Lieutenant-Governor Stewart L. Woodford. — Legislature of 1867. — Governor's Message. — Enlarged Locks on the Erie and Oswego Canals. — Adoption of Fourteenth Constitutional Amendment prohibiting Slavery. — Election of Roscoe Conklin as United States Senator. — Establishment of Free Schools throughout the State. — Additional Normal Schools. — State Constitutional Convention. — Reorganization of the Judiciary. — Renewal of Anti-Rent Disturbances. — Legislature of 1868. — Governor's Message. — State Debt.

xx   CONTENTS.

— Constitutional Convention. — Its Proceedings. — Organization of the Cornell University at Ithaca. — Election of Governor Hoffman and Lieutenant-Governor Beach. — Election of President Ulysses S. Grant and Vice-President Schuyler Colfax 306–310

CHAPTER IX. — ADMINISTRATION OF GOVERNOR JOHN T. HOFFMAN.

Legislature of 1869. — Governor's Message. — Finances of the State. — Common Schools. — Election of Ex-Governor Fenton as United States Senator. — Adoption of the Fifteenth Constitutional Amendment securing Colored Suffrage. — Submission of the new Constitution to the People. — Its Rejection, with the Exception of the Judiciary Article. — Democratic Triumph at the Fall Elections. — Legislature of 1870. — Governor's Message. — Revocation by the Legislature of its Consent to the Fifteenth Constitutional Amendment 310–314

CONCLUSION. — GENERAL RECAPITULATION.

General Survey of the History of the State. — Its Prominent Statesmen. — Governors. — Judges. — Chancellors. — Lawyers. — Legislators. — Senators and Representatives in Congress. — Cabinet Officers. — Presidents, Vice-Presidents, Judges of the Supreme Court of the United States, and Foreign Ministers. — Its Representatives in the Army and Navy. — Scientific and Literary Men. — Discoverers and Inventors. — Representatives of the Press. — Distinguished Clergymen. — Historians. — Poets. — Philanthropists — Educators. — Physicians. — Railroads, Canals, and Internal Improvements. — Valuation of Real and Personal Estate. — Exports and Imports. — Public Schools. — Colleges, Academies, and other Seminaries of Learning. — Normal Schools. — Charitable and Benevolent Institutions. — Churches, Cathedrals, and Places of Public Worship. — The City of New York 315–325

APPENDIX.

CONSTITUTION OF THE STATE OF NEW YORK 327
COUNTIES AND POPULATION OF THE STATE 358
TABLE OF DUTCH, ENGLISH, AND STATE GOVERNORS OF THE STATE . 362
TABLE OF LIEUTENANT-GOVERNORS OF THE STATE 364
TABLE OF SPEAKERS OF THE STATE ASSEMBLY 366
LIST OF RAILROADS IN THE STATE, WITH THEIR EXTENT AND COST 368
LIST OF CANALS OF THE STATE, WITH THEIR EXTENT AND COST . 369

INTRODUCTION.

1. The State of New York, one of the Thirteen original States of the American Union, is bounded on the north by Canada, from which it is separated by Lake Ontario and the St. Lawrence River; east by Vermont, Massachusetts, and Connecticut, from the former of which it is separated by Lake Champlain; south by New Jersey and Pennsylvania; and west by New Jersey, a part of Pennsylvania and Lake Erie, — that lake and the Niagara River separating it from Canada on the western side.

2. From the northern to the southern extremity of the State, its length is 311 miles between the fortieth and forty-fifth degrees of north latitude, and from east to west, between the seventy-first and seventy-ninth degrees of longitude, it extends 412 miles, — comprising an area of 50,519 square miles, or 32,332,160 acres, of which somewhat more than one half is under cultivation for agricultural purposes.

3. Its present population is about four millions, of whom one fourth are of foreign birth, chiefly from Ireland, Germany, and England. It is divided into sixty counties and about nine hundred and fifty towns and cities. Its principal cities, in the order of their population respectively, are New York, Brooklyn, Buffalo, Albany, Rochester, Troy, Syracuse, Utica, Oswego, Poughkeepsie, Auburn, Schenectady, Hudson, and Binghamton. The capital is at Albany, on the west bank of the Hudson.

4. The chief rivers of the State are the Hudson, Mohawk, Delaware, Genesee, Oswego, and Susquehannah, with the St.

Boundaries. — Extent. — Population. — Chief cities. — Rivers.

Lawrence on the north and the Niagara on the west. It possesses a sea-coast from the Atlantic on its southeasterly border along Staten and Long Island of 246 miles, a lake-coast of 352 miles, and 281 miles of navigable rivers.

5. Its principal lakes, exclusive of Lakes Erie, Ontario, and Champlain, are Lakes George on the east; Cayuga, Seneca, Canandaigua, Crooked, and Chautauque on the west; and Skaneateles, Oneida, and Otsego in the centre and south. The great cataract of Niagara, and the Genesee Falls at Rochester, the Portage, Trenton, Taghkanic, Kaaterskill, and Cohoes Falls, form prominent portions of the scenery.

6. The Alleghany Mountains enter the south and southeastern parts of the State in two distinct ridges from New Jersey and Pennsylvania, forming the Highlands, the Shawangunk, Cattskill, and Helderberg Mountains, and in the northern and northeastern parts of the State the Adirondack range of mountains constitute a branch of the great Apalachian system.

7. There are several important mineral and medicinal springs in the interior of the State, the chief of which are those at Ballston, Saratoga, Richfield, Clifton, and Sharon, the extensive saline deposits at Syracuse and Salina, from which from seven to ten millions of bushels of salt are annually manufactured, and various petroleum and gas springs in the western portion of the State.

8. Among the most important public works are the enlarged Erie and Champlain Canals, with their numerous locks and aqueducts, connecting Lake Erie with the waters of the Hudson and Lake Champlain, with eleven tributary canals in different sections of the State; the Croton Aqueduct for the supply of water to the city of New York, extending over a distance of forty miles from the Croton River in Westchester County, and spanning the Harlem by the magnificent High Bridge, built of stone, 1,450 feet in length, 114 feet above tide-water, and with fourteen piers varying from fifty to eighty feet in height; and the Niagara and Lewiston Suspension Bridges.

9. The geological features of the State present a series of

Lakes. — Falls. — Mountains. — Mineral, medicinal, and salt springs. — Public works.

rocks older than the coal formation, and terminating in the lowest member of that deposit, near the Pennsylvania line. They consist of the unstratified crystalline or primary, the stratified non-fossiliferous, and the older secondary fossiliferous rocks. Red sandstone occurs in the southern portions bordering on New Jersey; the great metamorphic belt passes along the eastern line; granite, with abundance of iron ore and limestone, is found in the northern and northeastern sections of the State, and marble in large quantities in the southeastern.

10. The climate and soil of the State are eminently favorable to the cultivation of the various grasses, wheat, oats, Indian corn, rye, garden vegetables, flowers, and fruit of every description indigenous to the northern temperate regions. The vast forests in the northern section afford nearly every variety of timber; and the numerous lakes and rivers furnish an ample supply of fish.

Geological features. — Climate, soil, and productions.

FIRST PERIOD.

INDIAN OCCUPANCY. — THE IROQUOIS, OR FIVE NATIONS.

1. Long before the white man made his appearance, the territory now constituting the State of New York was occupied by roving tribes of Indians, engaged in continual and bloody wars with each other and with neighboring tribes, and obtaining a subsistence mainly by hunting, fishing, and predatory incursions.

2. One portion of them, known as the LENNI LENAPE, or ALGONQUINS, occupied the southeastern portion of the State, chiefly on the banks of the Delaware River; another, and far

---

The Algonquins or Delawares.

the most numerous, known as the IROQUOIS, occupied the entire region between the Hudson River and Lakes Erie and Ontario. A portion of the MOHEGAN tribes, including the Pequods, were found upon Long Island; and the MANHATTANS upon the island of that name, now constituting the city of New York, and the lower portions of Westchester County bordering on the Hudson.

3. The IROQUOIS were originally separate tribes or nations, consisting of the Mohawks, Oneidas, Onondagas, Cayugas, and Senecas. In consequence of the perpetual inroads made upon them by the Algonquins or Delawares, the Adirondacks, Hurons, Eries, and Ottawas of Canada, these tribes, probably as early as the middle of the sixteenth century, formed themselves into a league or confederacy, since known as the FIVE NATIONS; expelled the Adirondacks from their hunting-grounds in Canada, defeated the Hurons and the Ottawas, extirpated the Eries, humbled the Delawares, and carried the terror of their arms as far west as the Mississippi River and southerly to the Gulf of Mexico.

4. The Iroquois Confederacy was the most celebrated and powerful of all the Indian leagues on the continent; and in its leading features strongly resembled the Confederation of States long afterwards established. Each tribe was independent of all the others, except so far as related to the general purposes and object of the league. The head-quarters of this formidable body were established on the banks of the Onondaga Lake, near the site of the present city of Syracuse; and here annually, or as often as the common interest required, its councils were held.

5. Hither, summoned by trusty and faithful messengers, came the sachems and leading warriors of the various tribes from the banks of the Hudson and Mohawk and the shores of the Ontario, Erie, Oneida, Cayuga, Seneca, and Onondaga Lakes, to consult in solemn conclave upon the general welfare, to smoke the pipe of peace, or to dig up the tomahawk and hatchet, and plan the savage war-path against the common enemy.

6. Here, from time to time were heard the eloquent and spirit-stirring appeals of the ATOTARHO, or presiding officer, of the sage

---

Mohegans. — Manhattans. — The Five Nations, — their origin, confederacy, conquests. — Character and objects of the confederacy. — Its chiefs, sachems, and orators.

HIAWATHA, the fierce and stormy THAYANDENAGA of the Mohawks, the noble and solitary LOGAN of the Cayugas, the eloquent RED JACKET of the Senecas, the chivalrous SKENANDOAE of the Oneidas, and the brave GARANGULA of the Onondagas, with others whose daring exploits and tried wisdom and sagacity entitled them to the confidence and regard of the confederacy.

7. Here, too, came the accredited representatives of the "Tortoise" the "Bear" and the "Wolf" tribes of the respective nations, to mingle their counsels with those of their brethren:—

> "By the far Mississippi the Illinois shrank
> When the trail of the TORTOISE was seen on the bank;
> On the hills of New England the Pequod turned pale
> When the howl of the WOLF swelled at night on the gale;
> And the Cherokee shook in his green smiling bowers
> When the foot of the BEAR stamped his carpet of flowers."
>
> STREET's *Frontenac.*

8. The confederacy owed its immediate origin to the necessity of combining its forces for the protection or defence of the separate tribes composing it, against the perpetual assaults and inroads of its enemies. Three of the wisest and most venerated chiefs,—ATOTARHO, after whom the presiding sachems were named, TOGANAWETAH, and HAH-YOH-WOUT-HAH, were regarded as its projectors and founders, and revered as possessed of preternatural qualities.

9. The traditions of the Iroquois concerning these great chiefs are exceedingly interesting and romantic. Toganawetah is described as a young man of remarkable beauty and unknown origin. After the formation of the confederacy he predicted its final dissolution by the "White Throats,"— a people of whose existence they had never heard, but for whose certain advent they watched until their fears were realized by the fulfilment of the prophecy.

10. Toganawetah, having uttered his solemn and mysterious warning of doom from the "Pale Faces," suddenly disappeared and was seen no more. Hah-yoh-wout-hah soon afterwards ascended to heaven in the presence of the assembled multitude, " amidst bursts of the sweetest melody, in a snow-white canoe

---

The Tortoise, Bear, and Wolf Tribes.—The founders of the confederacy.—Traditions of the Iroquois.

suddenly shot down from the sky, rising higher and higher until he melted away in the upper distance." Atotarho alone remained to place himself at the head of the confederacy on the banks of the Onondaga Lake, to govern and instruct his people, and transmit his name and authority to a long line of successors.

11. It was the belief of this primitive and simple people that when, after death, they reached the "happy hunting-grounds" the Great Spirit would provide for them the most delicious fruits known to their native forests, — chiefly the strawberry, which, as fast as consumed, would be eternally and unfailingly renewed. When one of their number is dying, with that calm and placid stoicism characteristic of the race, those around him are accustomed to say, "He is scenting the strawberry of the Great Spirit!"

12. Having in 1655 accomplished the subjugation of the Hurons and Algonquins in Canada and the vicinity of Lake Huron, these indomitable and fiery warriors attacked and conquered, two years later, the Miamis and Ottawas of Michigan. In the beginning of the ensuing century they prosecuted their conquests as far south as the waters of the Cape Fear River in North Carolina, and at a subsequent period nearly exterminated the Cherokees and Catawbas in South Carolina, Georgia, Alabama, and Tennessee.

13. In 1714 they were joined by the Tuscaroras of North Carolina, and from thenceforth assumed the title of the SIX NATIONS. They uniformly adhered to the British interests, or "Corlear" as they termed that nation, against "Yonondio," or the French; and on the revolt of the Americans in the Revolutionary struggle inflicted the most dire calamities on their former friends at Wyoming in Pennsylvania, and at Cherry Valley and the Mohawk settlements in New York.

14. At the period of the first settlement of New York, the aggregate number of this confederacy amounted to about forty thousand. Not more than seven thousand remain in existence, and of these a small remnant only is now to be found in the State.

The strawberry of the Great Spirit. — Conquests of the Iroquois. — Accession of the Tuscaroras. — Fidelity to the English. — Comparative numbers.

Minuit's Purchase of Manhattan Island.

SECOND PERIOD.

DISCOVERIES AND SETTLEMENTS.—THE DUTCH GOVERNMENTS.

CHAPTER I.

Discovery of the Hudson River.—First Settlement of the Province of New Netherlands.

1. The first Europeans who landed on the soil of New York were probably the crew of a French vessel under the command of John de Verrazzano, a Florentine, in the service of Francis I. of France. From the journals of the voyage preserved by him, it appears that about the middle of March, 1524, he arrived on the American coast in North Carolina, from whence, after proceeding south as far as Georgia, he sailed northward to the latitude of 41°, where he entered a harbor, which, from his

1524.

John de Verrazzano.

description, was probably that of New York. He seems to have remained there about fifteen days, visited by the Indians, and trafficking with them.

2. After an interval of nearly a century, SAMUEL CHAM- 1609. PLAIN, a French navigator, on the 4th of July, 1609, while descending the St. Lawrence River and exploring its tributaries, discovered the lake which bears his name. A few days subsequently, uniting his forces with the Hurons, Algonquins, and other Indian tribes in the vicinity, he enabled them by the use of fire-arms, hitherto unknown to the natives, to obtain a decisive victory over their hereditary enemies, the Iroquois.

3. Early in 1609, HENRY HUDSON, an English navigator, after the failure of two expeditions in the employ of a company of London merchants for the discovery of a nearer passage to Asia, offered his services to the Dutch East India Company in Holland; and on the 4th of April set sail for China in the yacht *Half Moon*, with his son, and a crew composed of English and Dutch sailors. After several ineffectual attempts to accomplish his object, he entered Delaware Bay in August, and on the 3d of September found a safe anchorage at Sandy Hook.

4. On the succeeding day he proceeded up the present New York Bay along the Jersey coast, sending from time to time his boats on shore, and receiving the visits of the natives, who came on board in great numbers, clad in loose furs, singing their wild songs, and in the most friendly manner offering to traffic with the strangers in exchange for pipes, tobacco, maize, beans, and oysters. For several days this mutual interchange of friendly civilities was continued; and on the 12th of September Hudson entered through the Narrows the river which bears his name, and sailed up its broad channel as far as the present site of Manhattanville.

5. On the 13th and 14th, passing the present site of Yonkers, he proceeded up as far as the Highlands, anchoring in the neighborhood of West Point; and on the evening of the 17th landed just above the present site of Hudson, where on the ensuing day he had a pleasant interview with the natives. On the 19th he

---

Samuel Champlain. — Henry Hudson. — His employment by the Dutch East India Company. — Entrance into New York Bay. — Intercourse with the Indians. — Discovery of the river.

reached the present site of Kinderhook, from whence, after having sent a small boat up the river to a point a little above Albany, he commenced on the 23d his return voyage.

6. During his trip up the river he was frequently visited by the Indians who came in considerable numbers on their boats, and manifested the most friendly disposition. On his return, however, several attempts were made a little below the Highlands, by the natives, to attack his crew, and in the effort to repulse them some ten or twelve were killed. On the 4th of October he set sail for Europe, and in the ensuing year engaged in another voyage for the discovery of the northwest passage to Asia, in which, near the straits in British America which now bear his name, he was abandoned by his mutinous crew and perished miserably.

1610. 7. Stimulated by the favorable accounts given by Hudson on his return to Holland, another vessel was equipped, during the succeeding year, for the fur-trade with the Indians on the banks of the newly discovered river; and this adventure having proved successful, HENDRICK CHRISTIANSEN and ADRIEN BLOCK in 1612 fitted out two additional
1612. ships for the same purpose, which were speedily followed by three others under the command of Captains DeWitt, Volckertsen, and May. The island of Manhattan was made the chief depot of the trade, and Christiansen received the appointment of agent for the traffic in furs during the passage of the vessels to and from Holland. He immediately set about the construction of a small fort with a few rude buildings, on the southern extremity of the island, thus laying the first foundations of the future city.

1614. 8. Adrien Block, having lost one of his vessels by an accidental fire, set about the construction of another, which he completed in the spring of 1614, and immediately commenced an active exploration of the neighboring country. Passing by the upper waters of the East River into Long Island Sound, and the outlet of the Housatonic River, he ascended the Connecticut to the head of navigation,— thence returning to

---

Voyage up the Hudson to Albany.— Return to Europe.— His death.— Expeditions from Holland in the fur-trade.— Adrien Block.— Foundation of New York City.

the Sound, he reached Montauk Point and the present Block Island; then, turning his course eastward, he explored the Narragansett Bay, Rhode Island, Nahant Bay, and the intervening islands, and, leaving his vessel at Cape Cod in charge of Cornelis Hendrickson, embarked for Holland in one of the ships on its way from Manhattan.

9. On the 11th of October a charter was granted by the States-General, conferring upon the merchants engaged in these expeditions the exclusive right of trading in the new territories situated between the fortieth and forty-fifth degrees of north latitude, for four voyages to be completed within three years; and giving to this entire region the name of New Netherlands. In the mean time Cornelissen Jacobsen May had explored the southern coast of Long Island, visited Delaware Bay, and given his name to its northern cape, while Hendrick Christiansen had ascended the Mauritius, as the Hudson River was then termed, to a point a little below Albany, where he established a fort and warehouse on Castle Island, calling it Fort Nassau. Shortly afterwards, however, Christiansen was murdered by a young Indian in his employ, and Jacob Eelkins was appointed to succeed him as agent. An association of merchants was formed under the title of the United New Netherlands Company, and the trade in furs with the Indians was vigorously prosecuted.

10. In the spring of 1617, a solemn council of the chiefs and warriors of the several Iroquois tribes, and the representatives of the New Netherlands, was held at a place called Tawasentha, near the present site of Albany, and a formal treaty of alliance and peace entered into between them. Protected by the provisions of this treaty the trade with the Indians became so flourishing and profitable that on the expiration of the charter of the Company in 1618 its renewal was refused by the States-General. Permission was, however, given by special license for a temporary continuance of their operations. 1617.

11. In 1620 Captain Thomas Dermer, an Englishman in the service of Sir Ferdinando Gorges, appeared at 1620.

Exploration and discoveries. — New charter. — Association of merchants. — United New Netherlands Company. — Council with the Indian tribes at Tawasentha. — Treaty of alliance. — Progress of the fur-trade. — Refusal to renew the charter. — English claims to the territory.

Manhattan on his voyage to New England, and laid claim to the entire territory occupied by the Dutch traders, upon the ground of prior discovery and occupancy. On the representation of his employers, James I., the English monarch, granted Gorges and his associates a charter of exclusive jurisdiction over all the territories in America between the fortieth and forty-eighth parallels of latitude, and the English ambassador at the Hague was directed to remonstrate against the intrusion of the Dutch occupants.

1621. 12. This remonstrance was, however, unheeded; and in June, 1621, the States-General granted a new charter to the Dutch "West India Company," conferring upon them exclusive jurisdiction for a period of twenty-one years over the Province of New Netherlands, with full and ample powers to trade with the natives from Newfoundland to the Straits of Magellan, to appoint governors subject to the approval of the States, to colonize the territory, erect forts, and administer justice throughout the entire territory. The executive management of the association was intrusted to a board of nineteen directors, one of whom was to be appointed by the Government and the remaining eighteen by the Company, distributed through five separate Chambers in different cities of Holland.

1623-5. 13. The Amsterdam Chamber, to which had been specially assigned the charge of the Province of New Netherlands, sent out a vessel under the command of Cornelissen Jacobsen May as director, with thirty families, consisting chiefly of Walloons or French Protestants, with the view of laying a permanent foundation for the projected colony. Eight of these families settled at Manhattan, others took up their abode on the Jersey shore, the Connecticut River, and as far up the Mauritius or Hudson River as the present site of Albany, where they built Fort Orange, four miles above Fort Nassau. George Jansen de Rapelye, with a few Walloon families, occupied a portion of Long Island in the vicinity of Walloon's Bay.

Charter to Sir Ferdinando Gorges and his associates. — The West India Company. — Colonization of New Netherlands. — Cornelissen Jacobsen May the first director. — Settlements at Manhattan. — Fort Orange and Long Island.

Reinforced by other accessions to their number, the Manhattan settlement in 1625 amounted to some two hundred persons, and the work of colonization was fairly commenced. May was succeeded in the directorship in 1625 by William Verhulst, who remained, however, only for about one year.

CHAPTER II.

Administration of Peter Minuit.—Purchase and Settlement of Manhattan Island.

1. In May, 1626, Peter Minuit arrived at New Netherlands as Director-General, and immediately effected the purchase of the island of Manhattan, of the Indians, for goods and trinkets to the value of sixty guilders, or about *twenty-four dollars*. An interchange of friendly relations was established with the English settlement at Plymouth, and arrangements for a mutual trade were entered into. In 1628 a church was organized with fifty communicants, under the auspices of Jonas Michaelius, a clergyman from Holland. The colony grew apace, and the traffic in furs with the surrounding Indian tribes was, for a time, quietly, industriously, and profitably pursued by the incipient colony. _{1626.} _{1628.}

2. The germs of future trouble soon, however, began to make their appearance. The murder of a Westchester Indian, who had visited the settlement for the purpose of trade, by three of Minuit's farm servants, had aroused a spirit of revenge which awaited only a favorable opportunity for its gratification. Notwithstanding the fact that the authorities at Manhattan were entirely ignorant of the commission of this rash outrage, and disclaimed all participation in it, the native tribes sullenly brooded over the unprovoked injury, and patiently bided their time for a bloody retribution.

3. In the mean time, the slow growth of the colony 1629.

Peter Minuit.—Purchase of Manhattan Island.—Establishment of friendly relations with the English colonists at Plymouth.—Organization of a church.—Murder of a Westchester Indian.

induced the States-General, on the recommendation of the Assembly of Nineteen, to adopt an ordinance granting to any member of the Company who should within four years establish a colony of fifty persons, exclusive of children under fifteen years of age, the privilege of selecting, with the title of Patroon, a tract of land, outside of the island of Manhattan, sixteen miles in length on one side, or eight miles on each side of any navigable river, and extending as far inland as the proprietor should choose.

4. The sole conditions, except that of colonization, imposed upon the grantees were: satisfaction to the Indians for the lands selected, the maintenance of a minister and schoolmaster, and the payment of a duty of five per cent on all trade carried on by them, exclusive of that in furs, which the Company reserved to themselves. The Company on their part agreed to strengthen the forts at Manhattan, to protect the colonists against all attacks from the Indians or English, and to supply them with a sufficient number of negro servants for an indefinite period of time. This was the first introduction of slavery into the province.

5. The Company also encouraged the emigration of individual settlers by offering them the grant of as much land as they could cultivate, with an exemption from taxation for ten years; precluding them, however, as well as the settlers under the Patroons, from any voice in the government of the colony, and from the manufacture of any linen, woollen, cotton, or other cloth. The Patroons were a species of feudal lords, with full powers over their tenants, the appointment of all local officers, and unrestricted privileges of hunting, fowling, and fishing.

6. Under these grants large tracts of land on each side of the Hudson, including the present counties of Albany and Rensselaer, were secured by Kilian Van Rensselaer, a director of the Company, under the title of Rensselaerwyck; and another director, Michael Pauw, appropriated Staten Island and a large tract in New Jersey, including the present Jersey City and Hoboken, to which he gave the name of Pavonia. A large por-

---

Grants of territory to Patroons and other settlers. — Introduction of slavery. — The Rensselaerwyck Patroons.

tion of the manorial estate conferred upon Van Rensselaer still remains in the possession of his descendants, and the descendants and successors of the original tenants, held by them under nominal rent charges.

7. The settlement at Manhattan in the mean while continued in a prosperous condition; its internal and foreign commerce was steadily increasing; a large vessel of eight hundred tons was built and despatched to Holland; settlements on the Brooklyn shore and in the interior of Long Island were springing up; and immigrants of every shade of religious faith, attracted by the liberal inducements offered by the Dutch Government and by the free toleration of their theological opinions, were flocking to the settlements.

8. A controversy having arisen between the Company and the Patroons, originating in the interference of the latter in the fur-trade, from all participation in which they were excluded by the terms of their charter, Minuit, who was suspected of favoring their pretensions, was in 1632 recalled. The ship in which he had embarked for Holland having been detained on her return voyage by the English authorities at Plymouth as an illegal trafficker in English goods, a correspondence ensued between the representatives of the two governments in reference to their respective claims to the title of the New Netherlands.

1632.

9. On the one hand, the Dutch relied upon the discoveries of Hudson; the subsequent immediate occupation of the territory by themselves, ratified and confirmed by charter; the establishment of forts and garrisons for its protection; the purchase by them of the land from the natives, and the failure of the English to occupy any portion of the territory claimed. The latter relied upon the prior discovery of Cabot, and the patent to the Plymouth Company granted by James I., covering the territory in question, — ignoring and denying the validity of any title procured from the Indians, who had themselves a mere possessory claim, — and offering to permit the continued occupation of the province by its present colonists, with a full guaranty of all their rights of property and person, on condition of the transfer of their allegiance to the English Crown.

Progress of the colony at Manhattan. — Controversy between the Company and Patroons. — Recall of Minuit. — English claims.

10. A definitive settlement of the controversy was, however, deferred to a future period, and the vessel released. Minuit subsequently returned to America during the administration of Governor Kieft, and, under the auspices of Queen Christina of Sweden, laid the foundation of a Swedish colony on the Delaware River by the erection of a fort, which he named after his royal patroness, where, in 1641, he died and was buried.

CHAPTER III.

Administration of Wouter Van Twiller.

1633. 1. In April, 1633, the new Director-General, WOUTER VAN TWILLER, arrived at Manhattan with a small military force and a Spanish vessel captured on the voyage from Holland. Among the passengers were EVERARDUS BOGARDUS, a clergyman, and ADAM ROELANDSEN, the pioneer schoolmaster of the colony. Van Twiller had previously visited the province with a view to the selection of lands under the patroon grants, and had married a niece of Killian Van Rensselaer. With the exception of the influence, and knowledge of the country, thus obtained, he seems to have been thoroughly incompetent to the discharge of the duties imposed upon him.

2. The fort at New Amsterdam, which had been commenced several years before, was completed, a guard-house and barracks for the soldiers erected, and a church and parsonage built, under his direction. An angry controversy soon sprung up between Bogardus and the Governor, in which the citizens generally took part, growing out of his administration of the affairs of the province. Bitter recriminations passed between the parties, — the anathemas of the Church were hurled upon the devoted head of the Director, who, in turn, denounced his reverend antagonist, — and the strife was prolonged to the close of his brief administration.

Swedish settlement on the Delaware by Minuit. — Erection of Fort Christina. — Death of Minuit. — Governor Van Twiller. — His character. — Controversy with Bogardus. — Adam Roelandsen. — Rebuilding of the fort. — Erection of a church.

3. In the mean time Jacob Eelkins, a former agent of the Company at Fort Orange, who had been dismissed from their employ, arrived at Manhattan as supercargo of an English vessel engaged in the fur-trade. The Governor refused to permit the vessel to proceed without the production of a suitable license from the Company. Eelkins declined exhibiting his commission, and claimed the right to trade with the natives as an Englishman to whom the territory legitimately belonged, and after displaying the English flag, and firing a salute in honor of the English king, proceeded up the river in defiance of the guns of the fort.

4. Van Twiller immediately summoned a meeting of the citizens at the square before the fort, now the Bowling Green, and after collecting their sentiments, and indulging in much bravado and festive display of loyalty to the government of the Prince of Orange, despatched an armed force to Fort Orange, whither Eelkins had already repaired, erected a tent, and was engaged in trading with the natives. The soldiers proceeded, on their arrival, to demolish his tent, take possession of his wares, and reconduct his vessel to Fort Amsterdam, whence it was sent to sea, with a warning henceforth to cease from intermeddling with the Dutch trade.

5. The Governor, soon after entering upon the duties of his administration, had despatched Jacob Van Corlaer and other agents to purchase of the Pequod Indians a tract of land on the Connecticut River, near the present site of Hartford. Upon this tract they built and fortified a redoubt, which they named Fort Good Hope. Against this invasion of their territory the Plymouth and Massachusetts colonies, through Governor Winthrop, sent an earnest remonstrance to Van Twiller, to which he returned a courteous reply, proposing a reference of their respective claims to their several governments.

6. The Plymouth colonists, however, having secured from the Indians a small tract in the vicinity of the fort, sent Lieutenant William Holmes with a sufficient force to take possession and commence an English settlement on the present site of Windsor.

Jacob Eelkins's visit to Manhattan. — Defiance of the authority of the Governor. — Van Twiller's proceedings. — Difficulties between the Dutch and English colonists on the Connecticut.

Van Corlaer ineffectually endeavored to oppose their progress, and Van Twiller sent a force of seventy soldiers to dislodge them. The Dutch commander, however, intimidated by their bold bearing, withdrew without any attempt at their expulsion.

7. Van Twiller met with better success in expelling a band of English intruders from the Virginia colony, who, headed by George Holmes, had taken possession of Fort Nassau. The Governor promptly despatched an armed force to South River, which dislodged the occupants and brought them back as prisoners to Fort Amsterdam, whence they were returned to Point Comfort just in season to intercept a party of their countrymen intending to join them. This energetic display of spirit secured to the province the undisputed control of the South River colony.

1636 - 7. 8. After purchasing on his own account, in conjunction with Jacob Van Corlaer and others, a tract of fifteen thousand acres of land, now comprising the flourishing town of Flatlands, to which he afterwards added the islands now known as Governor's, Blackwell's, and Randall's, thus rendering himself the wealthiest landholder in the province, he involved himself, with characteristic recklessness and impetuosity, in a quarrel with Van Dincklagen, one of the ablest members of his Council. The latter had complained of his rapacity, and in return had been deprived of his salary, removed from his office, and sent a prisoner to Holland on a charge of contumacy.

9. Van Dincklagen made so strong a representation of the inefficiency and corruption of the Governor, that the States-General urged the Amsterdam Chamber to recall him and reinstate his councillor, with which request the Chamber, after some delay, reluctantly complied. Prior, however, to his recall, the West India Company had effected the purchase of Pavonia from its patroon, which conferred upon them possession of and jurisdiction over the Jersey shore and Staten Island. The patroonship of Rensselaerwyck was therefore the only property of this description remaining in the province.

Invasion of Fort Nassau and its reconquest. — Rapacity and wealth of Van Twiller. — Controversy with Van Dincklagen. — Recall of Van Twiller. — Purchase of Pavonia.

CHAPTER IV.

Administration of Wilhelm Kieft.

1. On the 28th of March, 1638, Wilhelm Kieft arrived at Manhattan as the successor of Van Twiller in the government of the colony. He was a man of considerable energy of character, — irritable, capricious, and injudicious, and wholly deficient in that firmness, prudence, and cool discrimination so necessary to his difficult position. His previous career as a merchant at Amsterdam, and subsequently in the employ of the Government, had been stained with dishonor and criminal rapacity, and his administration of the new duties devolved upon him was a stormy and disastrous one; marked by the assumption of dictatorial powers, and distinguished chiefly for rashness, improvidence, and sanguinary contests with the surrounding Indian tribes. *1638.*

2. Immediately on his accession he surrounded himself with a Council entirely devoted to his own interests, and obedient in all things to his will. With characteristic activity he set about the reform of a variety of abuses which had crept into the public service under the lax administration of his predecessor. He prepared a code of laws and regulations strictly prohibiting all illegal traffic under heavy penalties, establishing rigid sanitary observances, and repressing all forms of vice and immorality.

3. He soon became involved in difficulties with the Swedish colonies on the Delaware and the English settlements on the Connecticut. His remonstrances, however, against the intrusion of the Swedish settlers on territory claimed by the Dutch, were disregarded both by the colonists and the States-General, who were unwilling to offend so powerful a neighbor; and he was reluctantly compelled to turn his attention in another direction.

4. A new charter of privileges was conferred upon the colonies by the Company: restricting the patroon rights of occupancy to four miles of frontage on navigable rivers and eight miles inland; granting two hundred acres of land to every *1639.*

Wilhelm Kieft. — His character and antecedents. — Reform of abuses. — Code of laws and regulations. — Difficulties with the Swedish colonists. — New charter of privileges.

six settlers who should transport themselves to the colony at their own expense; giving the right of choosing their own magistrates to all villages and cities thereafter to be established; relinquishing the monopoly of the Indian trade in exchange for a moderate duty; and making a liberal provision for individual settlers. The Reformed Dutch religion was recognized as the established faith of the province, with full toleration, however, to all other sects; and no discrimination, except an oath of fealty to the Dutch Government, was permitted to exist between foreigners and other citizens.

5. Attracted by these inducements, the colonization of the province rapidly increased, both from Holland and the New England and Virginia colonies. The cultivation of tobacco was introduced; new fruit-trees and other flowering plants and garden vegetables were domesticated; and the internal affairs of the colonists were prosperous beyond any previous experience. Large tracts of land on Long Island in the vicinity of the present Newtown, purchased for the Company by the Governor, were brought into cultivation; a settlement was commenced at Gravesend by Anthony Jansen Rapelye, the brother of the founder of the Walloon Colony; and other purchases were made of valuable farms in the vicinity of the city.

1640. 6. In the spring of 1640 Kieft, also in behalf of the Company, purchased of the Indians all the remaining territory comprised within the present limits of Kings and Queens Counties, and De Vries soon after established another colony at Tappan. These were followed in the ensuing year by a colony on the Hackensack River, by Vander Voorst, and on all that part of Staten Island not already in possession of De Vries, by Cornelius Melyn. A few scattered settlements had been effected on the eastern part of Long Island, at Southampton. Southold and Greenport, under English grants, and a few years later the towns of East Hampton and Setauket, were founded under the same authority, without any attempts at disturbance on the part of the Dutch Government.

7. An expedition was during this year fitted out at New Haven by George Lamberton, a merchant, with fifty families,

---

Internal prosperity of the colony. — Progress of settlements on Long Island.

for a settlement on the shores of the Delaware. Touching at Manhattan, the emigrants were forbidden by Kieft to prosecute further their enterprise. They, however, disregarded his threats, and proceeded on their voyage. Kieft, indignant at this defiance of his authority, organized a force for their summary expulsion; but, being prevented by Indian disturbances at home, deferred the enterprise until the following year, when with the aid of the Swedes he succeeded in breaking up the settlement and sending back the English with their goods to New Haven. Lamberton, who persisted in trading at the South River, was arrested and compelled to pay full duties on his cargo. Demands for satisfaction on the part of the English colonies, and continued annoyances ensuing from the refusal on the part of Kieft, induced the latter finally to proclaim an ordinance of non-intercourse with the Connecticut colony.

8. Negotiations were now opened for the purchase of the territory in the neighborhood of the Dutch post on the Connecticut River; but all terms being refused, both parties appealed to their respective governments for redress. The pendency of the civil war in England, however, prevented a settlement of the difficulties; and the English colonists continued for some time longer to harass and disturb their Dutch neighbors.

9. In July, 1640, Kieft sent an armed force against the Raritan Indians, belonging to the Delaware tribe in New Jersey, for an alleged robbery on Staten Island, by a portion of the tribe. Although these Indians were entirely innocent of the offence, ten of their warriors were ruthlessly slaughtered and their crops and other property destroyed. This severe chastisement soon provoked a bloody retaliation. The plantation of De Vries, on Staten Island, was attacked, his dwelling burned, and four of his planters killed. Other outrages speedily followed, and the foundations were thus laid for a vindictive contest, which for a time threatened the extermination of the infant colony. 1640.

10. Satisfaction having been refused by the chiefs of the offending tribes, a general declaration of war against the savages was resolved upon. Previously, however, to engaging in active hostilities, Kieft deemed it prudent to convoke a 1641.

Lamberton's expedition to the Delaware. — Proceedings of Kieft. — Attack upon the Raritan Indians. — Burning of De Vries' plantation. — Indian War.

general council of the principal citizens, who, on the 28th of August, 1641, nominated a select committee of twelve of their number to act as their representatives. This committee, while making every preparation for the impending conflict, exerted, in conjunction with the officers and agents of the Company, the utmost efforts for the peaceful settlement of the controversy.

1642. 11. Kieft, however, succeeded, in the commencement of the ensuing year, in obtaining a reluctant consent from the representative Council for the immediate adoption of vigorous measures for the chastisement of the Indians. He at once despatched a party of eighty men up the river, with orders to exterminate by fire and sword the neighboring Westchester tribe, a member of which, in retaliation for a murder committed twenty years before by Minuit's farm servants, had slain in cold blood an unoffending citizen, and was protected and justified by the tribe. The Indians, however, on learning their danger, sued for peace, promising to deliver up the murderer.

12. Pending these negotiations, two other murders were committed by the Indians, and satisfaction was promptly demanded by the Governor. In the mean time a band of Mohawks made a descent upon the river Indians, and, after killing and capturing many of their number, compelled them to flee for succor to the Dutch at Manhattan. More than a thousand of the hapless fugitives encamped on the Jersey shore at Pavonia, while the residue crossed the river, and appealed to the colonists for protection against their enraged and relentless enemies. A favorable opportunity was thus afforded for the restoration of friendly relations between the settlers and the natives; but it was frustrated by an act of wanton and disgraceful treachery and cruelty unparalleled in the annals of civilized humanity.

1643. 13. The faction in New Amsterdam in favor of a war of extermination against the Indians, supported by the influence of the Governor, succeeded in obtaining from that officer full authority to avail themselves of the helpless condition of the fugitives thus thrown upon their hospitality, by a general and indiscriminate massacre. In defiance of the most ur-

---

Formation of a representative committee. — Expedition against Westchester Indians. — Attack of the Mohawks upon the river tribes. — Massacre of the Indians at Pavonia and Corlaer's Hook.

gent remonstrances of the leading citizens, at midnight on the 25th of February, 1643, this inhuman and revolting outrage was perpetrated under the immediate sanction of the Governor, and eighty of the Indians at Pavonia — men, women, and children, surprised in the midst of their unsuspecting slumbers — were despatched by the muskets of their enemies or driven into the river to perish. A similar massacre was at the same time perpetrated at Corlaer's Hook, upon the confiding and unconscious savages there.

14. These atrocious deeds reflect indelible infamy upon the memory of Kieft, who was solely responsible for their commission. Well had it been if the swift retribution for their enormity could have fallen only upon him and his inhuman advisers and instruments! All the neighboring tribes immediately concentrated their forces for avenging this outrage upon their brethren, and openly proclaimed an unrelenting war against the devoted colonists. They took possession of the swamps and morasses of the island, lay in wait to shoot down the settlers at their work, to drive off their cattle, burn their dwellings, capture their wives and children, and devastate their possessions. Universal terror prevailed. The white settlements on every hand were attacked, and the colonists were reduced to despair.

15. Overtures of peace, preferred by Kieft, who too late began to repent his rashness, were scornfully rejected. Bitter recriminations passed between his cowardly advisers and himself; and the persecuted colonists heaped the most contumelious reproaches upon his head for his agency in bringing about the deplorable condition in which they found themselves. They even threatened his deposition and arrest as a prisoner, and talked of sending him in chains to Holland. De Vries alone, who had thrown the whole weight of his influence in opposition to the infatuated policy of the Governor, retained the confidence as well of the colonists as their maddened opponents, the savages.

16. Early in the spring, however, a white flag approached the fort, and through De Vries and Olfertson, who alone dared to confront the Indians who bore it, an interview took place with the sachems of the surrounding tribes, followed by a treaty providing for a temporary truce. In August the war

was again renewed, a new representative Council summoned by the Governor, an alliance entered into with the Long Island tribes, and energetic preparations made for offensive military operations, under the charge of Captain John Underhill.

17. The Indians on their part renewed their savage attacks upon all the neighboring settlements. The outlying farms were ruthlessly sacked; the plantation of the celebrated Anne Hutchinson on the East River near Hell Gate burned, and herself, and her whole family, with one exception, murdered; and throughout Westchester and the adjoining settlements, on Long Island and the Jersey shore, indiscriminate plunders and massacres were of daily occurrence. The sole place of safety for the hunted colonists was the fort at New Amsterdam, where some two or three hundred defenders, with their wives and children, were collected to resist the constant attacks of fifteen hundred armed and maddened savages. De Vries, finding himself ruined, and helpless, notwithstanding his great influence with the Indians, to avert the calamitous results of Kieft's reckless folly, abandoned the colony and returned to Holland.

1644. 18. The aid of the New Haven colony was in this emergency unsuccessfully invoked by the Council; and after an earnest and pressing appeal to Holland for assistance in this their hour of sore distress, the colonists sent out several expeditions against the Indian villages. The chief of one of the friendly Long Island tribes at Hempstead having fallen under suspicion of treachery to the whites, Kieft, without any effort to ascertain the truth of the charge, despatched a force of one hundred and twenty men with orders to exterminate the tribe. These orders were promptly carried into effect with circumstances of revolting barbarity and cruelty. Upwards of a hundred warriors were slaughtered, and two prisoners, conducted to Fort Amsterdam, put to death with excruciating tortures.

19. Underhill was then ordered with a hundred and fifty men on an expedition against the Connecticut Indians at Greenwich, who were surrounded at midnight, while celebrating one of their annual festivals, and put to the sword.

Truce with the Indians. — Renewal of the war. — Military preparations of the colonists. — Devastations of the Indians. — Murder of Anne Hutchinson. — Helpless condition of the settlers. — Massacre of Long Island Indians. — Massacre at Greenwich of Connecticut Indians.

Nearly two hundred of their number were killed, and the residue forced into their wigwams, which were immediately fired, and their hapless occupants either burned or shot in their efforts to escape. Eight only, of six hundred men, women, and children, escaped the fearful slaughter and conflagration. This sanguinary battle virtually terminated the war, although desultory hostilities continued down to the fall of the succeeding year, 1645, when a final treaty of peace and amity was concluded at the Bowling Green, and a day of general thanksgiving proclaimed. 1645.

20. At this period scarcely a hundred men were left on Manhattan Island, and such of the neighboring colonists as survived the calamities of the war had been reduced to poverty and destitution. Cattle, farms, provisions, and dwellings were destroyed, and everything bore tokens of a long, perilous, and deadly struggle with an infuriated and savage foe. A reinforcement of Dutch soldiers, forwarded by Stuyvesant, then Governor of Curaçoa, were billeted upon the citizens, and the expense of their clothing supplied by the imposition of an excise tax. Indignant at the enforcement of this additional burden, the Council demanded the recall of Kieft, denounced him as the author of the war, and petitioned for the allowance to the citizens of a voice in the municipal government.

21. Their memorial met with a favorable reception. Kieft was ordered home, new regulations for the government of the province were made, and its administration confided to new hands. On his outward voyage, the late Governor perished by shipwreck, leaving behind him a melancholy record of abused power and perverted opportunities of usefulness. With him were two of the members of the Council, under sentence of banishment by the new Director on charges preferred by Kieft, and Dominie Bogardus, who was on his way to answer similar charges preferred by the new Council. The two former were rescued and subsequently returned with honor to the colony. Bogardus and eighty others, including the Governor, went down with the ill-fated vessel. 1647.

Treaty of peace. — General thanksgiving. — Reduced condition of the colony. — Arrival of reinforcements. — Excise tax. — Indignation of the citizens. — Recall and death of Kieft.

New Amsterdam in 1656.

CHAPTER V.

Administration of Peter Stuyvesant.

1. Peter Stuyvesant, the newly appointed Director, took possession of the government on the 11th of May, 1647. On his arrival he was greeted with a hearty and cordial reception by the citizens, to which he responded by reciprocal professions of interest and regard. He had for several years been in the Company's service as Director of their colony at Curaçoa, and was distinguished for his energy and bravery. Having lost a leg in an attack on the Portuguese settlement at St. Martin's, he had been obliged to return to Europe for surgical aid, whence, still retaining his former commission, he was sent to the charge of the Province of New Netherlands.

1647.

2. Immediately on his accession he organized a representative Council of nine members from a list of eighteen presented to him by the inhabitants of the province, and gave his assent to

---

Peter Stuyvesant. — His reception, antecedents, and character. — Representative Council.

various important provisions for the regulation of trade and commerce. By a conciliatory and just treatment of the Indians so recently in revolt he speedily gained their affection and good-will, and by his judicious measures for their mutual protection restored peace and harmony among all classes.

3. To adjust the controversy which was still pending between the Dutch and English governments respecting the territory claimed by each on Long Island and at the mouth of the Connecticut River, Governor Stuyvesant assented to the appointment of two arbitrators on each side, who assigned to New England all that portion of Long Island comprising the present Suffolk County, and all that portion of Connecticut situate east of a specified line nowhere less than ten miles east of the Mauritius or Hudson River. The Dutch remained in possession of their territory at Fort Good Hope.

4. The terms of this arrangement were very unacceptable to the people of the Manhattan colony, who loudly complained of the Governor's course, accusing him of partiality to the English interest and injustice to their own. They demanded, moreover, an independent municipal government, such as had been bestowed upon the neighboring settlement at Brooklyn, the principal provisions of which were copied from those of the cities of Holland.

5. On the 4th of April, 1652, this petition was acceded to by the Company, and a burgher government established at Manhattan, consisting of a fiscal agent, to be appointed by the Company, and two burgomasters and five inferior magistrates elected by the people, who were to form a municipal court of justice, subject to the appellate jurisdiction of the Supreme Court of the Province. 1652.

6. Constant intrigues, in the mean while, were in progress between the New England colonies and the English settlers on Long Island, covertly fostered by the English Government under Cromwell, having for their ultimate object the conquest of the Dutch province. Stuyvesant was accused of 1654.

Regulations for trade and commerce. — Treatment of the Indians. — Adjustment of boundaries between the New England and Dutch colonies. — Dissatisfaction of the people. — Establishment of burgher governments at Manhattan and Brooklyn. — Intrigues of the English for the conquest of the province.

having plotted with the Narragansett Indians for the destruction of the English. This charge was indignantly denied, and was wholly unsupported by proof; and the General Court of Massachusetts discountenanced all efforts to involve the two colonies in war. Cromwell, however, was induced to fit out an expedition against New Amsterdam, when the restoration of peace between England and Holland put an end, for the time being, to all further proceedings in this direction.

7. With a view, however, to counteracting the growing influence of the English settlers, increased municipal powers were bestowed upon the several corporations on Long and Manhattan Islands, and the demands of the inhabitants for a more extended participation in the government acceded to by Stuyvesant, notwithstanding the remonstrances of the Company, and even in opposition to his own judgment.

1655. 8. In the ensuing year the Governor, under the direction of the Company, reconquered the Swedish forts on the Delaware from the Swedes who had captured them, and the Dutch Government again resumed possession of the territory, with honorable terms to the inhabitants.

9. During the absence of the troops on this expedition the slumbering hostility of the Indians against the settlers again broke out. A woman belonging to one of the neighboring tribes having, a few years previous, been detected in stealing, was shot by one of the inhabitants of the city; and the warriors of the tribe availed themselves of the departure of the troops to revenge the murder. On the morning of the 15th of September two thousand armed savages landed at Fort Amsterdam before daybreak, and spread themselves over the town, on pretence of searching for some missing Indians.

10. The inhabitants, however, suspecting their object, treated them with great civility and succeeded in persuading them to leave town in the evening and cross over to Governor's Island. They soon returned in force, shot the murderer of the woman and tomahawked another citizen, when they were again forced back to their canoes by the startled inhabitants. Crossing the Hudson, they made a descent upon Pavonia and Hoboken,

---

Extension of municipal powers. — Reconquest of the Swedish forts on the Delaware. — Renewal of Indian hostilities.

slaughtering men, women, and children, and burning houses, barns, and crops. Thence they proceeded to Staten Island, where they repeated their merciless and bloody work. One hundred of the settlers were killed, and a still greater number captured, and twenty-eight farms and crops were laid waste. The Long Island settlements were next threatened, and general consternation prevailed.

11. An express was immediately forwarded to the Governor, who at once returned to the city. Instead, however, of proceeding to the adoption of violent measures with his formidable and victorious foes, he prudently resorted to conciliatory counsels, kind words, and liberal presents, while at the same time displaying the utmost energy in placing the city on a footing of military defence. Pacified by his gifts and overawed by his display of force, the Indians soon relinquished their prisoners and entered into negotiations for peace.

12. With the restoration of peace, both at home and abroad, the prosperity of the colony rapidly and steadily advanced. 1656. The population of New Amsterdam consisted at this period of about one thousand inhabitants, occupying one hundred and twenty dwelling-houses. The average price of the best city lots was fifty dollars, and the average yearly rent of the best houses about fourteen. There being but one public school in the city, and the Governor having declined authorizing the establishment of a private institution, application was made to the Company for a Latin teacher by several of the burghers who were desirous of giving a classical education to their children, alleging in support of their request that by this means "New Amsterdam might finally attain to an academy, the credit of which would redound to the honor of the Company." The request was complied with, and a flourishing Latin school established by Dr. Alexander Carolus Curtius, who was soon afterwards succeeded by Dominie Ægidius Luyck, the private family tutor of Governor Stuyvesant.

13. The continued encroachments of the New England colonies and the long and vexatious controversies respect- 1664.

Attack upon Pavonia, Hoboken, and Long and Manhattan Islands.— Prudent conduct of the Governor. — Restoration of peace. — Flourishing condition of the colony.

ing the territorial boundaries fixed by conflicting grants of the two governments, occupied a large share of the time and attention of the Governor. In 1664 Charles II. of England granted by letters patent to his brother, the Duke of York, all the territory from the Connecticut River to the shores of the Delaware, embracing the entire possessions held by the Dutch. The Duke immediately sent an English squadron under the command of Colonel Richard Nicolls, to enforce his claim. The fleet anchored in the bay in August, and demanded the surrender of the city and government.

14. Governor Stuyvesant peremptorily refused to capitulate, and for several weeks resisted the popular clamor for surrender. The evident weakness, however, of the fortifications, and the strength of the dominant English faction, finally induced him reluctantly to yield; and on the 3d of September, 1664, the English flag was hoisted upon the public buildings. Early in October the government of the colony was transferred to Nicolls, and the names of New Netherlands and New Amsterdam were changed to "New York," and that of Fort Orange to "Albany." Stuyvesant himself, after a brief visit to Holland, returned to the city where so large a portion of his active life had been spent, took possession of his farm, now traversed by the "Bowery," and died in August, 1682. His remains still repose in the vaults of St. Mark's Church, in Tenth Street.

15. Soon after the surrender of the colony to the English, all that portion of New Netherlands now constituting the State of New Jersey was conveyed by the Duke of York to Lord Berkeley and Sir George Carteret, and a separate proprietary government established. The settlements on the Delaware pertained to the New York colony until their purchase by William Penn in 1682, when they were annexed to Pennsylvania; and Long Island was purchased by the Duke of York, in disregard of the claims of the Connecticut colony, and became annexed to New York, where it has since remained. Staten Island had been purchased by the Dutch Company in 1661 from its owners, and several small settlements on that territory and on Long Island effected.

Controversies respecting boundaries. — Grant of patent to the Duke of York. — Arrival of an English fleet, and surrender of the colony to Colonel Nicolls. — Death of Governor Stuyvesant. — Transfer of New Jersey. — The Delaware settlements. — Purchase and annexation of Long Island.

New York City Hall in 1679, cor. Pearl Street and Coentijs Slip.

THIRD PERIOD.

ENGLISH GOVERNMENT TO THE PERIOD OF THE FRENCH AND INDIAN WAR.

CHAPTER I.

ADMINISTRATION OF GOVERNORS NICOLLS, LOVELACE, AND ANDROS.

1. COLONEL NICOLLS, soon after entering upon his official duties as Governor, remodelled the city charter, changing the form of the municipal government by placing the executive power in the hands of a mayor, aldermen, and sheriff, to be appointed by the Governor. The mayoralty was conferred upon Thomas Willett, one of the first Plymouth emigrants. The power to enact laws and impose taxes was retained in the hands of the Governor and his Council.

1665.

Governor Nicolls. — New city charter.

2. The titles of the owners of property throughout the province under the Dutch Government were formally confirmed by new grants, involving a heavy burden of expense upon the proprietors. This, together with the increase of taxation consequent upon the organization of a new government, the strengthening and repair of the forts, and preparations for defence against an apprehended invasion from Holland, rendered the new administration somewhat unpopular; and in 1668, Governor Nicolls asked for and obtained his recall. Having engaged in a subsequent war with Holland, he was killed in a naval engagement in 1672.

1668.

3. He was succeeded in the government of the province by Colonel FRANCIS LOVELACE, whose administration proved even more unacceptable than that of his predecessor. To the remonstrances of the people and their protest against taxation without representation he turned a deaf ear, denouncing their complaints as scandalous and seditious, — fit only to be burned by the hands of the common hangman. "The people," he informed them, "should have liberty for no thought but how to pay their taxes."

4. War having been declared in 1672 by England against Holland, the Dutch promptly availed themselves of the opportunity to regain their lost possessions in America. A squadron of five ships was despatched in the summer of 1673 for the reconquest of the province and city of New York. Lovelace, without making any suitable preparations for defence, placed the fort in the hands of Captain John Manning, and proceeded to Albany for the settlement of some Indian difficulties in that quarter.

1672.

1673.

5. On receiving information of the approach of the fleet, he returned to the city, and set about vigorous measures for resistance, which, however, were speedily abandoned, and he again left the city. On the 29th of July the squadron made its appearance off Sandy Hook, and on the succeeding day anchored at Staten Island. The Governor was again sent for, and Manning hastily made every preparation for defence. Not being seconded

---

Confirmation of Dutch titles. — Recall and death of Nicolls. — Francis Lovelace. — His arbitrary measures. — War between England and Holland. — Despatch of a squadron for the reconquest of New York.

in these efforts by the inhabitants, either of the city or province, resistance was apparently hopeless.

6. The city having been summoned to surrender by the officers of the squadron, a heavy cannonade was opened against the fort without being returned; and Captain Anthony Colve, with six hundred men, soon effected a landing, and ranged themselves before the fort preparatory to taking possession of the city. Manning attempted a parley, and ineffectually endeavored to open a negotiation with the commander; but in the absence of any authority for definite proposals, he was compelled to surrender the fort, with permission to the garrison to retire with the honors of war. The city was again in possession of the Dutch Government under the name of New Orange; several of the English soldiers were sent to Holland as prisoners; and Lovelace returned with the squadron to Europe, leaving Captain Anthony Colve in command of the province.

7. Manning was subsequently, on its recovery, tried and convicted by court-martial for cowardice and treachery, and adjudged to have his sword broken over his head by the executioner in front of the City Hall, and to be incapacitated from thereafter holding any civil or military office in the gift of the Crown. Lovelace was also severely reprimanded by the English Government, and his estate confiscated. There seems no sufficient evidence against Manning to warrant so ignominious a punishment; but the English were smarting under a humiliating defeat, and were little disposed to mete out strict justice to those who in any way had contributed to its infliction.

8. During the brief administration of Colve the city and its defences were strengthened and placed upon an effective military footing, in apprehension of an effort for its recapture by the English. The claims of the Dutch to the entire province were reasserted and vigorously maintained. On the 9th of February, 1674, however, the territory was restored to the English by the provisions of a treaty with the States-General, and in November subsequently delivered up to their possession. A new patent for the territory, confirming the previous grant

1674.

Inefficiency of Lovelace and Manning. — Recapture of the city. — Return of Lovelace to Europe. — Proceedings against Manning and Lovelace. — Administration of Colve. — Restoration of the province to the English.

to the Duke of York, was issued, and Major EDMUND ANDROS appointed Governor.

9. Thus terminated, at the close of half a century from its commencement, the government of the Dutch over the city and province built up chiefly by their efforts and maintained by their care. Whatever may have been the defects of their administration of its internal and external affairs, measured by the more liberal standard of subsequent events, the social and domestic virtues of its primitive inhabitants, their indomitable patience and steady perseverance under the most discouraging trials and sufferings, and their strict honesty and integrity, simple manners, and blameless lives, have unquestionably exerted a powerful influence upon the character and civil and political institutions of the State which they founded.

10. Governor Andros pursued in his government the same arbitrary and oppressive course, under the directions of the Duke, as had characterized the administration of his predecessors, — repressing every effort on the part of the people for a share in the public councils, — and availing himself of every pretext for the increase of his power. He attempted the extension of his jurisdiction to the Connecticut River on the east, but, finding the people of that province prepared to dispute his claims by force, abandoned the undertaking. He however succeeded in planting a settlement and establishing a fort in Maine, between the Penobscot and Kennebec Rivers, and in adding to his territories Martha's Vineyard and Nantucket, and a small tract between the Delaware and Schuylkill.

1680.   11. In 1680 he was summoned to England to answer charges preferred by the proprietors of the New Jersey Government, of interference with their privileges. On his acquittal he again returned, with renewed instructions for the continuance of his oppressive measures. The resistance of the people, however, and the counsels of the celebrated William Penn,

1683.   induced the Duke to modify his pretensions; and in 1683 Andros was recalled, and Colonel THOMAS DONGAN appointed as his successor, with instructions to convoke a popular Assembly.

General characteristics of the Dutch Government. — Arbitrary measures of Andros. — Accession of territory. — Charges by New Jersey proprietors. Recall of Andros. — Thomas Dongan. — Concessions of the Duke.

CHAPTER II.

ADMINISTRATION OF THOMAS DONGAN.

1. IN accordance with his instructions, Governor Dongan, immediately upon his arrival, directed the call of a representative Assembly, which, consisting of ten councillors and seventeen representatives chosen by the people, and presided over by himself, convened in the city of New York, on the 17th of October, 1683. The first act of this body was to frame a Charter of Liberties, vesting the supreme legislative power in the Governor, Council, and people, in general assembly, conferring the right of suffrage on the freeholders without restraint, and establishing trial by jury. *1683.*

2. The imposition of any tax without consent of the Assembly, the quartering of soldiers or seamen on the inhabitants against their will, the declaration of martial law, or the questioning of any person professing faith in God, by Jesus Christ, for any differences of opinion in religious matters, were prohibited. Assemblies were directed to be convened at least triennially, and the delegates were apportioned according to population, for which purpose the province was divided into twelve counties, with twenty-one representatives, which number was afterwards increased to twenty-seven.

3. The Duke of York having succeeded to the English throne under the title of James II., many arbitrary exactions were again imposed upon the colony, — representative governments discouraged, freedom of the press prohibited, and a general feeling of insecurity induced. Strong efforts were made for the introduction of the Roman Catholic religion against the convictions of the people. All the offices of government, including the highest, were filled by Catholics. Governor Dongan was instructed to favor the introduction of Catholic priests among the Iroquois tribe of Indians; but apprehensive of the ambitious designs of the French for the extension of their *1685.*

Governor Dongan. — Representative Assembly. — Charter of Liberties. — Accession of James II. — Arbitrary measures of the King.

influence in this quarter, he effectually resisted the adoption of this policy. These tribes continued faithful to the English alliance, and successfully defended themselves against the invasions of the French.

4. During the past twenty years, the confederated Iroquois tribes, availing themselves of their knowledge of the use of fire-arms, acquired from their intimacy with the Dutch colonists, had renewed their hereditary warfare with the Hurons, defeated and extirpated the Eries, south of the lake of that name, and obtained a complete ascendency over all the hostile tribes from the Kennebec to the Mississippi and Missouri Rivers.

5. They had, moreover, held at bay the French forces in Canada; thrice repelled with severe loss the invasions of Champlain, and in their turn attacked the territory of New France. Though defeated and repulsed in this undertaking, they continued their hostilities in the face of the utmost power of the French authorities, — disregarding all efforts at conciliation, and declining the mediation even of the Jesuit missionaries, with whom they were on the most friendly terms, — until they had obtained an unquestioned superiority, and had even laid siege to Quebec.

6. The English colonies, in the mean time, had strengthened and confirmed their alliance with the tribes, notwithstanding the explicit instructions forwarded from the home government to preserve friendly relations with the French. In 1684 a council of chiefs and warriors met the governors of New York and Virginia at Albany, where the "pipe of peace" was smoked, the hatchet permanently buried, and the chain of concord brightened and its links firmly riveted. The arrival of a messenger from De la Barre, the French governor of Canada, had only the effect of confirming their resolutions, and stimulating their hostility to their ancient enemies.

7. De la Barre, immediately on his return, set in motion a formidable army of six hundred French soldiers, four hundred Indians, and seven hundred Canadians, with the view of attacking the English fort on the southern shore of Lake Ontario;

Adhesion of the Iroquois to the English, and resistance to the French. — Conquests of the Iroquois. — Alliance with the English. — Council at Albany. — Invasion of the French.

but, after crossing the lake and disembarking his troops, he found himself compelled by the unhealthiness of the season and his fruitless efforts to encounter his foes to offer terms of peace, which were haughtily accepted, and he was allowed to depart, leaving his allies at the mercy of their implacable enemies.

8. He was succeeded in his command in the ensuing year by Denonville, with a reinforcement of French troops. The attempt to establish a fort at Niagara was resisted by Governor Dongan, who claimed the entire territory south of the Great Lakes as belonging to England, and was rendered futile by the active and watchful hostility of the confederated tribes.

9. In 1687, Lamberville, the missionary to the Onondagas, was employed by the French to decoy the Iroquois chiefs into Fort Ontario, where they were arrested, put in irons, sent to Quebec, and from thence to Europe, and chained to the oars in the galleys at Marseilles. Lamberville, as the unconscious instrument of this treachery, was protected by the chiefs of the tribe from the vengeance of the warriors. 1687.

10. In the mean time the Seneca country was overrun by the French troops without serious resistance, and a fort erected at Niagara. The Senecas and the Onondagas in their turn made a descent upon the fort; and peace was finally proposed, through the mediation of Dongan, on condition of the ransom of the French prisoners, the restoration of the spoils taken from the Senecas, and the destruction of the fort. These propositions having been rejected, the Iroquois flew to arms, and twelve hundred warriors immediately started for Montreal. This display of energy on the part of the tribes secured the acceptance of the terms proposed, and the abandonment by the French of the entire region south of the Great Lakes.

11. Governor Dongan, in the mean time, having become obnoxious to the English monarch by his undisguised efforts in favor of the Protestant interests of the province against the intolerant policy of the King, was recalled, and FRANCIS NICHOLSON, the deputy of Sir Edmund Andros, who 1688.

Failure of De la Barre. — Denonville. — Lamberville's treachery. — Fort at Niagara. — Mediation of Dongan. — Abandonment of the Iroquois country by the French. — Recall of Dongan and appointment of Nicholson.

had been commissioned as Governor both of New England and of New York, assumed, in August, 1688, the temporary charge of the government.

1689. 12. Intelligence was, however, soon received of the abdication of James II. and the succession to the English throne of William and Mary, the Prince and Princess of Orange. Under these circumstances the authority of Nicholson as the representative of the deposed king was questioned by a large portion of the inhabitants of the city and province; and the respective adherents of the late and present sovereigns, stimulated by their religious dissensions and their political views, ranged themselves into parties known as democratic and aristocratic.

13. On the one hand it was contended that the change of government in England in no respect affected the existing condition of affairs in the province, and that the commission to Andros by James, and the delegation of his power to Nicholson, remained unrevoked, and in full force, until the pleasure of the new monarchs should be known. On the other hand it was maintained that the entire government, including that of the colonies, was overthrown by the revolution; and that, as no individual was invested with authority in the province, the power reverted to the people, who might designate the proper persons for its exercise until the will of the sovereigns should be expressed.

14. Among the principal adherents to the former of these views were the Governor himself and most of the wealthy and aristocratic of the citizens, including Van Cortlandt, the Mayor, Nicholas Bayard, commander of the city militia, Frederick Philipse and others of the municipal authorities, and members of the Council; while the great mass of the people, including the officers and members of the five train-bands, under the command of Colonel Bayard, were enthusiastic advocates of democratic opinions. These views were also countenanced by the inhabitants of Long Island, who deposed their magistrates, chose others in their stead, and despatched a large body of militia to New York to seize the fort.

15. The popular party was headed by Jacob Leisler, senior captain of the city train-bands, and one of the oldest and wealthiest of the inhabitants, a zealous opponent of the Catholic faith, and a man of great energy and determination of character. At first he declined countenancing the attempt to gain possession of the fort, where the public funds were deposited; but this enterprise having been achieved without resistance, he repaired thither with forty-seven men, and was cordially welcomed by the citizens as their leader. Nicholson in the mean while had returned to England.

CHAPTER III.

Administration of Jacob Leisler and Governors Sloughter and Fletcher.

1. Leisler, on entering upon his assumed powers as captain of the fort in behalf of the new sovereigns, proceeded at once to strengthen its defences by the erection of a battery of six guns beyond its walls. This was the origin of the public park since known as the "Battery." In the absence of the Governor, a Committee of Safety, chosen by the citizens, invested Leisler with the command of the city and province, while the Mayor and other official dignitaries retired to Albany. 1689.

2. In November, Milborne, the son-in-law and private secretary of the new commander, was despatched to Albany with an armed force, to secure the recognition of his authority in the northern provinces, as well as to protect them, in the event of such recognition, from the threatened assaults of the Indians in their neighborhood. This enterprise was, however, fruitless, as these provinces declined to sanction his usurpation of power.

3. A despatch from the Prince of Orange was received in December, at the fort, directed to the late Governor, or, in his absence, to such person as might be in charge of the government, empowering him to take the chief command of the province.

Jacob Leisler. — The fort and battery. — Committee of Safety. — Opposition in the northern portion of the province. — Recognition of the Leisler government by William and Mary.

Under this authority Leisler proceeded to the formal organization of the executive department, dissolved the Committee of Safety, appointed a council of advisers, and assumed the entire civil and military command of the city and province.

1690. 4. In February, 1690, during the war between the English and the French, known in history as "King William's War," a party of some three hundred French and Indians attacked and burned the city of Schenectady on the Mohawk, killed sixty of the inhabitants, who were aroused at midnight from their slumbers, and took thirty prisoners. The imminence of the peril from these deadly onslaughts of their savage enemies induced the speedy recognition, by the northern provinces, of the authority of Leisler, who with their assistance engaged with great vigor in the expeditions against the French and Indians. He organized and fitted out the first man-of-war fleet ever despatched from the port of New York, and actively co-operated with the authorities of Massachusetts and Connecticut in an unsuccessful effort for the reduction of Montreal and Quebec.

1691. 5. At the commencement of the ensuing year Richard Ingoldsby arrived from England with intelligence of the appointment of Colonel HENRY SLOUGHTER as Governor, and, without producing any credentials of authority, demanded the surrender of the fort, which was refused by Leisler, who, however, expressed his readiness to yield the government to Sloughter on his arrival. This event occurred in March, and Leisler immediately sent messengers to him for orders. These messengers were detained, and Ingoldsby was despatched to the fort with verbal directions for its surrender, which at first were disregarded, but on the succeeding day complied with by Leisler, who, with Milborne and others, were immediately arrested, and imprisoned, and the two former tried, convicted, and condemned to suffer death under a charge of treason.

6. Governor Sloughter long hesitated to enforce this sentence by issuing his warrant for its execution, chiefly on the ground

---

Formal assumption of the administration. — Burning of Schenectady. — Naval expedition against Quebec and Montreal. — Arrival of Ingoldsby. — Governor Sloughter. — Refusal of Leisler to surrender the government. — Arrest of Leisler and Milborne.

of its manifest injustice, and the absence of a fair and impartial trial. When, however, all attempts to procure his signature had proved fruitless, the enemies of Leisler and Milborne took advantage of a feast to which the Governor was invited in May, to obtain his consent when under the influence of wine, and before his recovery from intoxication the prisoners were executed.

7. In June the treaties between the Iroquois and the inhabitants of the province were renewed at a council held with the chiefs of the confederated tribes at Albany; a popular Assembly was convened by the Governor, and a liberal constitution formed under his sanction and approval. On the 2d of August, the life and administration of Sloughter were ignominiously brought to a sudden close by a severe attack of illness induced by intemperance.

8. He was succeeded by BENJAMIN FLETCHER, a man of moderate abilities, strong passions, and aristocratic tendencies, averse to religious toleration, and opposed to all popular concessions. He, however, prudently listened to the counsels of Major Schuyler, of Albany, in reference to his treatment of the Indian difficulties; and under the leadership of that gallant and intrepid officer the English and their faithful allies of the Five Nations signally defeated the French in the vicinity of Lake Champlain and drove them beyond the St. Lawrence. *1692.*

9. In 1693 the first printing-press was established in the city by William Bradford of Philadelphia, who was employed by the city government to print the corporation laws. A few years subsequently, as will hereafter be seen, he established the pioneer newspaper of the city, an enterprise which proved eminently successful. *1693.*

10. Governor Fletcher next addressed himself to a vigorous effort for the introduction into the province and city of the English Church and the English language. Strange as it may seem, the majority of the inhabitants still spoke the Dutch language,

---

Trial and execution. — Treaties with the Iroquois. — Formation of a liberal constitution. — Death of Sloughter. — Accession of Benjamin Fletcher. — Defeat of the French. — William Bradford establishes the first printing-press.

and regarded the Dutch Church as the established Church of the province. They were accordingly naturally averse to any change in these respects.

11. The Governor, however, succeeded in procuring from the Assembly, in September, 1693, an act, the provisions of which, though admitting of a more liberal construction, were interpreted by him as authority for the recognition of the Protestant Episcopal instead of the Dutch Church as the establishment. Under this act Trinity Church was erected and organized in 1696, and opened for worship in February of the ensuing year.

<small>1696.</small> 12. In June, 1696, Count Frontenac, then Governor-General of Canada, assembled an army near Montreal for an expedition against the Iroquois, whose animosity against the French had been uniformly displayed since the earliest settlement of the province. His army was composed of the regular troops and such of the Indian tribes as were allies of the French and hereditary enemies of the Iroquois. With these forces he ascended the St. Lawrence, coasted the eastern waters of Lake Ontario, ascended the Oswego River, and encamped upon the borders of Onondaga Lake, whence he penetrated into the wilderness in search of his enemies.

13. Finding their principal village deserted, and discovering no trace of their footsteps, he retraced his march, only to find that his path had been waylaid by his subtle foes, who continued to harass his progress until he had finally crossed their <small>1697.</small> territories. In the following year the war between England and France was terminated by the peace of Ryswick.

14. At about this period an organized system of privateering on the high seas between Europe and America prevailed extensively, and was even believed to be connived at and encouraged by the European governments for the annoyance of the commerce of their enemies. The American coasts suffered severely from these depredations, which soon assumed the form of piracy with all its attendant horrors. The merchant-vessels of New York were destroyed within sight of the harbor itself, and ships were boldly seized while lying at anchor near the wharves.

Church controversy. — Trinity Church. — Invasion of Frontenac. — Termination of King William's War. — Piratical depredations.

15. Repeated and pressing complaints were made to the provincial and municipal authorities, and the suppression of this iniquitous traffic was loudly demanded. But the provincial and municipal authorities were themselves suspected of participating directly or indirectly in the profits of these buccaneering expeditions; and among others the Governor himself was seriously implicated. The English Government found itself compelled to resort to vigorous measures for the suppression of these flagrant abuses; and in 1695 Fletcher was recalled, and Earl Bellamont, an Irish peer, appointed in his stead, with instructions to rid the seas of their piratical occupants.

CHAPTER IV.

Earl of Bellamont, Lord Cornbury, and Lieutenant-Governor Ingoldsby.

1. It was not until 1698, that the Earl of Bellamont, who was also subsequently commissioned as Governor of Massachusetts, and was distinguished for capacity and integrity, assumed his position as the successor of Fletcher. A stock company for the suppression of piracy was organized in England under the direct patronage of the King and many of the nobility, and an armed vessel fitted out for this purpose and placed under the command of the celebrated Captain WILLIAM KIDD, one of the boldest and most successful ship-masters of New York.

1698.

2. This vessel, in April, 1696, sailed from Plymouth, England, and, after recruiting at New York, proceeded on its course to the East Indies and Africa. The commander, however, finding his crew favorable to such an enterprise, abandoning his original undertaking, entered upon a bold and daring career of piracy along the coasts of Malabar and Madagascar, returning to New York in 1698 with an immense booty, large portions of which were concealed on the eastern shores of Long Island.

3. He then proceeded openly to Boston, where he was

Fletcher recalled. — Appointment of Earl Bellamont. — Earl of Bellamont. — Captain Kidd.

arrested, by the orders of the Governor, on a charge of piracy and murder, and transported to England for trial, convicted and executed in 1701. His treasures, so far as discovered, were secured by Bellamont, who was himself suspected, although without apparent cause, of a secret participation in his nefarious enterprises.

1699. 4. Lord Bellamont on his arrival attached himself at once to the democratic or Leislerian party, with whom he was a great favorite, having interested himself in England in the reversal of the attainder against Leisler. On the 18th of May, 1699, a new Assembly was convened, strongly democratic in its composition, which, after receiving assurances of his favorable disposition, voted him a revenue for six years, and passed vigorous acts for the suppression of piracy, and for a general indemnity to State offenders. Under the latter act the families of Leisler and Milborne were reinstated in their possessions. Their remains were also disinterred with great ceremony and deposited in the Dutch church in Garden Street, attended by an immense concourse of people, including the Governor himself.

5. On the death of Bellamont, which occurred soon after, Lieutenant-Governor Nanfan temporarily succeeded to his authority. Colonel Bayard, the inveterate enemy and persecutor of Leisler, and the author of the act under which he was condemned and executed, was himself arrested, tried, and convicted for a similar offence in vilifying the administration of Nanfan, inciting the soldiers to rebellion, and other treasonable acts. He, with John Hutchins, another offender, was sentenced to death, but reprieved by the Governor until the King's pleasure should be known. On the arrival of Cornbury, however, the newly appointed Governor, he was released, the Leislerian party discountenanced, and their opponents taken into favor.

1702. 6. EDWARD HYDE, subsequently created Lord CORNBURY, assumed in May, 1702, the duties of Governor of the combined provinces of New York and New Jersey, the latter having been added to his jurisdiction by surrender of the

---

Political views of Bellamont. — Proceedings of the Assembly. — Reversal of attainders of Leisler and Milborne. — Reinterment of their remains. — Death of Bellamont. — Lieutenant-Governor Nanfan. — Trial and conviction of Bayard. — Arrival of Cornbury.

patent of the proprietors. A revenue of seven years was voted him, his salary doubled, and the expenses of his voyage reimbursed by the Assembly, which was devoted to his interests. A public dinner was given him, and the freedom of the city formally bestowed in a gold box. The members of his suite, the soldiers of the garrison, and all citizens unable to purchase their freedom, were also made freemen, with the rights of suffrage, of trade, and of holding office.

7. The corporation of the city, having resolved upon the establishment of a grammar-school, in the absence of any suitably qualified teacher in New York directed a petition to be forwarded to the Bishop of London, entreating him to forward them a native-born English teacher, of good learning, pious life and conversation, and good temper. Lord Cornbury's influence in the matter was urgently but ineffectually requested. It was not until 1705 that the school was finally established and Andrew Clarke appointed master.

8. The administration of Lord Cornbury was chiefly distinguished for its intolerance, licentiousness, dishonesty, and misrule. He engaged, in direct opposition to his instructions from the Queen, in a systematic persecution of all religious denominations dissenting from the Church of England, plundered the public treasury, involved himself in private debts, and opposed every effort on the part of the representatives of the people for the security of their rights and the growth of free institutions. He was finally, in 1708, recalled, through the pressure of popular sentiment, and cast into prison by his creditors, where he remained until released by the accession of his peerage, on the death of his father. John Lord Lovelace was appointed his successor, but retained the office a little more than a year, when he died, leaving the government in the hands of Lieutenant-Governor Ingoldsby. *1708.*

9. In 1709, during Queen Anne's War, a military and naval force of eighteen hundred men was fitted out in the combined colonies of New York and New Jersey, to proceed against Montreal by way of Lake Champlain. The expedition *1709.*

Honor to Lord Cornbury. — Establishment of a grammar-school. — Character of Cornbury. — Lord Lovelace. — Richard Ingoldsby. — Queen Anne's War.

was, however, after proceeding as far as Wood Creek, abandoned, in consequence of the absence of effective co-operation on the part of England, and mismanagement on that of Ingoldsby, who was accordingly removed. In 1711 another expedition of four thousand men was organized in these two provinces, in conjunction with Connecticut, to co-operate with an English fleet under the command of Sir Hovenden Walker in an attack upon Canada, which also proved a failure, entailing upon the provinces, however, a heavy burden of debt, and seriously embarrassing their resources for several years.

1711.

CHAPTER V.

ROBERT HUNTER, WILLIAM BURNET, AND JOHN MONTGOMERIE.

1. EARLY in the summer of 1710 ROBERT HUNTER arrived in the province with a commission as Governor, bringing over with him three thousand Germans, natives of the Palatinate, driven from their homes by the persecution of Louis XIV. of France. Several of their number took up their abode in New York City, where they erected a Lutheran church; others settled upon Livingston's Manor on the Hudson, on the tract now known as the German Flatts; but the greater part found permanent homes in Pennsylvania, where their descendants still reside.

1710.

2. The new Governor was a man of superior abilities and excellent character; but, conceiving himself bound by his instructions to support the claims of the Crown, and repress the growing spirit of insubordination in the province, he at once attached himself to the aristocratic party, and strengthened its influence by every means in his power. His Council was selected from the ablest, wealthiest, and most influential men of the colony. He secured the warm support of Lewis Morris, one of the greatest landholders in the combined provinces of New York and New Jersey, the son of Richard Morris, an officer in

---

Expeditions against Canada. — Arrival of Governor Hunter. — German immigrants. — Character of Hunter. — His energetic administration. — Lewis Morris.

Cromwell's army, who had emigrated to America and purchased a manor ten miles square, in the neighborhood of Harlem, to which he gave the name of Morrisania, and where his son now resided.

3. The unsuccessful expedition for the conquest of Canada, in which the Governor, with the sanction of his Council and the Provincial Assemblies, entered with great zeal and enthusiasm, produced a discouraging effect upon his subsequent measures, and seriously impaired his influence with the people. His request for a permanent appropriation for the support of the government was met by a decided and persistent refusal of the Assembly, which could only be prevailed upon to furnish supplies for a single year. The Indian tribes had become distrustful and unreliable; and a rumored insurrection of the negroes had created a riotous panic in the city, resulting in the firing of several buildings, the death of many white citizens, and the arrest and execution of nineteen of the negroes. 1711-12.

4. The war between England and France having been terminated by the treaty of Utrecht, the contest between the Governor and the Assembly on the question of supplies was again renewed, and after a protracted struggle a government revenue was secured, independent of the people, for the term of three years. A Court of Chancery was established and confirmed. Lewis Morris was appointed Chief-Justice of the province, and taxes on British imports and tonnage duties on foreign vessels were imposed. In 1719 failing health compelled the Governor to return to England, leaving the government in the hands of Peter Schuyler, the eldest member of the Council. 1715. 1719.

5. During the brief period which elapsed before the arrival of Governor Hunter's successor the affairs of the province were successfully administered by Schuyler, whose long familiarity with public affairs, and especially the high regard in which he was held by the Indian tribes, enabled him to carry on the government to the general acceptation of the people. 1720.

Expedition against Canada. — Effect of its failure. — Contest between the Governor and the Assembly. — Court of Chancery. — Chief Justice. — Taxes on imports and tonnage duties. — Return of Governor Hunter to England. — Peter Schuyler.

He succeeded in completely restoring the relations of amity and concord between the Iroquois and the English, which had previously been seriously interrupted.

6. William Burnet, son of the celebrated Bishop Burnet of England, arrived on the 17th of September, 1720, as Governor of the two provinces, and immediately entered upon his duties. He was a man of fine talents, popular in his manners, and frank and upright in all his dealings. The Assembly convened five years previously was retained in office, and signalized his accession and complaisance by voting him a revenue for the ensuing five years. He took into his counsels, such men as Lewis Morris, Cadwallader Colden, Peter Schuyler, Gerardus Beekman, Abraham De Peyster, and William Smith, through whose influence he succeeded in gaining, and for a considerable period retaining, the public confidence.

1722. 7. To counteract the efforts which the French were secretly making through their agents — the Jesuits, missionaries, and others — to secure a monopoly of the Indian trade along the northern and western frontiers, Governor Burnet, in 1722, with the sanction of the Assembly, commenced the erection of a trading-post at Oswego, with the design of following it up with a line of similar posts extending from the great northern lakes to the mouth of the Mississippi. A convention of deputies from the several provinces assembled at Albany, and forwarded to the King a memorial strongly urging the adoption of this policy, which, however, failed to receive the royal assent, and was reluctantly abandoned.

1724. 8. A powerful opposition had in the mean time sprung up against his administration, originating in the disaffection of a large party of merchants and others interested in the French trading policy; and the Assembly, imbued with this spirit, had withdrawn its confidence from its former favorite, 1727. and refused the renewal of supplies except for a period of three years. The Governor in 1727 dissolved this body:

Renewal of friendly relations with the Indian tribes. — Arrival of G1 ernor Burnet. — His character and popularity. — French missionaries a˙ traders. — Trading-post at Oswego. — Convention of delegates at Alban — Memorial to the King. — Abandonment of the undertaking. — Opp˙ tion to the Governor in the Assembly.

but its successor proved still more unyielding and refractory, and was in its turn dissolved. Through the influence of his persevering enemies Burnet was transferred, on the accession of George II., to the government of Massachusetts, and the law prohibiting the French trade repealed.

9. During this administration the first public newspaper was established in the city of New York, by William Bradford, the government printer, under the title of the New York Gazette. It was published weekly, at first on a half-sheet, increased during the following year to four pages. 1729.

10. The successor of Governor Burnet, John Montgomerie, entered upon his duties on the 15th of April, 1728, as Governor and Chancellor of New York and New Jersey. He was cordially welcomed by the citizens, presented with the freedom of the city in a gold box, and by the Assembly with a revenue for five years. The principal event of his brief administration was the grant, in 1730, of a new city charter. He died on the 1st of July, 1731, and was succeeded by Rip Van Dam, the eldest member of the Council, who discharged the duties of the office for thirteen months, when Colonel William Cosby, the new Governor, arrived. 1728-31.

CHAPTER VI.

Administration of Governor Cosby.— Trial of Zenger.

1. Cosby's administration was tumultuous, despotic, and exceedingly obnoxious to the people. His arbitrary and avaricious disposition kept him in continual collision with the various factions into which the city and province were divided; and his arrival at a period when liberal principles were rapidly attaining a decided ascendency, through the agency of the press and public discussion, plunged him at once into the vortex of popular dissension, and prepared the way for those decisive events which culminated in the American Revolution. 1732.

Transfer of Burnet to Massachusetts. — Repeal of the Prohibitory Act. — Establishment of the first newspaper. — Governor Montgomerie. — Rip Van Dam. — William Cosby.

2. His first act was the production of a royal order directing an equal division with himself of the salary of his immediate predecessor, Van Dam, during the brief period of his temporary administration. The latter expressed his assent to this arrangement, on condition that Cosby should reciprocate by an equal participation of the perquisites received by him since his appointment and previous to his assumption of office. In this demand he was supported by the popular voice, which refused to recognize the justice of heaping pecuniary emoluments upon favored foreigners, while depriving native-born officers of their vested rights.

3. Legal proceedings were accordingly instituted in the Supreme Court of the province by Cosby against Van Dam for the recovery of the amount claimed. As the Governor himself was, by virtue of his office, chancellor, and two of the other judges, De Lancey and Philipse, his personal friends, exceptions were taken by the counsel for the defence against the jurisdiction of the court. A majority of the judges, however, against Chief-Justice Morris, overruled the exceptions, and directed the payment to Cosby of half of Van Dam's salary. Morris was promptly removed from office, and De Lancey appointed in his place, without even the formality of consulting the Council.

4. These high-handed and arbitrary proceedings of the Governor roused the public indignation to a high pitch. The popular discontent at first vented itself in squibs, lampoons, and satirical ballads, levelled against the aristocracy, which speedily culminated in systematic attacks, through the columns of the New York Weekly Journal, edited by John Peter Zenger — against the Governor, Council, Assembly, and Court, arraigning them in the strongest terms for a violation of the liberties, rights, and privileges of the people, for the tyrannical assumption of arbitrary and despotic power, and for the perversion of their official stations to purposes of personal resentment and private emolument.

5. The Council in November, 1734, ordered these papers to be burnt by the hands of the common hangman, and a few day

---

Controversy with Van Dam. — Proceedings in court. — Arbitrary measures of Cosby. — Popular discontent. — John Peter Zenger.

afterwards Zenger was arrested and imprisoned on a criminal charge for publishing a seditious libel against the government. The grand jury having refused to find a bill of indictment for this offence, an information was, in January, 1735, filed against the prisoner by the Attorney-General, and after a protracted confinement he was brought up for trial on the 4th of August, 1735. His friends in the mean time, and an association known as the "Sons of Liberty" for the protection and advocacy of popular rights, had secured the services of the venerable Andrew Hamilton, of Philadelphia, then eighty years of age, but in full possession of all his faculties, as counsel for the defence.

1735.

6. This remarkable trial took place in the City Hall, before the judges of the Supreme Court, James De Lancey presiding as Chief Justice, Philipse as Judge, and Bradley as Attorney-General. The court-room was crowded to excess by an anxious and excited auditory, and the unexpected appearance of the venerable and eloquent counsel for the prisoner added intense interest to the scene. The plea of "Not guilty" having been interposed, and a jury impanelled, the publication of the alleged libel was boldly admitted, and full proof of its justification offered. The Attorney-General, however, resisted the introduction of this proof, on the ground that in a criminal proceeding for the publication of libellous matter the truth of the facts alleged was inadmissible in evidence. This objection was sustained by the Court.

7. Hamilton then proceeded to address the jury, and in an eloquent and brilliant speech confuted the assumption of the Court that "the greater the truth, the greater was the libel"; insisted that the jury were themselves the judges, not only of the facts, but of the law; that it was their peculiar province to pass upon all the circumstances and bearings of the alleged offence, and to determine for themselves its innocence or guilt; that they were the sworn protectors of the rights, liberties, and privileges of their fellow-citizens, violated in this instance by a most outrageous and vindictive series of persecutions; that it was for them to interpose between the tyrannical and arbitrary violations of law and justice and their intended victim; to assert

Prosecution for libel. — Trial of Zenger.

and uphold the freedom of speech and of the press, and to vindicate by their verdict the supremacy of the people over their wanton and powerful oppressors.

8. Notwithstanding the reiterated charge of the Court that they were judges of the facts only put in issue, and not of the conclusions of law upon those facts; that the truth of the alleged libel was a matter wholly beyond their jurisdiction; and that its publication having been admitted, and all evidence of the facts excluded, it was their imperative duty to convict the prisoner, the jury, after a brief deliberation, unanimously returned a verdict of "Not guilty." Amid the irrepressible applause of the vast crowd of spectators Hamilton was borne in triumph from the hall, and conducted to a splendid entertainment prepared for his reception. A public dinner was next day given him by the citizens, the freedom of the city presented by the corporation, and his departure signalized by the highest and most distinguished honors.

9. Thus terminated this exciting and important trial by the complete triumph of the popular cause, — the vindication of the right of the public press to pass upon the conduct of the public authorities, and to criticise, with entire freedom, their official proceedings, — and the assertion of the unalterable determination of the people to protect their champions and the defenders of their rights against all the assaults of power, and the machinations of tyranny and oppression. The organization effected for the successful accomplishment of these great objects was perpetuated and strengthened for the attainment at no distant period of a still more signal and important triumph.

1736. 10. Cosby, however, notwithstanding the severe repulse he had received through the acquittal of Zenger, still persisted with unyielding pertinacity in his arbitrary and rapacious proceedings. He directed a resurvey of the grants and patents of land in the province with the view of adding to his revenues by the fees, and destroyed several important documents intrusted to him for this purpose. His death on the 10th of March, 1736, put an end to his further proceedings; not, however, until he had once more signalized his inveterate hostility

---

Acquittal of Zenger. — Oppressive proceedings of Cosby.

to the people by the suspension, through his Council, of his former antagonist, Rip Van Dam, who, as the oldest member of the Council, would have been entitled to the administration on his decease.

CHAPTER VII.

ADMINISTRATION OF GEORGE CLARKE. — NEGRO PLOT. — ADMIRAL CLINTON. — SIR DANVERS OSBORNE. — JAMES DE LANCEY. — SIR CHARLES HARDY.

1. GEORGE CLARKE, the next in succession, was inducted into office by the Council, and on the 14th of October subsequently received a commission from England empowering him to act as Lieutenant-Governor until the arrival of Cosby's successor. He endeavored to ingratiate himself with both the aristocratic and the popular party. The Assembly was dissolved, and a new one called, which met in the ensuing summer, but could not be prevailed upon to grant a revenue for a longer period than one year. This precedent was thereafter steadily acted upon by the assemblies subsequently convened. The only act of importance passed during the session was one disfranchising the Jews residing in the province. 1737.

2. At this period New York City contained about ten thousand inhabitants, nearly one fifth of whom were negro slaves. Both the Dutch and English governments had systematically encouraged their importation into the colony, and the principal merchants of the city had engaged in the traffic as a prominent branch of trade and source of profit. The most stringent regulations for their control and subordination were enacted, and every transgression was severely punished; but their great number, thievish propensities, and occasional acts of insubordination, rendered the community sensitively alive to the possible dangers which might arise from their presence. This pervading feeling of insecurity required only a slight provocation to ripen into a general panic. 1741.

Cosby's death. — Exclusion of Van Dam. — George Clarke, Lieutenant-Governor. — Dissolution of Assembly. — Disfranchisement of the Jews. — Slavery in New York.

3. A trifling robbery which occurred in March, 1741, in the house of a merchant, and which was traced to some of the negroes, followed soon after by a series of incendiary fires in different quarters of the city, created a general alarm, and so inflamed the public mind, that numerous arrests were made, and a searching investigation instituted by the authorities, which, however, failed in discovering any reliable traces of the guilty perpetrators. Heavy rewards were offered by the Common Council for their arrest and conviction, together with a full pardon to any of their number who would reveal his knowledge of the conspiracy and denounce his associates. Many of the inhabitants removed their goods from the city, and every effort was made to obtain the faintest clew to the guilty authors of the outrages.

4. The Supreme Court of the province was specially convened for the investigation of the matter, and a grand-jury consisting of the principal inhabitants of the city charged with its consideration. Great numbers of witnesses were examined, and on the testimony of a negro girl, Mary Burton, who had been promised a full pardon, several of the negroes implicated by her were arrested, and, notwithstanding their terrified efforts to secure safety by criminating their innocent associates, were convicted and executed.

5. Other informers speedily appeared, and fresh victims to the popular fury were immolated in great numbers and in quick succession. The populace, maddened by excitement and thirsting for revenge, stimulated the authorities in the prosecution of their hasty inquiries, and even refused to permit any interference on their part with the fate of the condemned, even when, by a compliance with the terms of pardon, they had entitled themselves to immunity.

6. The general fury and panic, unappeased by the wholesale sacrifice of the negroes, soon extended to the white population. John Ury, a reputed Catholic priest and schoolmaster, was denounced by the girl Mary Burton, and notwithstanding his protestations of innocence, and the absence of all rational proof of guilt, was summarily condemned and executed. His arrest was

---

Origin of the negro plot. — Investigation by the authorities. — Public informers.

the signal for the implication of others of the whites; and the reign of terror was fearfully inaugurated throughout the city. The prisons were rapidly filled with the miserable victims of the popular delusion; and so great was their number that infection was averted only by the frequency of executions when pardons could not be effected.

7. From the 11th of May to the 29th of August, the day of the execution of Ury, one hundred and fifty-four negroes were committed to prison, fourteen of whom were burnt at the stake, eighteen hanged, and seventy-one transported. During the same period twenty-four whites were imprisoned, four of whom were executed. The implication by Burton of some of the principal inhabitants who were known to be innocent served to sober down the popular excitement, and restore the community to its wonted composure. The prisons were cleared, a day of general thanksgiving proclaimed, and the ordinary channels of business again resumed.

8. Upon the most candid and impartial survey of all the facts, no substantial justification seems to be afforded for the merciless persecution of the hapless victims of this terrible period. Both informers and witnesses were of the lowest and vilest character, their testimony vague and contradictory, and their inducements to falsehood strong and powerful. Nothing but the irrational panic pervading all classes could have attached any serious weight to the incredible and inconsistent statements of these frightened wretches, driven to perjury by the imminent fear of death, and encouraged in their successful devices by the applause of the terrified multitude. The whole fearful drama seems but a repetition, on a somewhat smaller scale and humbler surrounding, of the celebrated Titus Oates Plot; and the sole excuse for the harsh proceedings of the public authorities consists in their inability in the midst of the prevailing panic to discover the real authors of the crimes originally perpetrated.

9. In September, 1743, Lieutenant-Governor Clarke was superseded by Admiral GEORGE CLINTON, father of the Sir Henry Clinton who commanded the British troops during the subsequent Revolution. He met with a favorable reception,   1743.

Reign of terror. — Number of the victims. — End of the excitement. — Summary of the evidence. — Admiral George Clinton.

received the usual vote of supplies, coincided with the Assembly in all its measures, — among which was one limiting its term and that of its successors to a period of seven years, — and co-operated with that body in fitting out an expedition for the conquest of Canada, in the war then pending between France and England. He soon, however, became involved in a collision between the two leading political factions headed by De Lancey and Colden, which occasioned him no little vexation and embarrassment during the remainder of his term.

1748. 10. In 1748 he ineffectually urged upon the Assembly an appropriation for the support of the government for five years, with the view of again rendering the executive independent of that body. Soon afterwards he made himself obnoxious to the popular party by refusing to surrender for trial the captain of an English war-vessel which had fired upon a colonial vessel, killing one of its passengers, for omission to lower its flag in passing, as required by the regulations of the home government. The persistent refusal of the Assembly to comply with his reiterated demands for a permanent revenue, and the powerful opposition he encountered from all classes of the people, finally induced him, after proroguing the refractory Chamber, to tender his resignation and abandon the government.

1753. 11. He was succeeded on the 7th of September, 1753, by Sir DANVERS OSBORNE, with instructions for the maintenance of the royal prerogative, and the demand of a permanent revenue, to be disbursed solely by himself and his Council. On assuming the government, the corporation of the city presented him with an address of congratulation, at the same time expressing the hope that he would be as averse to countenancing, as they should be to permitting, any infringement upon their civil or religious liberties. A magnificent entertainment was given him by the city, accompanied with the strongest manifestations of popular regard.

12. A few days afterwards the Council was convened and the Governor's instructions were laid before them. On being informed by them that the Assembly would unquestionably refuse obedi-

---

Dissensions with the Assembly. — Popular discontent. — Resignation. — Sir Danvers Osborne. — His reception. — Proceedings of the Council.

ence to the royal commands, he appeared deeply dejected; and on the ensuing morning his body was found suspended by a handkerchief from the garden-wall of his lodgings. He had previously been subject to derangement, owing to domestic losses, and had once before attempted his life. By his death the government devolved upon Lieutenant-Governor JAMES DE LANCEY, who, by his recent persistent and successful opposition to the demands of the Crown, had rendered himself highly popular.

13. A striking change had occurred in the relative position of parties. The aristocratic faction, headed by De Lancey, Colden, Van Rensselaer, Philipse, Heathcote, and others, had now become the popular leaders, while their former opponents had ranged themselves under the royal banner. Hence the position of the new Governor was one of peculiar difficulty. Compelled by the instructions of his predecessor to carry out the policy of the Crown, he found himself at the same time pledged, as the leader of the popular party, to a policy diametrically opposite. While, therefore, he fulfilled the letter of his instructions by laying them before the Assembly, he at the same time urged upon the home government the propriety and necessity of concessions to the popular will.

14. In September, 1755, Sir CHARLES HARDY arrived at New York as Governor, and was received with the usual honors. De Lancey resumed his seat as Chief-Justice; but Hardy, fully conscious of his own deficiencies in the new and unaccustomed field of action which had been assigned him, abandoned all but its nominal duties to his predecessor, and by his return to England and resumption of his post in the navy, left the government again in his charge. 1755.

Suicide. — Accession of Lieutenant-Governor De Lancey. — His policy and its results. — Sir Charles Hardy. — His abandonment of the government and return to England.

Ruins of Fort Ticonderoga.

FOURTH PERIOD.

FROM THE FRENCH AND INDIAN WAR TO THE REVOLUTION.

CHAPTER I.

ADMINISTRATION OF LIEUTENANT-GOVERNOR DE LANCEY. — CAMPAIGNS OF 1754, 1755, AND 1756.

1. AFTER the capture of the Fortress of Louisburg, on Cape Breton Island, then (1745) in possession of the French, by the English fleet under Commodore Warren, and the combined colonial forces under William Pepperell, — a blow rendered the more severe by the vast expense and great strength of the works, — the French entered upon a course of vigorous operations to concentrate and extend their power in America, in opposition to the efforts of their hereditary enemies, the English,

1753.

Preparations of the French for opposing the extension of the British power in America.

who had already obtained so firm a footing. Having established a number of trading-posts and missionary stations among the Indian tribes occupying the depth of the wilderness along the entire valley of the Mississippi most remote from the white settlements, they prepared to assert their possessory claims by such efficient measures as seemed best adapted to the accomplishment of this object.

2. They built a strong fleet of vessels at Kingston, on the Canadian shore of Lake Ontario; strengthened Fort Niagara, at the confluence of the Niagara River with that lake; entered into friendly negotiations with the Delaware tribe of Indians on the east, and the Shawnees on the west of the Alleghany Mountains; and erected a formidable chain of fortifications, commanding the entire valley of the Mississippi and its tributaries from Canada to the Gulf of Mexico.

3. The collision between the Ohio Company, claiming an extensive tract of land on the Ohio River under the English Government, and the French, who were engaged in the erection of forts south of Lake Erie, caused the first military services of GEORGE WASHINGTON to be put in requisition by Governor Dinwiddie, of Virginia. St. Pierre, the commander of the fort to which Washington was despatched, refused to withdraw his troops from its occupation; and in 1754 an unsuccessful effort was made by the Ohio Company to erect a fort on the present site of Pittsburg, at the junction of the Alleghany and Monongahela Rivers. The workmen were driven from the ground by the French, who completed the fort and gave it the name of Fort du Quesne. *1753.* *1754.*

4. Washington, at the head of a body of provincial troops from Virginia, marched into the disputed territory, surprised and routed an advance party of French sent to intercept his approach, and after erecting a small fort, which he named Fort Necessity, and being reinforced by additional troops from New York and the Carolinas, proceeded with four hundred men on his route to Fort du Quesne. Hearing, however, of the advance of a large body of French and Indians, he returned to Fort Necessity, where he

---

Washington's mission to St. Pierre. — Its result. — Establishment by the French of Fort du Quesne.

was soon after attacked by a superior force, and compelled to capitulate after a severe and obstinate resistance, with permission to retire unmolested to Virginia.

5. The English Ministry, in the mean time, aware of the importance of the crisis, had forwarded instructions to their colonies to secure, if possible, the continued friendship and alliance of the Iroquois Indians, and to unite their efforts in the common defence. In accordance with this recommendation a convention of delegates from the respective colonies was held in Albany in the summer of this year, Lieutenant-Governor De Lancey presiding, a treaty with the Six Nations renewed, and a plan of confederation, similar to that subsequently adopted by the Continental Congress, submitted by the celebrated Dr. Benjamin Franklin, of Pennsylvania, and adopted on the fourth day of July. The colonial assemblies and the representatives of the British Government refused, however, to ratify the ordinance of the Convention; and the conduct of the war was confided to the English Parliament, with such aid as the colonies might find themselves able to furnish.

1755. 6. In 1755, General Braddock was sent over as Commander-in-Chief; and at a convention of the colonial governors three expeditions were resolved upon: one against Fort du Quesne, under Braddock himself; one against Niagara; and a third against Crown Point, on the western shore of Lake Champlain. The first was disastrous in the extreme, and the troops engaged in it were saved from total destruction only by the coolness and bravery of Washington. That against Crown Point was intrusted to General Johnson, afterwards Sir William Johnson, a member of the Council of New York.

7. In July, 1755, about six thousand troops from New England, New York, and New Jersey assembled, under the command of General Lyman, of Connecticut, at the head of boat navigation on the Hudson, fifty miles north of Albany, where a strong fortification, afterwards known as Fort Edward, was erected. General Johnson, immediately on his arrival in August,

---

Attack on Fort Necessity, by the French and Indians, and its capitulation by Washington. — Renewal of treaties with the Iroquois. — Convention at Albany, and plan of confederation of Dr. Franklin. — Events of 1755. — General Johnson's campaign. — Fort Edward.

with the main body of the troops, marched to the head of Lake George, where he established a camp preparatory to an attack upon Crown Point, situated on a tongue of land on the southern shore of Lake Champlain.

8. Baron Dieskau, the French commander, in the mean time, with two thousand men, chiefly Canadians and Indians, was approaching from Montreal by way of Lake Champlain; and, abandoning his first intention of attacking Fort Edward, marched directly to the English camp on Lake George. Colonel Williams was immediately despatched by Johnson, with a thousand Massachusetts troops and two hundred Mohawks, under their famous Sachem Hendricks, to intercept the French. After proceeding a few miles, however, the detachment fell into an ambuscade; both Williams and Hendricks were slain, and their comrades fell back in good order upon the camp, hotly pursued by the enemy.

9. Early in September, Dieskau advanced with his forces to the English camp, where, intrenchments having been hastily thrown up, he was received with a spirited fire of musketry and artillery. The Canadian militia and Indians fled to the shelter of the surrounding forests, and the approach of reinforcements under General Lyman from Fort Edward, together with the loss of their leader, Baron Dieskau, who was severely wounded, compelled them to withdraw to the fortifications of Crown Point. Johnson, after having erected a fort called William Henry on the site of his camp, and strengthened Fort Edward, dispersed the residue of his troops, and returned in October to Albany. For his services in this campaign the King bestowed upon him the order of knighthood, and presented him with a large sum of money.

10. The expedition of Shirley against Niagara and Frontenac was unsuccessful. The prevalence of heavy storms, sickness in the camp, desertion of the Indians, and other casualties, prevented any efficient action until the lateness of the season rendered it advisable to relinquish the enterprise. Leaving a suffi-

---

Camp on Lake George. — Attack by Dieskau. — Williams and Hendricks slain. — Dieskau's attack upon the English camp. — Its repulse. — Forts Edward and William Henry. — Johnson's promotion. — Failure of the expedition against Niagara by Shirley.

cient garrison at Oswego under Colonel Mercer, the remainder of the troops were reconducted to Albany, and their commander returned to Massachusetts.

1756. 11. The campaign of 1756, planned by a meeting of the several colonial governors at New York in December preceding, comprised an attack upon Crown Point with ten thousand men, Niagara with six thousand, Fort du Quesne with three thousand, and Quebec and the other French settlements in Canada with two thousand. Shirley was superseded in his command, in the spring of 1756, by Lord Loudoun, Governor of Virginia, with General Abercrombie as his lieutenant.

12. Early in June the latter arrived with General Webb and several regiments of British troops. General Winslow, of Massachusetts, was assigned to the command of the expedition against Crown Point, and with a force of seven thousand men awaited the arrival of Loudoun at Albany, where Abercrombie was engaged in settling vexatious questions of rank between the officers of the regular and provincial troops, and controversies with the citizens growing out of the billeting of the soldiers upon them. Loudoun did not make his appearance until the latter part of July; and before preparations for the commencement of the campaign could be completed, the advance of the season and the successes of the French had rendered them nugatory.

13. In the mean time an attack was made upon Oswego by a body of French troops under De Lery, who penetrated to the fort at the Oneida portage, gained possession of it, and, destroying its stores, returned to Montreal with thirty prisoners. De Villiers, also, with eight hundred men, established a camp in May near the mouth of Sandy Creek, from whence he was enabled to intercept all supplies and reinforcements for the town. Four of the Six Nations — the Onondagas, Oneidas, Cayugas, and Mohawks — sent an embassy to Montreal with a declaration of neutrality and a petition for protection, which met with a favorable response.

14. The Marquis de Montcalm, the successor of Dieskau in

Campaign of 1756. — Arrival of Lord Loudoun, Abercrombie, and Webb. — Dilatory proceedings. — Abandonment of the attack upon Crown Point. — Attack upon Oswego. — Neutrality of a portion of the Iroquois tribes.

the command of the French army, after strengthening the defences of Fort Carillon at Ticonderoga, proceeded, early in August, with three regiments from Quebec and a large force of Canadians and Indians, to the attack of Fort Ontario, which was in charge of Colonel Mercer, Shirley being in command of the principal fort, Oswego, on the west bank of the river, nearly opposite. The fort was gallantly defended for several hours by its garrison, when, their ammunition having been expended, they spiked their guns and retreated to Fort Oswego.

15. Montcalm immediately occupied the height, and turned such of the guns of the fort as were still serviceable upon the remaining fortress. Colonel Mercer was shot down, and a formidable breach made in the walls. On the succeeding day (August 14), as Montcalm was making preparations for storming the intrenchments, the garrison, about sixteen hundred in number, capitulated. One hundred and twenty cannon, six vessels of war, three hundred boats, three chests of money, and stores of ammunition and provisions, with fourteen hundred prisoners, fell into the power of the conquerors as the spoils of victory.

16. After demolishing the forts, Montcalm returned to Canada, leaving the entire region of the Six Nations open to the incursions of the French. A thousand of the regular troops were billeted by Loudoun upon the citizens of New York, notwithstanding the remonstrances of the authorities against this invasion of their rights and privileges under the common law as Englishmen. Overawed by the threats of Loudoun, a subscription was raised by the magistrates, and the demand reluctantly complied with.

Montcalm attacks Forts Ontario and Oswego. — Surrender of the garrison. — Death of Mercer. — Quartering of troops in New York.

CHAPTER II.

SIEGE OF FORT WILLIAM HENRY. — CAPTURE OF TICONDEROGA, CROWN POINT, NIAGARA, FORT DU QUESNE, QUEBEC, AND MONTREAL. — GOVERNORS COLDEN AND MONCKTON.

1. After an ineffectual effort on the part of Lord Loudoun to capture Louisburg, Montcalm, towards the close of July, 1757, proceeded, with a force of about seven thousand whites and two thousand negroes, to lay siege to Fort William Henry, then under the command of Colonel Monro, with three thousand troops. General Webb was at Fort Edward with four thousand men; and with this combined force Colonel Monro deemed his position impregnable. To the demand of Montcalm, on the 4th of August, for surrender of the fort, he returned a defiant answer, and the siege progressed.

1757.

2. An express was despatched by Monro to Webb for reinforcements, which was repeated during the ensuing six days, without eliciting any action on his part other than an advice to capitulate, which was intercepted by the French and forwarded to Monro. Under these discouraging circumstances, and having exhausted his means of defence, that gallant officer sent a flag of truce to Montcalm, with the view of negotiating terms of surrender.

3. The French commander, after a council with the Indians, consented to allow the English to depart from the fort with the honors of war, — delivering up all their prisoners and leaving all their military stores, with a pledge not to serve against the French for eighteen months, — and to furnish an escort for their departure. On the 9th of August this arrangement was carried into effect, — the French took possession of the fort, and the English retired to their intrenched camp.

4. The Indians, meanwhile, having procured from the English the means of intoxication, spent the night in feasting and revelry, and when, on the ensuing morning, the English were preparing for their march to Fort Edward, commenced an in-

---

Siege of Fort William Henry. — Treachery of Webb. — Negotiation for a surrender. — Surrender of the fort.

discriminate attack, plunder, and massacre. In spite of all the efforts of Montcalm and the officers under his command, a large proportion of the defenceless troops were slain or taken captives, and only about six hundred of the whole number succeeded, after encountering the utmost peril, in reaching Fort Edward. Four hundred were rescued by Montcalm from the French camp and sent under a heavy escort to rejoin their comrades, and an officer was despatched by him to ransom the captives. The fort and its appendages were destroyed.

5. The campaign of 1758 commenced under more favorable auspices. William Pitt had succeeded to the reins of government in England, and under his instructions Lord Loudoun was recalled from the command in America, and General Abercrombie appointed in his place. A strong naval force was sent out under Admiral Boscawen, and twelve thousand additional troops forwarded for the defence of the colonies. To these the latter added nearly thirty-five thousand men, of which New York furnished about three thousand, so that on the arrival of Abercrombie he found an effective army of nearly fifty thousand men at his disposal. *1758.*

6. Three several expeditions were speedily organized. General Amherst, with the English troops under the intrepid James Wolfe, was assigned, in conjunction with the naval armament of Boscawen, to the conquest of Louisburg; General Forbes to that of Fort du Quesne and the Ohio Valley; and to Abercrombie himself, with Lord Howe as his lieutenant, was intrusted the capture of Ticonderoga and Crown Point.

7. General Amherst, with a fleet of twenty-two ships of the line and fifteen frigates, and ten thousand effective men, disembarked in front of Louisburg on the 8th of June, and entered vigorously upon the siege of that important fortress. It was not, however, until the 26th of July, that its French defenders, finding further opposition futile, surrendered the town and fort, together with the islands of Cape Breton and St. John (now Prince Edward) and their dependencies, leaving the English masters of the entire territory nearly to the mouth of the St. Lawrence.

Massacre of the garrison by the Indians. — Noble exertions of Montcalm for their rescue. — Destruction of the fort. — Campaign of 1758. — Organization of forces, and plan of the campaign.

8. Meanwhile Abercrombie, with seven thousand regulars, nine thousand provincial troops, and a heavy train of artillery, was thundering against the fortifications of Ticonderoga, then occupied by Montcalm with an inferior force. The gallant Lord Howe, on his march from Lake George, had been attacked and slain by a scouting-party of the enemy. Abercrombie, on the 8th of July, was severely repulsed in an attack upon the fort, and after a bloody conflict of several hours' duration was compelled to retreat to Lake George.

9. The French fort at Frontenac was then attacked by General Bradstreet, aided by a detachment of three thousand men sent by Abercrombie, and a hundred and fifty warriors of the Six Nations. On the 26th of August it was surrendered, with a large collection of military stores for Fort du Quesne, and nine armed vessels. Bradstreet, after destroying the fort, returned to Rome, where he built Fort Stanwix. Abercrombie, having garrisoned Fort George, returned to Albany with his remaining forces, and was soon afterwards superseded in his command by General Amherst.

10. Fort du Quesne, on the 24th of November, surrendered under an attack of the provincial troops, commanded by Washington, though nominally under the control of General Forbes. Its name was changed to that of Fort Pitt, in honor of the great English minister, whose energetic counsels had infused so much spirit into the affairs of the colonies, and contributed so largely to the triumph of its arms.

1759. 11. Abercrombie having been succeeded by General Amherst, twenty thousand provincial troops were, early in the spring, placed at his disposal, and a large land and naval force of regulars sent over from England. General Wolfe was directed to ascend the St. Lawrence and attack Quebec; Amherst himself undertook the conquest of Ticonderoga, after which he was to seize Montreal and unite his forces with those of Wolfe before Quebec; and General Prideaux was to capture Fort Niagara, and proceed to Montreal.

Attack upon Fort Ticonderoga. — Death of Lord Howe. — Repulse of the English. — Retreat to Lake George. — Attack upon Fort Frontenac by Bradstreet. — Recall of Abercrombie and appointment of Amherst. — Capture of Fort du Quesne. — Amherst succeeds Abercrombie. — Plan of the campaign.

12. Ticonderoga was abandoned by the French without a struggle, on the 26th of July. Crown Point surrendered soon afterwards, and was occupied by Amherst, who strengthened its defences by the erection of a strong and impregnable fortress. Prideaux appeared before Niagara on the 17th of July, and, having been mortally wounded on the same day by the bursting of a gun, was succeeded in command by General Johnson. The garrison, in expectation of reinforcements, held out for three weeks. On the 25th, however, after a severe conflict, the fort and its dependencies were compelled to surrender, notwithstanding the accession of an additional force of nearly three thousand French and Indians.

13. General Wolfe, with eight thousand troops, landed, on the 27th of June, upon Orleans Island, a few miles below Quebec. The town was strongly defended by the French troops, and its approaches were held by Montcalm in person at the head of the main army. After several ineffectual efforts to gain possession of the city, it was determined, at a council of war, to attempt the Heights of Abraham, a level plateau, three hundred feet above the water, in the upper part of the town.

14. At sunrise on the morning of the 13th of September the whole English army stood in battle array upon the plains in front of the heights, and being immediately confronted by the French, a general and fierce battle ensued. Wolfe, severely wounded, led the van, and at the head of his men received another bullet in his breast, which compelled his removal to the rear. Monckton, who succeeded him in command, was also mortally wounded, and replaced by Townshend. Montcalm also fell, and the order for retreat was given by the French. Amid the shouts of victory, and the acclamations of the conquerors, Wolfe's gallant spirit passed away at about the same time with that of his heroic but defeated opponent. On the 18th the city was formally surrendered to the English.

15. Montcalm's successor, Levi, made an ineffectual effort, in the spring of the succeeding year, to recapture Quebec; and on its failure the French forces under Vaudreuil

1760.

Capture of Ticonderoga, Crown Point, and Niagara.— Siege of Quebec. — Death of Wolfe and Montcalm.— Surrender of the city.

were concentrated for the defence of Montreal. Early in September, Amherst arrived before the city at the head of ten thousand troops; Johnson followed with a thousand Indian warriors, Murray with four thousand troops from Quebec, and Colonel Haviland with three thousand from Crown Point.

16. Vaudreuil, conscious of his inability to resist this formidable force, on the 8th of September, signed a capitulation surrendering Montreal and all other French posts in Canada. It was not, however, until 1763 — the interval having been spent in naval warfare, where the English were almost uniformly successful — that a definitive treaty of peace between the two nations was concluded, by which France ceded to England all her American possessions.

1760. 17. On the morning of the 30th of July, 1760, Lieutenant-Governor De Lancey was found dead in his study, from the effects of a chronic disease, and the government devolved upon the venerable Cadwallader Colden, now seventy-three years of age. Governor Colden had long been intimately familiar with public affairs, and possessed superior literary and administrative abilities. He entered upon his new duties, however, at a most critical period in the history of the province and of the nation, and found himself utterly incapable of resisting the progress of events tending rapidly to the dissolution of the existing form of government.

1761. 18. His administration was temporarily interrupted in October of the following year by the arrival of a commission for General Robert Monckton, then commanding a military force on Staten Island. His public announcement on the assumption of his duties, that he had no instructions, and hoped never to have any, was highly acceptable to the people. The new Assembly gave him a warm reception, and the usual honors were conferred upon him.

19. His administration opened under the most favorable auspices, had he only the ability and the disposition to profit by them. The English Government had conceded to the colonies many of the rights so long and pertinaciously withheld, had

---

Capture of Montreal. — Naval warfare. — Treaty of peace. — Death of Governor De Lancey. — Administration of Cadwallader Colden and Robert Monckton.

abandoned its demands for a permanent revenue, and had left them in most respects, financial and otherwise, to their own guidance. Occasional aggressions on their rights were still inflicted and impatiently endured ; and judicious legislation and prudent administration alone were requisite to have insured permanent peace and continued union.

20. The independence of the Judiciary was, soon after his accession, threatened by the appointment of Pratt, a lawyer of Boston, as the successor of Chief-Justice De Lancey, to hold his office "at the King's pleasure," instead of as formerly " during good behavior." The Assembly regarded this innovation as inconsistent with the rights and liberties of the province. Monckton himself disapproved of it, and even Colden advised against it ; and Pratt, while accepting the office, was forced to concede and keenly to feel the repugnance of the people to the proposed tenure. The Presbyterians and Congregationalists were also jealous of the favor shown by the officers of the Crown to Episcopacy, especially in the government of the college, which was placed under Episcopal direction.

21. The Assembly having refused to provide for the salary of the Chief-Justice, unless he should receive an independent commission, the Board of Trade advised that the income for the royal quit-rents should be applied to this object. This course was accordingly adopted, and the Judiciary were subjected to the power and influence of the Crown, who named the judges, removed them at pleasure, fixed their salaries and paid them from funds beyond the control of the colonial legislature. 1762.

The independence of the Judiciary assailed.

Washington's Head-quarters at Newburgh, on the Hudson.

FIFTH PERIOD.

THE REVOLUTIONARY WAR.

CHAPTER I.

THE STAMP ACT. — FIRST COLONIAL CONGRESS. — SONS OF LIBERTY. — SIR HENRY MOORE. — LIBERTY POLE.

1. The relations which, during a period of upwards of a century, had existed between the American colonies and the English Government, had been generally of a peaceful nature. With the exception of occasional remonstrances on the part of the representative Assemblies of the provinces against various enactments of Parliament, and regulation of the Boards of Trade, affecting injuriously the manufactures, commerce, and navigation of the colonies, an uninterrupted spirit of loyalty prevailed among them, and voluntary contributions of men and money were cheerfully and promptly furnished

1763.

Relation between the colonies and the home government.

whenever the military exigencies of the parent government rendered such aid necessary or desirable.

2. The imposition upon them of forms of government and executive officers not of their own choice, or without in any manner consulting their wishes or inclinations; the vexatious restrictions upon their domestic and foreign trade by the prohibition, except under high duties and onerous regulations, of the importation and exportation of articles necessary to their prosperity and welfare; and various arbitrary and tyrannical enactments, affecting their civil, religious, and social rights and privileges, had hitherto failed sensibly to weaken their regard for the institutions and their attachment to the government with which they had so long been familiar. But the time had finally arrived when patience and unquestioning submission to the increasing exaction of arbitrary power had ceased to be virtues. Their experience in self-government, and the gradual growth among them of a representative democracy, had prepared them for the firm and manly assertion of their rights, and taught them the value of freedom.

3. Their prompt and lavish expenditure of blood and treasure during the war just closed had materially contributed to procure for the mother country a vast and valuable accession to her territory in America, and to expel from her possessions the enemy who had apparently obtained so firm a footing. Thirty thousand of the bravest soldiers of the colonies, and a debt of thirteen millions of pounds, had been the price ungrudgingly paid for the conquests which had added such signal lustre to the Crown of Great Britain. The arrogant and insatiable demands of a tyrannical government, however, required additional sacrifices, and nothing less than the abject concession of unlimited powers over their persons and property would satisfy the haughty ambition of the English aristocracy.

4. Notwithstanding the repeated and persistent refusal of the provincial Assemblies to recognize the right of the English Parliament to impose taxes upon them without their own consent, Lord Grenville, then at the head of the British Ministry, submitted, in 1764, a proposition for the raising of

1764.

Restrictions upon commerce and navigation. — Sacrifices of the colonies, and demands of the government.

a permanent revenue upon the colonies, by the establishment of stamp duties, and taxation of various articles of foreign produce. During the sessions of that and the succeeding year various enactments were made in conformity with these suggestions; and in contemptuous disregard of the earnest remonstrance of the colonies, the celebrated Stamp Act was passed on the 22d of March, 1765, to take effect on the first day of November subsequently.

<small>1765.</small>

5. By the provisions of this act all legal and mercantile documents and contracts, newspapers, pamphlets, almanacs, &c., were required to be written or printed on stamped paper, upon which a duty was to be imposed payable to officers appointed by the Crown. Its promulgation created a general feeling of indignation throughout the colonies, accompanied by a determination, at all hazards, to resist or evade its enforcement. In New York the obnoxious act was publicly paraded through the streets of the city, with a death's head affixed, bearing the significant inscription, "The Folly of England, and the Ruin of America." Similar demonstrations were made in Boston, Philadelphia, and other principal cities and towns.

6. On the 7th of October the FIRST COLONIAL CONGRESS, consisting of twenty-eight delegates from nine colonies, assembled at New York, and remained in session for two weeks. The body was presided over by Timothy Ruggles of Massachusetts, and after mature consideration adopted a Declaration of Rights, drawn up by John Cruger of New York; a calm and temperate, but firm and decided, statement of grievances in the form of a Memorial to Parliament, prepared by Robert R. Livingston, also of New York; and a Petition to the King, by James Otis of Massachusetts.

7. These documents asserted the inalienable right of the inhabitants of the several colonies to all the privileges of free-born Englishmen; the protection of life, liberty, property, and person; exemption from all taxes, restrictions, and imposts not voluntarily assumed by themselves or assented to by their representatives freely chosen; and denounced in glowing terms the

---

Passage of the Stamp Act. — Its reception in the colonies. — Proceedings at New York. — Proceedings of the first Colonial Congress. — Its composition and officers. — Declaration of Rights and Memorial to Parliament.

continued and systematic invasion of these rights and privileges, under pretence of law, by a body in which they were wholly unrepresented. Protesting their unimpaired confidence in the wisdom and justice of Parliament, and their earnest desire for a continuance of the friendly relations hitherto existing between the two countries, they respectfully demanded the repeal of the obnoxious acts complained of, and the discontinuance in future of all similar arbitrary legislation.

8. On the 1st of November, the day on which the Stamp Act was to go into effect, the shops, stores, and public offices of the city were closed; the flags of the vessels in the port were floating at half-mast; the bells of the several churches were tolled, and numerous other manifestations of the public discontent and sorrow were displayed. All business was suspended, the courts were closed, and the city was clothed in mourning. Meanwhile the obnoxious stamps had reached the city, and been deposited in the fort for safe-keeping by the direction of Governor Colden, who had recently succeeded Monckton in the administration of the province.

9. McEvers, the agent appointed by the Crown for the distribution and sale of the stamps, intimidated by the manifestations of the popular feeling on every hand, had resigned his commission; the association of the "Sons of Liberty," headed by Isaac Sears, John Lamb, Alexander McDougall, Francis Lewis, Marinus Willett, and other patriotic leaders, had been revived, and an engagement entered into by the merchants generally to cease all importation of goods from Great Britain while the act remained in force. Handbills were circulated throughout the city, warning all people against the purchase or use of stamps at their peril.

10. In the evening two organized companies, under the lead of the Sons of Liberty, paraded the streets, one of which proceeded to the Commons, the site of the present City Hall, where they suspended an effigy of the Governor with the stamped paper in his hands, and other contemptuous devices; while the other proceeded to the fort with another effigy of the obnoxious Governor, broke open the stable of his residence, and

---

Arrival of the stamps. — The 1st of November. — Proceedings of the Sons of Liberty. — Demonstration of the Sons of Liberty.

taking from it his carriage and, placing in it the effigy, returned in triumph to their associates on the Commons, from whence, consolidating their ranks, they took up their march in strict order and unbroken silence to the fort.

11. Here they found the troops, under the command of General Gage, drawn up on the rampart for their reception, and the muzzles of the cannon aimed directly at their ranks. The British commander, however, prudently reserved his fire; and the procession, being denied admission to the fort, repaired to the Bowling Green, tore down the wooden palisades, and contented themselves with burning the carriage with its effigy and other accompaniments. Some of their more violent associates, disregarding the remonstrances of their comrades, proceeded to the residence of Major James, a British officer, who had rendered himself obnoxious to the populace, broke open and rifled the house, and burned the furniture, carrying off the royal standard in triumph.

12. The next evening the people again assembled at the Commons with the intention of renewing the attack upon the fort and gaining possession of the stamped paper. Governor Colden, however, anticipated their action on this occasion by sending a communication to the city authorities, declaring his intention not to issue any of the stamps while he remained in office. Not content with this assurance, another demonstration was made on the ensuing evening, and the Governor, having failed in his efforts to place the stamps under military protection, delivered them up in due form to the Mayor and Corporation, taking from them a receipt for their safe-keeping. This proceeding quieted the popular leaders for the time, and restored order to the city.

13. In the mean time, the Committee of Correspondence, appointed by the citizens, through their Chairman, John Lamb, had addressed circular letters to the merchants of the sister-cities of the colonies, inviting their co-operation in the non-intercourse policy, which was promptly acceded to by all. They had also drafted articles for a general union and confederation of the colonies in resistance to the arbitrary measures of the

---

Attack on the fort. — Riotous proceedings. — Governor Colden delivers up the stamps. — General non-intercourse agreement. — Articles of confederation proposed.

Crown, and providing for the assembling of a general Congress in the event of persistence in these measures. These articles were also unanimously approved and adopted.

14. A new supply of stamps soon after arrived in the province, with the new Governor, Sir HENRY MOORE, and Peter De Lancey, Jr., who had been appointed stamp distributor in the place of McEvers. The Governor having peremptorily declined any interference with the obnoxious stamps, they were deposited with the others in the City Hall, and De Lancey advised by a committee of the Sons of Liberty to follow the prudent example of his predecessor, with which he was fain publicly to comply. A similar course was pursued towards a Maryland official who had sought the protection of Governor Colden, and taken shelter on Long Island.

15. The new Governor met with a favorable reception from the citizens and the public authorities, who were highly pleased with his liberal views and ready concessions to the popular sentiment. The Assembly which convened on his arrival confirmed the proceedings of their delegates in the Colonial Congress, and adopted resolutions in favor of the policy inaugurated by that body. About the same time, Captain Christian Jacobsen, of the ship Hope, arrived from Holland, having refused to bring over additional stamps.

16. The Sons of Liberty, on information that stamps designed for Connecticut were concealed on board the vessel bringing over the Governor, instituted a vigilant search ; but finding that they had been transferred to another vessel, repaired on board and took ten packages from the hold, which they conveyed to the ship-yards and burnt. They also resorted to the most vigorous measures for the repression of all sales of stamped paper within the province.

17. So odious had the act become in all the colonies, and so determined and effective was the opposition to its enforcement, that its repeal was procured on the 20th of February of the ensuing year, at the instance of the Marquis of

1766.

Arrival of Sir Henry Moore as Governor.— New supply of stamps.— Proceedings of the Sons of Liberty. — Reception of the Governor. — Proceedings of the Assembly. — Vigilance of the Sons of Liberty. — Repeal of the Stamp Act.

Rockingham, accompanied, however, by a declaratory act affirming the right of Parliament to tax the colonies for any purpose whatsoever. Its repeal was hailed in the city with acclamations of delight, and received with the utmost satisfaction by all the colonies.

18. Bells were rung, cannon fired, bonfires kindled, a public dinner given by the civic authorities, and the city illuminated in honor of the event. On the 4th of June following, the patriots again assembled on the Commons in honor of the King's birthday, and, after the most enthusiastic manifestations of loyalty, raised, near where the present City Hall stands, a LIBERTY POLE, on which were inscribed the words, "The King, Pitt, and Liberty." In defence of this standard, the first blood of the Revolution was soon destined to be shed.

CHAPTER II.

TAX ON TEA. — THE LIBERTY POLE. — SONS OF LIBERTY. — GOVERNOR COLDEN. — JOHN LAMB AND ALEXANDER McDOUGALL.

1. DURING the month of June a sharp controversy was maintained between the Governor and the Assembly in reference to the supplies required to be furnished by the citizens of New York to the troops under the command of General Gage, stationed in the city, nominally for its protection. The spirit of opposition manifested by the Assembly to the demands of the Governor was vigorously seconded by the people, and frequent collisions from time to time occurred between the occupants of the barracks on the Commons and the more violent of the patriotic leaders.

1766.

2. On the night of the 10th of August a party of soldiers from the barracks cut down the Liberty Pole erected on the Commons, and on the succeeding day attacked and dispersed a party of the citizens who had assembled to replace it, seriously

---

Rejoicings in the colonies. — Patriotic celebrations. — Erection of Liberty Pole. — Controversies between the Governor and Assembly. — The Liberty Pole cut down. — Disturbances between the soldiery and citizens.

wounding several of their number, among whom were Isaac Sears and John Berrien, prominent members of the Sons of Liberty. Although this violent proceeding of the soldiers was justified by their officers, the patriots were allowed to replace the pole a few days afterwards, without further molestation at that time.

3. On the 23d of September, however, the pole was again cut down, and again replaced on the next day by the inhabitants. This persistent determination of the citizens induced the Governor to prohibit all future attempts of the like nature on the part of the soldiery, and the most stringent measures were adopted by both the civil and military authorities to prevent their repetition.

4. The refusal of the Assembly to comply with the requisitions of the Governor for the provision of supplies for the military brought down upon them a severe censure from the Crown; and a spirited reply on their part was followed by a temporary prorogation. Rumors, however, of warlike preparation in England, and the menaces and persuasions of the Governor, induced them finally to consent to an additional appropriation, which, while it incurred the strong disapprobation of the patriotic party, failed to conciliate the Government. The legislative powers of the Assembly were suspended by Parliament, and instructions forwarded to the Governor prohibiting his assent to any act passed by them until a full compliance with the demands of the Crown should be obtained.

5. That body, however, disregarding the injunctions of the English Government, and supported by the general approval of the popular voice in their own and the neighboring colonies, continued their sessions as usual, and adopted strong resolutions declaring the arbitrary proceedings of Parliament suspending their legislative functions unconstitutional and void. Meanwhile Parliament, on the motion of Charles Townshend, Chancellor of the Exchequer, had unanimously passed a bill, early in 1767, imposing duties on all tea, glass, paper, painters' colors, and lead imported into the colonies. 1767.

Proceedings of the authorities. — Proceedings of the Assembly. — Suspension of legislative powers. — Resistance of the Assembly. — Tax on tea, &c.

6. This fresh invasion of their rights and privileges created a renewed excitement in all the colonies. Committees of correspondence were established throughout the provinces by the energetic and vigilant Sons of Liberty in New York, and the merchants of that city again assembled and unanimously renewed the non-importation agreement, pledging themselves to its strict observance during the continuance of the obnoxious duties.

7. On the 18th of March, previous to the arrival of intelligence of the proceedings of Parliament, the anniversary of the repeal of the Stamp Act was celebrated by the citizens with the utmost enthusiasm. On the succeeding night, however, the Liberty Pole on the Commons was again levelled to the ground by the soldiery. Another and a more substantial one, secured by iron bands, was on the next day set up in its place by the Sons of Liberty. Several ineffectual efforts were made for its destruction, all of which were counteracted by the vigilance of its patriotic defenders. The officers of the garrison finally interfered, and prevented the further continuance of these demonstrations.

1768. 8. The Assembly having been formally dissolved by the Governor in February, 1768, a new election was ordered, resulting in the return of representatives little less disposed to compliance with the demands of the government than their predecessors. On their meeting in October, in utter disregard of the royal injunction, they opened a correspondence with the Massachusetts Assembly, warmly sympathizing with their misfortunes; and after voting a liberal appropriation for supplies to the troops quartered in the city, coupled with a series of resolutions strongly declaratory of their rights, and denouncing their repeated infringement by Parliament, were dissolved.

1769. 9. On the 4th of April, 1769, another new Assembly was convened, and after renewing, at the earnest solicitation of the Governor, the appropriation for military supplies to the garrison, was prorogued. The Governor continued to exert his influence to the extent of his power for the repres-

---

Indignation of the colonies. — Proceedings of the Sons of Liberty. — Renewal of non-importation agreement. — Renewed efforts for the destruction of the Liberty Pole. — Proceedings of the new Assembly.

sion of all disloyal manifestations on the part of the inhabitants of the province and city; but his well-meant efforts at conciliation were suddenly ended by his death, which took place on the 11th of September, devolving the government again upon Cadwallader Colden.

10. The Assembly was again convened on the 21st of November; and through a coalition between the Governor and his former inveterate opponent, De Lancey, an additional appropriation of money for supplies was obtained. Inflammatory handbills were immediately circulated by the leaders of the popular party, openly charging the Assembly with a betrayal of the trust reposed in them by their constituents; and a large assemblage of citizens gathered on the Commons on the 18th of December, presided over by John Lamb, denounced the proceedings of the Assembly, and so far alarmed the members of that body and the Governor, that it was found necessary at the close of the session to force through, by a close vote, a bill for the issue of colonial bills of credit to the amount of one hundred and twenty thousand pounds, the interest to be applied to the support of the colonial government, which, early in January, 1770, received the prompt approval of the Governor.

11. In the mean time the Assembly, by a nearly unanimous vote, denounced the handbills as libellous, and offered a reward of one hundred and fifty pounds for the discovery of their authors. Lamb was arrested and brought before the House, where he boldly avowed the part he had taken in the proceedings of the public meeting, and justified it as the exercise of a right which, in common with every Englishman, he possessed. His associates among the Sons of Liberty fearlessly seconded his appeal, and avowed their approval of, and participation in, his acts, and their readiness to meet the consequences. This spirited behavior procured their discharge. Alexander McDougall, to whom the authorship of the handbills

1770.

Death of Governor Moore. — Colden resumes the government. — Coalition with De Lancey. — Vote of supplies to the troops. — Indignation of the people. — Inflammatory handbills. — Public meeting. — Passage of bill for issue of colonial bills of credit. — Arrest of Lamb. — Imprisonment of McDougall.

was traced, was arrested and imprisoned, when, for nearly two months, he was daily visited by crowds of his friends of both sexes, who regarded him as a martyr to the cause of liberty, and where he remained until, on indictment by the grand jury, he was admitted to bail in the ensuing April.

CHAPTER III.

BATTLE OF GOLDEN HILL. — DEMOLITION OF THE LIBERTY POLE. — NON-IMPORTATION AGREEMENT. — LORD DUNMORE. — BILLS OF CREDIT. — McDOUGALL AND GEORGE CLINTON.

1. On the evening of the 13th of January a renewed attack was made upon the Liberty Pole by a party of soldiers belonging to the garrison. Indignant at their failure to accomplish its overthrow before an alarm was given, and smarting under the hisses and jeers of the citizens gathered in front of Montagnie's tavern, the head-quarters of the Sons of Liberty in the immediate vicinity of the Commons, they commenced a furious attack upon the crowd, driving them into the house with their bayonets, and, sword in hand, proceeded to demolish the windows and furniture of the building, after which they retired.

1770.

2. An additional attempt was made on the evening of the 15th to effect the demolition of the popular standard, but again without success. The next evening, however, they accomplished their object, levelling the pole to the ground, sawing it into pieces, and piling them triumphantly in front of the hotel. The people were aroused by the discovery of this outrage, and a public meeting of the citizens was hastily convened at the Commons on the morning of the 17th.

3. Several thousands of the inhabitants of the city promptly responded to this call, and at noon the Commons were thronged by an excited multitude, while a party of seamen scoured the docks, piers, and warehouses, where the soldiers were employed as laborers, and compelled them to abandon their occupation

---

Riotous proceedings of the soldiers. — Demolition of the Liberty Pole. — Excitement of the people. — Public meeting of the citizens.

and return to their quarters. Resolutions were passed censuring in the strongest terms the riotous conduct of the soldiery, denouncing their presence in the city as unnecessary and dangerous, and discountenancing their employment by the citizens when off duty as detrimental to the interests of the laboring class. All soldiers appearing armed in the streets, or found out of their barracks after roll-call, were directed to be dealt with as enemies of the city.

4. On the ensuing day (January 18) two soldiers were arrested by Isaac Sears and another of the Sons of Liberty in the act of posting an inflammatory handbill prepared by their comrades, and conducted to the Mayor's office, where they were immediately followed by a party of twenty soldiers armed with cutlasses and bayonets, who demanded the immediate release of the prisoners. This demand was promptly resisted by Captain Richardson and other citizens, who defended the entrance and ordered the return of the soldiers to their barracks.

5. The crowd collected in front of the Mayor's office had, in the mean time, provided themselves with stakes from the carts and sleighs in the vicinity, and seemed not indisposed to measure their strength with their armed opponents in the impending contest. In apparent obedience to the orders of the Mayor the soldiers retired, closely followed by the citizens, as far as the summit of Golden Hill, as John Street was then called, between William and Cliff Streets. Here they were joined by a reinforcement from the upper barracks on the Commons, headed by an officer in disguise. He immediately ordered a charge upon the people, who, with the exception of a few in possession of clubs, were entirely unarmed. They succeeded, however, by their numbers, in steadily resisting the furious attack of the soldiers, and impeding their apparent return down the hill to the Mayor's office, until they were hemmed in by another body of soldiers from the upper barracks, while a third approached to the relief of their comrades from the fort.

6. The three parties, consolidating their forces by the junction of a portion of the assailants who had forced their way

---

Resolutions adopted. — Arrest of soldiers by the Sons of Liberty. — Proceedings at the Mayor's office. — Attempt at recapture of the prisoners by their associates. — Battle of Golden Hill.

through the unarmed crowd of citizens, commenced a furious attack upon the latter, severely wounding several of their number. Others, including women and children, not participating in the affray, were cut down and bayoneted, though none were mortally injured, and it was not until some time had elapsed that the contest was arrested by the interference of the officers of the garrison.

7. On the ensuing day the soldiers recommenced their assaults by thrusting a bayonet through the dress of a woman returning from market. About noon a party of sailors were attacked at the head of Chapel Street, now Park Row, opposite Beekman Street, and one of their number was run through the body. In the midst of the conflict the Mayor made his appearance, and attempted, without success, to disperse the infuriated soldiers. He then despatched a message to the officers at the barracks, but the messenger was intercepted by the troops, who refused to suffer him to proceed. A party of the Sons of Liberty, however, who had been engaged at playing ball in the neighborhood, came to the rescue and dispersed the soldiers.

8. In the afternoon another affray occurred between the soldiery and citizens on the Commons. The "Liberty Boys" again appeared in force, and after a severe conflict succeeded in driving the assailants to their barracks, after disarming a portion of their number, severely wounding others, and capturing and imprisoning one of the leaders in the affair of the preceding day.

9. Thus terminated the earliest contest in which blood was shed, which ushered in the American Revolution; and although no lives are known to have been lost, yet the firm stand made by the mass of the citizens, unarmed and undisciplined, against an armed and trained foreign soldiery imposed upon them against their will, sufficiently served to indicate the irrepressible spirit which animated the colonists, and to warn their haughty oppressors of the danger of persistence in their fatal policy.

10. Governor Colden in his despatches to the English Government, detailing the events we have related, attributed their oc-

---

Renewal of the conflict. — Its termination by the Liberty Boys. — Governor Colden's despatches.

currence to the violence of party faction, promoted by the enemies of the Crown, chiefly Dissenters or Independents from New England of republican principles, while the friends of Government were chiefly connected with the English, Lutheran, and Dutch churches, with a sprinkling of Presbyterians. The repugnance of the popular leaders to the demands of the Crown for the support of the soldiers is specially adverted to, and high commendation bestowed upon the officers and magistrates for their exertions in quelling the disturbances.

11. The petition of the Sons of Liberty for permission to erect another Liberty Pole in the place of the one cut down having been refused by the Common Council, Lamb and his associates purchased a site near the former one, and on the 6th of February planted it firmly, with the inscription "Liberty and Property," amid the acclamations of the people and the cheering strains of music. The Sons of Liberty established their headquarters on the present site of the Herald office, in a building to which they gave the appropriate name of Hampden Hall.

12. On the 29th of March a final attack was made upon the Liberty Pole by the soldiers who were about embarking for Pensacola, whither they were desirous of transporting a portion of its timber as a trophy. The Liberty Boys speedily rallied to its defence, driving its assailants to their barracks. Reinforced, the party, fifteen in number, returned with forty of their comrades, and charged the citizens, who retreated to their hall, which was immediately surrounded by the soldiers, and an entrance by force attempted, with infuriated denunciations of vengeance. The alarm-bell was rung, the citizens flew to arms, and, apprehensive of a recurrence of the conflict at Golden Hill, the officers of the garrison hastened to withdraw their forces. The troops embarked on the 3d of May without their coveted prize, which remained thenceforth unmolested until the occupation of the city by the British in 1776, when it was again levelled by the orders of the infamous Provost-Marshal Cunningham.

13. Soon after the departure of the troops, the Sons of Liberty, learning of the visit of one Rogers, a Boston merchant,

---

Erection of a new Liberty Pole. — Hampden Hall. — Renewed attack upon the Pole. — Its successful defence. — Its final fate.

who had been posted by his fellow-citizens for a violation of the non-importation agreement, and suspecting his intentions, paraded his effigy in procession through the streets, suspended on a gallows, and with four or five thousand citizens proceeded to his residence with the view of further honors. Finding him absent, and being informed of his contemplated departure for Philadelphia, they apprised their brethren there of his intentions, requesting at their hands a worthy welcome. Rogers, however, deferred his visit, and returned terrified to Boston.

14. The act of Parliament of 1767, imposing additional duties on the colonies, having been repealed with the exception of the tax on tea, a general committee of one hundred of the leading inhabitants of the city and province was formed, and the non-importation agreement, so long and so faithfully adhered to by the merchants of New York at a heavy pecuniary sacrifice, was now restricted to the single article of tea. The patriotic Sons of Liberty, however, and their adherents among the popular party, declined to sanction this compromise, and continued their opposition to the principle still involved in the act, notwithstanding the diminution of the pecuniary demand.

15. On the 25th of October, Colden was superseded by Lord Dunmore. The Assembly was informed of the royal approval of the bill for the issue of colonial bills of credit, and the renewal of the required appropriations for the support of the troops. In January of the succeeding year, McDougall was brought before that body to answer to the indictment pending against him. On his refusal to acknowledge the authorship of the alleged libel, he was required by the Assembly to give a definitive answer. "The House has declared the paper a libel," he boldly replied, "and the law does not require me to criminate myself."

1771.

16. De Noyellis, the prosecutor, insisted that the House had power to extort an answer and to punish him for contumacy. "The House has power to throw the prisoner over the bar or out of the window," observed George Clinton, the future Gov-

---

Proceedings of the Sons of Liberty on the visit of a Boston merchant charged with violation of the non-importation agreement. — Repeal of duties except on tea. — Non-importation agreement. — Lord Dunmore. — Proceedings against McDougall.

ernor of New York, "but the public will doubt the justice of the proceeding." A written answer having been refused, on the allegation that it reflected on the dignity of the body, the intrepid Clinton indignantly exclaimed, "The dignity of the House would be better supported by justice than by overstrained authority." McDougall was recommitted to prison, where he remained but a short time before he obtained his release through the efforts of his friends.

CHAPTER IV.

GOVERNORS TRYON AND COLDEN. — TAX ON TEA. — THE "MOHAWKS" AND SONS OF LIBERTY. — BOARDING OF THE TEA-SHIPS.

1. LORD DUNMORE having been transferred to Virginia, WILLIAM TRYON was duly commissioned as Governor in his stead. On his arrival early in July, he was favorably received by the people, signalizing his accession, however, as did his predecessor, by a refusal to accept any income from the Assembly, preferring to rely for support exclusively upon his Majesty, and the disposition by the government of the colonial taxes. The quiet of the city and province remained undisturbed for a considerable period after Tryon's assumption of his duties, although the revolutionary spirit was rapidly increasing in depth and earnestness. [1771.]

2. The persistent refusal on the part of the colonies to import, purchase, or in any manner to use tea, the only remaining commodity on which an impost was demanded by the British Government, induced Parliament, on the urgent representations of the East India Company, to remit all export duties payable by the Company in England, and to insist only upon a tax of threepence per pound payable on its arrival in America. [1773.]

3. Large shipments of tea having been prepared for the colonies under the expectation that the trifling duties demanded by

the new act would secure a ready sale, the irrepressible Sons of Liberty again rallied their forces, sternly prohibiting the introduction under any pretence of the obnoxious article, and delegating an association of their number, known as "Mohawks," to superintend the arrival of ships freighted wholly or in part with this cargo.

4. Alarmed at these decided demonstrations of the popular leaders, the Tea-Commissioners appointed for New York at once resigned their commissions; and even the foreign tea-merchants began to doubt the expediency of shipments to the colonies; but being reassured by a renegade merchant of New York that all opposition would be promptly quelled by the new Governor, who was a man of decision and energy, they determined to venture upon the experiment.

5. On the 27th of November the Sons of Liberty formally renewed their organization and adopted a series of spirited resolutions, denouncing as enemies to the liberties of America any person aiding or abetting in any way the introduction, purchase, or use of tea, and declaring that whether the duties imposed by the act were paid in Great Britain or America, the liberties of the colonies were equally affected. On the 16th of December, the same day on which the Boston tea-party took place, these resolutions were again promulgated in immediate anticipation of the landing of a cargo from England. Governor Tryon made an ineffectual effort to secure its introduction by promising that after its formal reception the tea should be returned to the ships; but the excited inhabitants, headed by John Lamb, unanimously refused to permit its landing.

6. The ship, in the mean while, delayed by adverse winds, failed to make her appearance; and on the 7th of April of the ensuing year, Tryon, leaving the government again in the hands of Colden, set sail for England. On the 18th the long-expected vessel — the Nancy, Captain Lockyer — arrived off Sandy Hook with a cargo of tea for the port. The pilots, under the directions of the Vigilance Committee, detained the vessel in the Lower Bay, while several of the committee proceeded on board and took possession. The captain was per-

1774.

Spirited proceedings of the Sons of Liberty. — Colden resumes the administration. — Arrival of tea-ships.

mitted, under a strong escort, to consult with the consignee, who at once refused to receive the cargo, and advised its prompt return to England.

7. On the 22d, Captain Chambers, a recreant New-Yorker, arrived in the harbor with the ship London, and was immediately boarded by two of the members of the committee. On his assurance that he had no tea on board, and the exhibition of his papers, confirming this statement, he was permitted to proceed to the city. On reaching the wharf, the vessel was again boarded by the committee, who demanded a thorough search for the obnoxious article. Driven to bay by their determined vigilance, Chambers finally admitted the possession of tea, alleging, however, that it was his own on a private venture, and without the knowledge of the Company. At eight in the evening the vessel was again boarded by a vast crowd of the excited inhabitants, the hatches forced open, eighteen chests of tea brought upon deck, opened, and their contents emptied into the river. No attempt at disguise or concealment was made; and the people at an early hour quietly dispersed without further violence.

8. The next morning, in pursuance of a call of the Vigilance Committee, the citizens assembled in front of the Coffee House in Wall Street, where Lockyer was lodging, and amid the ringing of bells, firing of cannon, display of flags, and the music of the city bands, conducted him to a boat at the foot of the street, whence, with his companion Chambers, under the escort of a less ceremonious committee, he was taken on board the Nancy, and, accompanied by the vigilant representatives of the popular feeling three leagues beyond Sandy Hook, they took a polite leave of their entertainers and proceeded on their outward voyage.

9. On a meeting of the citizens on the 19th of May, in response to an invitation from the patriots of Boston for a renewal of the non-importation agreement, a corresponding committee of fifty-one of the leading inhabitants was formed, and a sub-committee, consisting of Alexander McDougall, Isaac Low,

---

New York "tea-party."—Proceedings of the Vigilance Committee and citizens.—Departure of the tea-ships.—Public meeting of citizens.—Committee of fifty-one.

James Duane, and John Jay, appointed to prepare an answer to the Bostonians. This committee, deeming a renewal of the non-importation agreement inexpedient under existing circumstances, recommended a General Congress of deputies from the colonies for the consideration of public affairs. At a public meeting on the 6th of July, presided over by McDougall, and at which Alexander Hamilton, then a youth of seventeen, and a student of King's College, made his first appearance as an orator, the non-importation agreement was renewed, notwithstanding the opposition of the committee, their recommendation of a Colonial Congress adopted, and resolutions strongly sympathizing with the Bostonians under the arbitrary tyranny of England unanimously passed.

10. The second Colonial Congress accordingly assembled at Philadelphia early in September, New York being represented by Philip Livingston, John Alsop, Isaac Low, James Duane, and John Jay, appointed by the committee of fifty-one, in conjunction with a committee of mechanics. This body adopted a Declaration of Rights and Privileges drawn up by Jay, protesting against standing armies and parliamentary taxation, and declaring the various obnoxious acts passed since the accession of the present monarch infringements of their rights and unconstitutional. They also leagued themselves into a non-importation association, pledging themselves to import no goods from Great Britain or its dependencies until the repeal of these acts.

1775. 11. The Assembly, although a majority of its members could not be prevailed upon to afford their sanction to the proceedings of the Colonial Congress, addressed, nevertheless, a strong remonstrance to Parliament against its harsh and severe treatment of the colonies, in terms so distasteful to that body that the ministry refused to receive it. On the 3d of April, 1775, the Assembly adjourned, and was never afterwards convoked. The first Provincial Congress, consisting of delegates from the several counties, assembled in their stead on the 20th of April, and appointed five delegates to the first Continental Congress, which convened at Philadelphia in the ensuing month.

Recommendation of a General Congress. — Second Colonial Congress. — Declaration of Rights. — Non-importation league. — Assembly. — First Provincial Congress. — First Continental Congress.

12. On the 22d of May the Provincial Congress, consisting of about seventy members, again convened at New York. Two regiments were authorized to be raised; bounties were offered for the manufacture of gunpowder and muskets; fortifications at Kingsbridge and the Highlands were projected, and Philip Schuyler and Richard Montgomery were recommended to the Continental Congress as Major and Brigadier Generals. After delegating their powers to a committee of safety they adjourned early in September.

13. A short time previous to these events the seventy-four-gun ship Asia had been ordered from Boston and anchored off the Battery, with her guns pointed against the city. The removal of the troops to Boston, preparatory to a large reinforcement, rendered the erection of additional barracks in that city necessary, for which the mutinous inhabitants declined furnishing the requisite materials. New York was applied to for aid; but the vigilant Sons of Liberty peremptorily forbade any efforts in that direction. A vessel was, however, fitted out for that purpose in the harbor; and the patriots, headed by John Lamb, Marinus Willett, and Isaac Sears, resolved to seize the ship and prevent her voyage. The citizens were requested to provide themselves with a supply of arms and ammunition. Sears, the principal instigator of this daring movement, was arrested and brought before the Mayor, but, on his refusal to give bail, was committed. On his way to prison, however, he was forcibly rescued by the people, and conducted in triumph through the principal streets of the city.

14. On the receipt, soon after, of intelligence of the battle of Lexington, all business was at once suspended; the patriotic Sons of Liberty took possession of the City Hall, distributed the arms and ammunition found there and at the arsenal among the citizens, a portion of whom organized a volunteer corps under the command of Samuel Broome, and assumed the temporary government of the city. They obtained possession of the Custom House, which they at once closed, laid an embargo upon the English vessels in the port destined for the

---

Second Provincial Congress. — Arrival of the Asia. — Disturbances in the city. — Receipt of news of the battle of Lexington. — Proceedings of the Sons of Liberty.

eastern colonies, and relieved them of eighty thousand pounds' worth of provisions and supplies for the British army.

15. On the 5th of May, a Provisional Government, consisting of one hundred of the principal inhabitants, was organized by the citizens, and the municipal affairs of the city placed under their absolute control until the Continental Congress should otherwise order. A large body of troops being on their way to the city, Lieutenant-Governor Colden was soon afterwards requested to use his influence with General Gage, then in command in the city, to prevent their landing. The Congress, however, recommended that permission for their landing should not be withheld, while no fortification should be allowed to be constructed, and all warlike stores be removed from the town, and a safe retreat provided for the women and children in the event of a siege.

16. In the mean time the patriots under the direction of their daring leader, John Lamb, having procured a vessel from Connecticut, had taken possession of a quantity of military stores belonging to the royal troops, at Turtle Bay, near the foot of the present Forty-Seventh Street on the Hudson, a portion of which was despatched to the army at Cambridge, and the residue reserved for future use. Some other demonstrations of the popular feeling occurring soon after, the Provisional Congress requested General Wooster to take up his head-quarters near the city, where he accordingly, early in June, encamped with his troops at Harlem.

17. The royal troops, having been soon afterwards ordered to repair to Boston, were permitted by the Provisional Government to depart, with the stipulation that they should take nothing with them but their own arms and accoutrements. Disregarding this express restriction, they proceeded to the place of embarkation in Broad Street with a large quantity of military stores belonging to the city. Here, however, they were met by Colonel Marinus Willett and John Morin Scott, who, notwithstanding the opposition of their leader and the remonstrances of the Mayor and Gouverneur Morris, who supposed full permis-

---

Provisional Government of the city. — Patriotic demonstrations. — Capture of ammunition at Turtle Bay. — General Wooster encamps at Harlem. — Embarkation of the royal troops for Boston.

sion had been given by the authorities, succeeded with the aid of the citizens, who had by this time assembled, in turning them back, and regaining the arms. Having secured the stores in a safe place, the soldiers were escorted to the wharf, where they embarked amid the hisses and execrations of the crowd.

CHAPTER V.

CAPTURE OF TICONDEROGA AND CROWN POINT. — WASHINGTON ASSUMES COMMAND OF THE ARMY. — GOVERNOR TRYON'S ABDICATION. — INVASION OF CANADA. — SIEGE OF QUEBEC AND DEATH OF MONTGOMERY.

1. ON the morning of the 10th of May, 1775, Colonel ETHAN ALLEN of Vermont, aided by Captain BENEDICT ARNOLD, having with a force of eighty-three men crossed over Lake Champlain from the Vermont shore during the preceding night, attacked the strong fortifications of Ticonderoga, and, after a brief conflict with the surprised garrison, demanded and effected its surrender "in the name of the Great Jehovah and the Continental Congress." One hundred and eighty-two cannon and a large quantity of military stores were captured with the garrison, as the result of this bold and daring enterprise. On the succeeding day, Colonel SETH WARNER, of Vermont, obtained possession of Crown Point, with its garrison and a hundred and eleven pieces of artillery. This gallant enterprise seems to have been originally suggested by Colonel John Brown of Massachusetts.

1775.

2. On the 25th of June, eight days after the battle of Bunker Hill, WASHINGTON, having been commissioned by the Continental Congress as Commander-in-Chief of the American armies, passed through New York on his way to his headquarters at Cambridge, whither he was escorted by the provincial militia, and where, on the 3d of July, he assumed the command. Tryon on the morning of the day Washington left the city resumed his official duties as Governor, and was accorded a

---

Recapture of arms by the citizens. — Capture of Ticonderoga and Crown Point — Washington assumes command of the army. — Return of Governor Tryon.

favorable reception by the Mayor and Corporation; although such was the changed sentiment of the city, that, while nominally according him all the respect due to his position, the Provincial Congress in their midst secured their ready and implicit obedience.

3. Three thousand men were ordered by the Continental Congress to be raised by the colony of New York as her quota of the troops for the public defence. Four regiments were accordingly raised under the authority of the Provincial Congress, and placed under the command of Colonel Alexander McDougall, Gozen Van Schaick, James Clinton, and Colonel Holmes. John Lamb was appointed to the command of an artillery and Marinus Willett of an infantry company. Sears and others of the "Liberty Boys" joined the ranks.

4. The Provincial Congress, desiring the guns of the fort on the Battery for the fortifications of the Highlands, and regarding their present position as unfavorable to the patriotic cause, directed their removal accordingly. Captain Lamb, on the night of the 23d of August, proceeded to the execution of this order with a party of the Sons of Liberty and a number of citizens, including Alexander Hamilton. While thus engaged a shot was fired from a barge of the ship-of-war Asia, stationed near the shore; and on the fire being returned by Lamb, killing one of the crew and wounding several others, a heavy cannonade was opened upon the town by the ship, inflicting considerable damage upon the buildings near the Battery and severely wounding some of the inhabitants. The Liberty Boys, undismayed by this formidable attack, coolly persevered in their work until it was completed and the guns safely removed.

5. The commander of the Asia, on the ensuing day, forwarded a despatch to the Mayor, demanding satisfaction for the murder of one of his crew. A desultory correspondence followed the receipt of this demand, when the Provincial Congress put an end to it by declaring that, as the Asia had seen fit to cannonade the city, she must henceforth obtain her sup-

---

Organization of four regiments as the quota of New York. — Removal of the guns on the Battery. — Cannonade of the city by the Asia sloop-of-war. — Disposition of the demands for satisfaction of the cannonade of the Asia.

plies from some other source. Meanwhile the Governor, finding his position growing daily more unsatisfactory and perilous, determined to abandon the city, and took refuge on board the Asia. His organ and that of the royalists — Rivington's New York Gazette — having excited the ire of the patriots, Captain Sears, with a party of light-horse, on the 4th of December proceeded to its demolition, destroying the press and scattering the types. The proprietor sailed for England, whence, however, on the occupation of the city by the British troops, he returned and resumed the publication of his journal.

6. On the 27th of June the Continental Congress directed General Philip Schuyler to repair to Ticonderoga, and in conjunction with Colonels Arnold and Hinman to place the fortifications at that post in a complete state of defence, and afterwards, if found practicable, to take military possession of St. John's, Montreal, or any other portions of Canada which he might deem important to the interests of the colonies. Schuyler, under these instructions, reached Ticonderoga on the 18th of July, and, after making suitable provisions for its defence, despatched an agent to Canada to ascertain the disposition of the inhabitants, and the number and condition of the royal forces.

7. General Montgomery, with a force of twelve hundred men, left Crown Point on the 31st of August, and being joined on the 4th of September by Schuyler, with about a thousand troops, the latter advanced on the 6th against St. John's, but, meeting with a formidable opposition, withdrew and re-embarked his troops on the succeeding morning. Having been reinforced by seven hundred men from New York and Connecticut, a second attempt upon St. John's was made, under the command of Montgomery on the 10th, which was again frustrated by the cowardice of the troops. General Schuyler being compelled by sickness to return to Ticonderoga, Montgomery assumed the command of the expedition on the 16th, and on the same day was joined by Colonel Seth Warner, with one hundred and seventy Green Mountain boys. On the 19th of October the fort at Chambly, twelve miles below St. John's, was captured by Majors Brown and Livingston.

Governor Tryon's abdication. — Demolition of Rivington's press. — Preparations for an invasion of Canada.

8. It was not, however, until the 2d of November, that St. John's was surrendered, after a series of misfortunes and miscarriages which would have discouraged a less determined spirit. Five hundred regulars and one hundred Canadians, with forty pieces of artillery and a quantity of naval stores, fell into the hands of the victors. Two parties sent to the relief of the fort by General Carleton, the British commander, one of which was headed by himself, were defeated by Colonel Warner and Majors Brown and Livingston. Major John André, whose subsequent history is well known, was one of the prisoners taken at the fort. Colonel Allen, in the mean time, acting wholly without authority from Schuyler or Montgomery, had involved himself in a series of disastrous failures in an attack upon Montreal, resulting in his capture and prolonged imprisonment.

9. General Montgomery then proceeded to Montreal, which city, after intercepting and defeating a strong naval and military force under the command of Generals Carleton and Prescott, was surrendered to him on the 12th of November. In the mean time General Washington had, about the middle of September, despatched Arnold with a force of about two thousand men, by the route of the Kennebec River, against Quebec. After incredible hardships and fatigue the troops reached Point Levi, opposite the city, on the 8th of November, and, having been strengthened by the arrival of reinforcements from St. John's, crossed the river on the 13th, and were drawn up on the Plains of Abraham, where they awaited the answer of the garrison to their repeated demands for surrender.

10. Learning, however, of the approach of an armed vessel to the relief of the city, Arnold on the 19th withdrew his forces a short distance up the river, to await the arrival of Montgomery, who on the 3d of December joined him with a strong reinforcement. The combined army immediately moved down the river to Quebec, and on the next day took up their position opposite the city, where vigorous preparations had been made by Carleton, who had escaped from Montreal, for their reception. A spirited but ineffectual bombardment was kept up for several days by the besiegers, when on the 16th a definitive plan of

---

Siege and capture of St. John's. — Disastrous expedition of Allen. — Siege of Quebec by Arnold and Montgomery.

operations was arranged by Montgomery for a final and decisive assault.

11. In consequence, however, of the treachery of deserters, a change in this plan became necessary. Major Brown and Colonel Livingston were intrusted with the execution of two feints on the upper town; Arnold, with Lamb's artillery, was ordered to attack the suburbs on the north; while Montgomery in person was to attack the lower town, with the consolidated forces, upon their junction.

12. At five o'clock in the morning of the last day of December, in the midst of a furious storm of wind and snow, the troops took up their respective lines of march. Montgomery, at the head of his detachment, descended from the Heights of Abraham toward the lower town, where, encountering a block-house of hewed logs, flanked by a strong stockade, with his own hand he sawed off the posts of the latter, and at the head of his party entered the opening. At that moment the occupants of the block-house discharged against the assailants a three-pounder loaded with grape, instantly killing every person who had entered, with the exception of the French guide, including General Montgomery and both his aids. The remainder of the party, appalled by this disaster, immediately fell back hastily and retreated to their quarters.

13. Meanwhile the intrepid Arnold led his men through a succession of heavy snow-drifts to the foot of the cliff on the St. Lawrence, where a battery was erected for the defence of the suburbs. Advancing to its attack at the head of his troops, he was disabled by a musket-shot in the knee, and conveyed from the field. Captain Morgan, assuming the command, carried the battery, amid a storm of musketry and grape-shot, and immediately commenced an assault upon a second battery, which he also carried after a fierce contest of three hours. Carleton, however, with a heavy force, now appeared in his rear, and the gallant Morgan, finding himself unsupported and surrounded was compelled to surrender, leaving a hundred and fifty of his heroic band killed or wounded, and a large number of prisoners, including Captain Lamb, Major Ogden, Aaron Burr, and Captain Oswald.

Death of Montgomery, and defeat of Captain Morgan.

14. General Carleton, after making suitable provision for the disposition of the dead and wounded, with a chivalry which reflects high credit on his character, directed special honors to be paid to the remains of his gallant enemy, General Montgomery, which were buried, under the personal superintendence of the Lieutenant-Governor, within the walls of the city. Forty-two years later they were removed, by order of the Legislature of New York, to St. Paul's Church in the city of New York, where they now repose under a monumental tablet, erected under the directions of Congress as a lasting record of his bravery and worth.

1776. 15. Colonel Arnold assumed the command of the remaining troops, and having withdrawn from the immediate neighborhood of the city, awaited the arrival of General Wooster, who, in April of the ensuing year, renewed the siege. After a series of ineffectual efforts to effect an entrance, the troops, on the approach of General Burgoyne early in May, with heavy reinforcements, hastily retreated, leaving their stores and sick in the hands of the enemy. Thus terminated this bold and daring but disastrous invasion of Canada, — a result due more to the insubordination and want of discipline of a portion of the troops, the absence of necessary supplies, and the inefficiency of some of the officers, than to any deficiency in its conception, or want of ability or heroic bravery in its gallant commanders.

Honors to the memory of Montgomery. — Continuance of the siege by Arnold and Wooster. — Arrival of Burgoyne, and retreat of the American troops.

CHAPTER VI.

DECLARATION OF INDEPENDENCE. — INVESTMENT OF THE CITY OF NEW YORK BY THE BRITISH. — BATTLE OF LONG ISLAND. — RETREAT OF THE AMERICANS TO HARLEM HEIGHTS AND KINGSBRIDGE. — EXECUTION OF NATHAN HALE. — BATTLE OF WHITE PLAINS. — CAPTURE OF FORTS WASHINGTON AND LEE. — RETREAT THROUGH NEW JERSEY.

1. GENERAL WASHINGTON having, about the middle of March, 1776, forced the British troops under Howe to evacuate Boston, whence they sailed for Halifax, and apprehensive of an intended attack upon New York by the forces under Sir Henry Clinton, made immediate preparations for the defence of that city. General Charles Lee, who had commanded the American forces since the departure of Wooster in January, having been ordered to Charleston, General Putnam was assigned to duty in his place. Clinton, aware of the spirited preparations for his reception, passed down the harbor with his troops, and proceeded south to the attack of Charleston.

1776.

2. General Washington, with the main body of his army, arrived in the city in April, and proceeded to fortify the town and its vicinity, together with the passes of the Highlands on the Hudson. On the 25th of June General Howe appeared before the city with a fleet from Halifax, and on the 2d of July took possession of Staten Island on the south, where he was soon after joined by his brother, Admiral Lord Howe, with a fleet and a large land force from England, and by Sir Henry Clinton with the troops under his command.

3. In the mean time a committee of Congress, consisting of Thomas Jefferson of Virginia, John Adams of Massachusetts, Benjamin Franklin of Pennsylvania, Roger Sherman of Connecticut, and Robert R. Livingston of New York, had reported a DECLARATION OF INDEPENDENCE, which, on the FOURTH OF JULY, was unanimously adopted by the delegates of all the late Colonies, now forming the THIRTEEN UNITED STATES of America. This declaration was enthusiastically approved on the 9th of July by

---

Preparations for the defence of New York. — General and Lord Howe and Sir Henry Clinton invest New York. — Declaration of Independence.

the Fourth Provincial Congress of New York, at their meeting at White Plains, and effective measures of defence were inaugurated.

4. The city of New York was now invested by a formidable army of twenty-five thousand veteran troops, under the command of an able and experienced general, and heavy reinforcements from England and the Continent were daily expected. By the possession of the city, with its harbor and adjacent islands, and the consequent command of the Hudson, a free communication with Canada was expected to be secured, and the separation of the Eastern from the Middle States effected. To meet this powerful force, Washington had at his command au undisciplined militia of about seventeen thousand effective men.

5. Several abortive efforts at accommodation having been made by the British commanders, a force of ten thousand men, with forty pieces of artillery, were, on the 22d of August, landed on the southern shore of Long Island, near the villages of New Utrecht and Gravesend, a few miles below the city, and in three divisions marched to the attack of the American camp at Brooklyn, commanded by General Putnam, with a force of about five thousand men. The left division of the British army, under General Grant, took the route by the Narrows towards Gowanus; the right, under Generals Clinton and Cornwallis, that leading to the interior of the island, and intersecting the road leading from Bedford to Jamaica; and the central division, under De Heister, chiefly composed of Hessians, that by the village of Flatbush, on the south of the range of hills connecting the Narrows with Jamaica.

6. On the morning of the 27th, Clinton, advancing from Flatlands, had succeeded in gaining possession of the Jamaica pass, near the site of the present East New York, intrusted to the command of General Sullivan, and, with his entire force, descended, by the village of Bedford, into the plain between the hills and the American camp. Grant, moving along the shores of the bay, attacked Lord Stirling on the present site of the Greenwood Cemetery. De Heister, advancing on the Flatbush road, the patrols assigned to guard the passes having been rash-

---

Approved by Provincial Congress at White Plains. — Plan of the campaign. — Forces of the combatants. — Battle of Long Island. — Disposition of the forces.

ly withdrawn by Putnam's order, engaged Sullivan, while Clinton gained a position in his rear. Sullivan immediately ordered a retreat to the American lines at Brooklyn; but being pressed by Clinton and driven back upon the Hessians, after losing a great portion of his force, he was compelled to surrender.

7. Cornwallis, in the mean while, taking the road to Gowanus, attacked Stirling, who was made prisoner, together with most of his command, many of their number having been drowned while attempting to escape across the Gowanus Creek. The victory on the part of the British was decisive. Five hundred Americans were killed or wounded, and upwards of a thousand taken prisoners and confined in the prison-ships at New York, where, for a long period, they endured extreme hardships and privations. The British loss was comparatively trifling. On the night of the 29th, Washington silently, and under cover of the darkness and a thick mist, drew off the remainder of his troops to New York, unperceived by the enemy.

8. On the 12th of September, Washington, with the broken and dispirited remainder of his forces, retreated to Harlem Heights on the upper part of the island, where he fortified himself and awaited the attack of the British. With the view of obtaining authentic information of their movements, Nathan Hale, a young officer in Colonel Knowlton's regiment, was despatched to the enemy's camp on Long Island, in disguise. After possessing himself of full intelligence of their strength and plans, he was intercepted on his return and conveyed to General Howe's head-quarters, then in New York, where he was tried and convicted as a spy, and executed at daybreak on the ensuing morning, with circumstances of contumely and insult reflecting deep disgrace on their heartless agents.

9. In the mean time, under cover of the fire of the British ships, Howe, on the 15th, landed at Kip's Bay, at the foot of the present Thirty-Sixth Street on the East River, driving before him two brigades of Connecticut militia stationed in the neighborhood for its defence, to the intense and passionate indigna-

---

Defeat of the Americans. — Withdrawal of the troops to New York. — Retreat to Harlem Heights. — Arrest and execution of Nathan Hale as a spy. — Howe effects a landing at Kip's Bay. — Cowardly retreat of Connecticut troops.

tion of Washington, who arrived on the ground just in season to witness, without being able to prevent, their ignominious flight. Seeing that further occupation of the island was impracticable, Putnam received orders to evacuate the city, and the troops at Harlem were removed to Kingsbridge, at its upper extremity. Silliman's brigade, which by some mischance had been left behind, was extricated from its perilous position by the bravery and address of Colonel Burr, then an aid of Putnam's. On the next day a severe skirmish ensued between the contending forces at Harlem, in which the Americans were victorious, with the loss of two brave officers, — Colonel Knowlton of Connecticut and Major Leitch of Virginia.

10. General Howe, with the design of gaining the rear of the American army, leaving a strong force in possession of the city, and sending three armed vessels up the Hudson to intercept all communication with New Jersey, transferred the main portion of his forces, now amounting to 35,000 men, to a point in Westchester County, in the vicinity of Throg's Neck on the Sound, sixteen miles north of the city. Washington, comprehending his designs, and leaving a garrison of three thousand men in Fort Washington on the Hudson, under command of Colonel Magaw, withdrew the residue of his forces to White Plains, on the left bank of the Bronx River.

11. Here the American army took post on the high grounds northwest and northeast of the village, and on the lower ground between, extending from the Bronx on the right to Horton's (now Willett's) Pond, on the left, having the village in their front, and the rocky height known as Chatterton's Hill on the southwest, separated from the right of the lines by a narrow marsh, through which the river flowed. The enemy, meanwhile, having advanced to Scarsdale, within four miles of White Plains, where they remained for three days, marched, on the morning of the 28th of October, in two columns, to the attack, General Clinton with the British troops commanding the right, and General Howe, with the Hessians under De Heister, having charge of the left.

12. Driving before them the pickets and advance parties,

Washington's indignation. — Evacuation of the city. — Skilful extrication of Silliman's brigade. — Skirmish at Harlem. — Advance of the British to Throg's Neck. — Retreat of Washington to White Plains.

the division of De Heister encountered at Hart's Corners, about a mile south of the lines, a battalion of two thousand American troops, under General Spencer, who gave them a temporary check. They speedily rallied, however, and gained a position south of Chatterton's Hill, in front of which intrenchments had been hastily thrown up by the Americans, and placed in charge of General McDougall, at the head of his brigade. Colonel Haslett's Delaware regiment, which had been ordered to his support, was thrown into confusion by the Hessian fire, and replaced by the Maryland and one of the New York regiments on the extreme right of the line.

13. General Howe, abandoning his original intention of attacking the main body on the heights and plains north of the village, concentrated his force against McDougall. A sharp cannonading was kept up for upwards of an hour. The enemy, in three divisions, steadily ascended the hill, attacking simultaneously the regiments stationed on its southern and northern slope and on the summit, as well as the right flank which was assailed by the Hessians. An attempt to turn McDougall's left was promptly defeated. After an obstinate contest, General McDougall's troops were forced to give way, with the loss of about sixty men killed and an equal number wounded, with forty prisoners. The remainder of the force retreated in good order.

14. On the ensuing night, General Washington drew back his lines, ordered fresh reinforcements, and so strengthened his position that no renewal of the attack was attempted. On the 31st he retired to North Castle, about two miles north, where he remained until early in November, when the enemy withdrew their forces to Kingsbridge, preparatory to a contemplated attack on Fort Washington, which was speedily invested.

15. This important fortress occupied a prominent position on the Hudson River, between the present One Hundred and Eighty-First and One Hundred and Eighty-Sixth Streets, the highest point on the island, and completely commanding the navigation of the river. It was supported and defended by a series of strong redoubts, batteries, and other works, on the north and south, extending across the entire island at that point, covering the

Battle of White Plains.

Harlem River, and that portion of Westchester County between its eastern shore and Long Island Sound.

16. General Knyphausen, with a large body of Hessian and English troops, amounting in all to five thousand men, attacked the fort on the 16th of November, which, after a gallant defence by the garrison, under Colonel Magaw, with about three thousand men, was compelled to surrender, with the loss of fifty men killed and about one hundred wounded, the remainder being captured. Two days afterwards, Fort Lee, on the opposite shore of the Hudson, fell into the hands of Lord Cornwallis, with its garrison of six thousand men, and a quantity of baggage and military stores. And the remainder of the American army fell back through New Jersey to Trenton, where, on the 8th of December, they crossed the Delaware into Pennsylvania.

17. Events, meanwhile, of considerable importance, were transpiring on the northern frontier. General Gates, — to whom the command of the troops lately engaged in the disastrous expedition against Canada had been assigned, — apprehensive of an immediate attempt to recapture Crown Point and Ticonderoga, abandoning the former by the advice of a council of officers, concentrated his forces at the latter point, where in August he constructed a squadron of small vessels, and placed them on Lake Champlain under the command of General Arnold. Carleton, on learning this intelligence, made similar preparations on his part to counteract the movement, whatever it might portend, and anchored his squadron opposite St. John's. Arnold, unaware of the strength of his opponent, fell back from his position opposite Crown Point to Valcour's Island, a short distance south of Plattsburg, where he anchored his fleet across the narrow channel between the island and the western shore of the lake, and awaited Carleton's approach.

18. On the morning of the 11th of October the enemy's squadron, consisting of a very superior force in ships, schooners, soldiers, and seamen, appeared off Cumberland Head to the northward, and, sweeping around the southerly point of Valcour's Island, took up a position directly south of the American fleet.

Capture of Forts Washington and Lee. — Retreat of the American army through New Jersey to Pennsylvania. — Naval combat on Lake Champlain between the British and American fleets.

Arnold immediately prepared for action, and at about eleven o'clock his schooner — the Royal Savage — and a few of the small boats got under way, the residue of the squadron remaining at anchor. The schooner was speedily disabled by the enemy's guns, and, to prevent her falling into his hands, run ashore by her captain and burnt. The action was continued with round and grape shot, on both sides, until night separated the combatants.

19. So severe were the injuries sustained by the American squadron in this desperate engagement, that an immediate return to Crown Point was deemed advisable; and notwithstanding the proximity of the enemy's vessels in their front, aided by the darkness of the night and the presence of a heavy fog, they succeeded in passing through the fleet undiscovered, and in reaching Schuyler's Island, ten miles distant, where they stopped for a short time for repairs. Resuming their course, and closely pursued by their disappointed adversaries, they reached Willsborough, about thirty miles north of Crown Point, on the morning of the 13th, and were shortly afterwards overtaken by the enemy's fleet, favored by a fresh northeasterly breeze.

20. The schooner Washington, which was first overtaken, after sustaining with great gallantry the fire of three of the British vessels, struck her colors, and General Waterbury and his men, who were on board, were taken prisoners. The Congress was next attacked, and sustained for five hours a spirited but unequal contest against a vastly superior force, when, having become a complete wreck, with her sails, rigging, and hull torn to shreds, Arnold run her into a creek on the eastern shore of the lake, and set her on fire, with the remaining boats by which he was accompanied. He then, after witnessing the completion of his work, marched his men through the woods to Chimney Point, reaching Crown Point at an early hour on the ensuing morning.

21. Of the fleet with which he sailed from Crown Point a few days before, only two schooners, a sloop, two galleys, and a gondola remained. The prisoners captured from the Washington were released on parole, and returned to Crown Point on

---

The American fleet disabled. — Its retreat and pursuit. — Return to Crown Point.

the next day. General Arnold was highly complimented in all quarters for his skill, bravery, and persistent courage in the face of so great odds; and the result of the combat was hailed as indicative of future naval triumphs on the part of the Americans, under less adverse circumstances.

CHAPTER VII.

FIRST STATE CONSTITUTION. — GEORGE CLINTON ELECTED GOVERNOR. — BARBAROUS TREATMENT OF PRISONERS IN THE CITY OF NEW YORK. — BURGOYNE'S CAMPAIGN. — MURDER OF JANE MCCREA. — BATTLE OF ORISKANY.

1. MEANWHILE the city of New York became, from the period of its occupation by the English troops, the head-quarters of the British army, under the command of General Howe. The patriotic inhabitants — such of them, at least, as had escaped capture and imprisonment — were compelled to abandon their abodes, which were occupied chiefly by officers of the army and hosts of Tories from the neighboring counties. The Provincial Congress adjourned to Kingston and other towns on the Hudson, where, in conjunction with delegates from the interior, they established a committee of safety, with John Jay at its head, and by spirited and patriotic addresses encouraged resistance to the common enemy. Westchester and Rockland, known as the neutral ground, were infested by "Cow-Boys" and "Skinners," — the former avowed Tories, and the latter indifferent to any principle other than plunder.

1777.

2. In March, 1777, General Howe despatched a strong force up the Hudson for the capture of the military stores of the Americans at Peekskill, which, on their approach, were promptly destroyed by the defenders under the command of General McDougall, and the party, without accomplishing their object, returned to New York. A short time afterwards Colonel Meigs, with one hundred and twenty men, attacked a British post at Sag Harbor, on the eastern extremity of Long Island,

---

Result of the conflict. — Occupation of New York. — The neutral ground. — Military stores at Peekskill. — Attack on Sag Harbor.

burned several vessels, store-houses, &c., and took ninety prisoners, for which he received the thanks of Congress.

3. In April of this year, a Convention of delegates, representing the several counties of the State, assembled at Kingston and formed the first State Constitution. By its provisions a Governor was to be elected by the people for a term of three years, and the legislative department vested in a Senate and Assembly, deriving their power from the same source. All inferior offices were to be filled by the Governor and a council of four senators, — one from each district; and to a Council of Revision, similarly constituted, was assigned the power to pass upon the validity and constitutionality of legislative acts. GEORGE CLINTON, of Orange County, already favorably distinguished for his patriotism and public and private worth, was elected Governor. John Jay was appointed Chief-Justice; Robert R. Livingston, Chancellor; and Philip Livingston, James Duane, Francis Lewis, and Gouverneur Morris, delegates to the Continental Congress.

4. During this period, and until nearly the conclusion of the war, the numerous prisons in the city of New York, and the prison-ships in its vicinity, were crowded with captives, whose ill-treatment and sufferings reflected a lasting disgrace upon the vile instruments by whom they were inflicted and upon the nation which permitted them. The City Hall, the Bridewell, situated on the Commons, the new jail in the Provost, many of the churches, the old Sugar-House, built in the days of Leisler, and other public buildings, were transformed into receptacles for the captured soldiers.

5. The Jersey prison-ship, and numerous other vessels in the bay, rivers, and harbor, were converted into loathsome dungeons for the sailors. The former, under the supervision of the infamous Provost-Marshal Cunningham, with his assistants, deputies, and commissaries, were subjected to the most inhuman and incredible barbarities; while the latter were huddled together in vast numbers in crowded hulks and miserable cabins, suffering all the horrors of pestilence, starvation, and tyrannical barbarity.

Constitutional Convention. — Election of Governor and appointment of State officers and Congressional delegates. — Barbarous treatment of prisoners. — The Sugar-House and Jersey prison-ship.

In one church eight hundred prisoners were incarcerated, of whom many died from sheer want of the necessaries of life, ill-treatment, and neglect; and in another three thousand were crowded together, large numbers of whom perished from disease and violence.

6. The atrocities which have consigned the memory of the old Sugar House to an eternal infamy were of a still deeper dye, and their horrible and revolting details are equalled only by the annals of the Bastile and the dungeon vaults of the European feudal ages. But even these were surpassed, if possible, in cruelty and criminality, in the Provost Jail, under the immediate charge of Cunningham, where the most brutal and barbarous treatment to prisoners of distinction of every grade was of daily occurrence. On board the prison-ships the same systematic outrages against the commonest dictates of humanity were continually perpetrated; nor did they cease, in these or the other prisons, notwithstanding the constant remonstrances of Washington, until the close of the war.

7. In accordance with the original design of separating the eastern and northern colonies from the southern and western by the occupancy of the Hudson River, General Burgoyne, in command of an army of seven thousand men, consisting of English, Germans, Canadians, and Indians, established himself, on the 16th of June, 1777, at Crown Point, and from that point proceeded on the 2d of July to invest Ticonderoga, sending out a detachment of about two thousand Canadians and Indians, by way of Oswego, to attack Fort Schuyler on the Mohawk.

8. General St. Clair, who commanded the post at Ticonderoga, with a force of about three thousand men, finding himself unable to hold the outworks against the superior forces brought to bear against him, withdrew to the defences of the fort. The British troops took post on the northwest; their German allies on the opposite side of the lake in the rear of Mount Independence, occupied by the Americans; while Mount Defiance, on the southern side of the outlet, which commanded the entire position, had been left unfortified from inability to furnish it with an effective garrison.

9. The British immediately availed themselves of this omis-

Plan and objects of the campaign. — Attack on Ticonderoga.

sion by planting their artillery on the summit of this height, at the distance of about a mile from the fort; and St. Clair, at once perceiving the futility of further resistance, evacuated the works on the evening of the 5th of July, crossed over to Mount Independence, and, sending his ammunition and stores to Skenesborough, a few miles up the lake, commenced his retreat to Fort Edward.

10. His movements, however, having been discovered by the enemy, through the accidental burning of a building on Mount Independence, he was pursued, his baggage, stores, and provisions seized and destroyed, and his rear division, under Colonel Seth Warner, overtaken at Hubbardton in Vermont, and, after a severe engagement, routed and dispersed. The victors, on the 7th of July, returned in triumph to Ticonderoga, over which the British flag was floating, while the dispirited remnant of the Americans, five days afterwards, reached General Schuyler's camp at Fort Edward.

11. That officer, finding himself unable to maintain his position with a very inferior force against a victorious adversary, sent a strong party to obstruct the route of the invaders, while he slowly retreated, with the residue of his command, down the valley of the Hudson to the mouth of the Mohawk. Here, with the aid of the distinguished Count Kosciusko, who was attached to his staff as engineer, he erected a series of strong intrenchments in the neighborhood of Cohoes Falls, and, reinforced by a large body of New England troops under General Lincoln, awaited, with an army of thirteen thousand men, the approach of the enemy.

12. General Burgoyne's march to Fort Edward was seriously impeded by the numerous obstructions thrown in his path by the party sent out to Skenesborough by Schuyler, and it was not until the 30th of July that his army, nearly destitute of provisions and exhausted by fatigue, reached their destination. On this march occurred the lamentable tragedy of the murder of Jane McCrea, a young woman consigned by her betrothed to a party of Indians belonging to the British army, for conveyance from

---

Retreat of St. Clair. — Retreat of General Schuyler. — Concentration of troops at the mouth of the Mohawk. — Kosciusko. — Murder of Jane McCrea.

Fort Edward to the British camp. The circumstances under which the murder was committed are involved in considerable obscurity; but there seems to be little doubt that the hapless girl was brutally shot down in a quarrel among her savage guides for the reward offered for her transmission to the camp.

13. On the 2d and 3d of August, Fort Schuyler, situated on the site of the present village of Rome, on the Mohawk, had been invested by a detachment of Burgoyne's army, commanded by St. Leger, numbering some seventeen hundred men, and consisting of a large number of Mohawk Indians under Brant, and of American Tories under Sir William Johnson and the infamous Butler. On the morning of the 4th active hostilities commenced, and were continued on the 5th. The fort was commanded by Colonel Peter Gansevoort. General Herkimer, with a force of about eight hundred men, marched to his relief, accompanied by Thomas Spencer, the faithful sachem of the Oneidas. Crossing the Mohawk at the present site of Utica, they encamped on the 5th at Oriskany, near the present village of Whitesborough, from whence General Herkimer sent messengers to apprise Colonel Gansevoort of their approach, and to concert measures of co-operation.

14. In consequence of the reckless impetuosity of the troops under his command and their entire disregard of discipline, Herkimer, seconded by Spencer and some of his most experienced officers, was desirous of remaining in his present camp until the arrival of reinforcements, or intelligence from the fort. The junior officers, however, strongly remonstrated against all delay, and an angry altercation ensued, in the course of which General Herkimer was stigmatized as a coward and a Tory. His indignant reply was a peremptory order to "March on!" and the command was immediately obeyed with the utmost precipitation and disorder, taking care, however, to send out an advanced guard and flanking parties to guard against surprise.

15. St. Leger having received information of his approach, sent forward a detachment under the command of Sir John Johnson, including the entire body of Indians, headed by Brant, to intercept his progress. At about two miles west of Oriskany an ambuscade was prepared by Brant along the margin

of a deep ravine, through which the advancing party were compelled to pass, and into which, followed by their baggage-wagons, they passed, and were immediately surrounded and hemmed in by their savage foe, shouting the war-whoop and pouring in upon their disorderly and panic-stricken columns a torrent of rifle-balls. The rear-guard, cut off from their advancing comrades, fled with precipitation, closely pursued by the Indians, by whom they were severely harassed, while the main body, recovering from their surprise, maintained the unequal contest with the skill and desperation of veterans.

16. Early in the action, General Herkimer was severely wounded by a musket-ball, which killed his horse and shattered his own leg. At his request he was placed upon his saddle at the foot of a tree, where he coolly continued to direct the battle, which raged with the utmost fury for nearly an hour, when it was interrupted by a heavy thunder-storm, which enabled the little band to gain a more favorable position. The struggle was again renewed, and just as the Indians were beginning to give way before the skilful and persistent attacks of the Americans, a reinforcement of Tories was sent by St. Leger to their relief, and the hand-to-hand contest continued with increased determination and ferocity on both sides.

17. The signal guns from the fort now announced a sortie from the garrison, which had been previously concerted by General Herkimer, and, a *ruse* of Butler's for deceiving the Americans by the appearance of relief having been detected, the Tory reinforcement were driven from their ground with great slaughter, followed by their associates and the Indians, who, perceiving the retreat of their allies, immediately fled in every direction, leaving the heroic band, after a contest of eight hours' duration, in possession of the field.

18. Meanwhile the detachment from the fort, under the command of Colonel Marinus Willett, made an impetuous attack upon St. Leger's advanced guard, and speedily succeeded in gaining possession of his camp, military stores, and baggage, without the loss of a single man, driving the Indians into the woods and compelling Johnson to a hasty retreat. Five British standards were captured and immediately hoisted on the flag-

Indian ambuscade.

staff of the fort, under the American colors. The siege was continued until the 22d, when the appearance of General Arnold with reinforcements from Schuyler induced the prompt withdrawal of the British and their savage allies. General Herkimer soon after died from the effects of his wound.

CHAPTER VIII.

First and Second Battles of Stillwater. — Victory of the Americans. — Surrender of Burgoyne at Saratoga.

1. General Burgoyne, weakened and discouraged as he was by the defeat at Bennington of an expedition sent into Vermont for supplies to his army, by the scarcity of provisions, and by the numerous obstructions which were interposed to his progress on every hand, still persisted in his determination to carry out the original plan of the campaign by effecting a union with the forces of Lord Howe, and thereby cutting off all communication between the eastern and the middle and southern colonies. With this view, on the 13th and 14th of September he crossed with his army to the western bank of the Hudson, and encamped on the heights and plains of Saratoga, on the ground now occupied by the village of Schuylerville, — the American army being stationed in the neighborhood of Stillwater, about nine miles distant.

1777.

2. On the 18th he advanced to a position within about two miles from the American camp, near what is now known as Wilbur's Basin, where, having strengthened himself by throwing up intrenchments and redoubts, and being further protected by a deep ravine in front, preparations were immediately made for an attack on the American lines. The right wing of his army consisted of light-infantry and grenadiers, supported by the Hessian riflemen and a body of Canadian Tories and Indians as skirmishers, and was placed under the command of General Frazer,

---

Termination of the siege. — Reinforcements from Arnold and Schuyler. — Retreat of the British. — Plan of the campaign. — Burgoyne advances to Saratoga. — Position of the armies.

Major Ackland, and the Earl of Balcarras; the centre, of English troops under Burgoyne in person and General Hamilton; and the left, of the artillery regiments and Hessians under Generals Riedesel and Philips.

3. The Americans occupied an advantageous position on Bemis's Heights, which they had taken care strongly to protect, by the erection of breastworks and redoubts. Its right, commanded by General Gates, who had recently superseded Schuyler, occupied the meadows between the heights and the river; and the left, under General Arnold and Colonel Morgan, occupied the heights and the high grounds to the west. A deep, closely wooded ravine also protected the front of the right wing, and, at a little distance north, another of a similar character intervened between the two armies.

4. On the afternoon of the 19th the enemy in three divisions advanced to the attack, — the centre crossing the ravine in a line directly in front of the American camp, the right around its head, and the left passing down the road skirting the river. Colonel Morgan's regiment of riflemen, led by Major Morris, encountered the advanced column, and after an impetuous attack were driven from the field with the loss of twenty men. Arnold was immediately despatched with two regiments to their relief; but notwithstanding his accustomed display of vigor and bravery, he was forced to retreat, Gates having refused the reinforcements which he required.

5. Arnold immediately, by a rapid countermarch, fell suddenly and with great precipitation upon the enemy's centre, commanded by Burgoyne himself, and, having been strengthened by the accession of several regiments belonging to his own division, — comprising the New York troops, under Colonels Pierre Van Courtlandt and the Livingstons, with the New Hampshire, Connecticut, and Massachusetts troops, — maintained the action for four hours, until darkness separated the combatants, when he retired in good order and without pursuit. The forces of the two armies were nearly equal, the superiority in numbers being with the enemy, who had thirty-five hundred men against Arnold's three thousand. The British loss was six

---

Battle at Bemis's Heights. — Arrangement of forces. — Repulse of Morgan and Arnold. — Renewal of Arnold's attack.

hundred killed and wounded, while the Americans' was only about half that number. The enemy retained possession of the field; and both parties strengthened their positions preparatory to a renewal of the battle.

6. Meantime an unfortunate and serious misunderstanding had sprung up between Generals Gates and Arnold, growing out of the removal of Schuyler; and an unpleasant interview, following the detachment of Morgan's riflemen and Dearborn's infantry from Arnold's division, had resulted in his removal from all command, and exclusion from head-quarters, the left wing being assigned to General Lincoln. So far was this bitter feud carried, that no mention was made by Gates, in his official despatches to the Commander-in-Chief, of the important part taken in the battle of the previous day by Arnold.

7. For upwards of two weeks following the battle of Bemis's Heights, or Stillwater, as it is more generally designated, the enemy's lines were incessantly harassed by sorties from the American camp, though no general engagement occurred. The supply of provisions and forage for the British was daily diminishing. The difficulties of a retreat to Canada, combined with the hazard of leaving Gates free to turn his army against Howe, inclined him to await communications from the latter; but the pressure of want, and the necessity of some movement to supply the deficiencies of the soldiery, rendered a second and decisive battle imperative.

8. On the 7th of October, accordingly, General Burgoyne, in the absence of all information from Howe, deemed it advisable to make a demonstration on the left of the American lines. A detachment of fifteen hundred regular troops, with a heavy battery of artillery and field-pieces, accompanied by Generals Philips, Riedesel, and Frazer, was moved, under his immediate command, to a position within three quarters of a mile of the left wing of the Americans, while Captain Frazer's rangers, the Indians, and Tory refugees, were directed to effect, if possible, a diversion of their attention from the operations on their flank.

Dissension between Gates and Arnold. — Arnold deprived of his command. — Unworthy conduct of Gates. — Temporary cessation of hostilities. — Embarrassing position of Burgoyne. — Active operations determined upon. — Movements of the enemy.

Their movements were, however, seasonably discovered, and Morgan was ordered by Gates to gain the high ground on their right, while General Poor, with the Eastern and New York regiments, advanced against their left.

9. By a sudden and rapid movement the attack was commenced on the extreme left of the enemy's line, where Major Ackland was in command, and soon reached the centre, while Morgan appeared on the right, and the action became general. Burgoyne finding himself unable effectually to resist this combined attack, attempted to form a second line in rear of the first, to secure the retreat of the latter; but, before this object could be effected, Major Dearborn had effected a breach in the enemy's left wing, compelling the right to rally to its relief.

10. In the execution of this movement, General Frazer received a mortal wound, and Burgoyne found it necessary to order a retreat of the main body, under cover of the forces of Generals Philips and Reidesel, and such assistance as he himself might be able to render with such troops as could hastily be collected. With great difficulty they were enabled to regain their camp, with the loss of six pieces of artillery and several of their men.

11. Arnold, notwithstanding orders to the contrary, had occupied his usual place at the head of his troops, and participated in the attack with his usual bravery and determined energy. Flying in hot haste from one part of the field to the other, he cheered on his men, everywhere received with the greatest enthusiasm, his orders carried out and his example emulated throughout the line. Chiefly by his indomitable spirit and gallant exertions the right and rear of the enemy's forces were carried and held by Lieutenant-Colonel Brooks, when the approach of darkness again put an end to the contest.

12. The Americans had, however, obtained a complete and brilliant victory. The British had been driven from the field with the loss of several of their best officers, six hundred men killed, wounded, and prisoners, and most of their artillery, ammunition, horses, and baggage. The American loss did not exceed one hundred and fifty killed and wounded, among the

---

Counter-movements of the Americans. — Second battle of Stillwater. — Bravery of Arnold. — Retreat of the British. — Victory of the Americans.

latter of whom was General Arnold, who, just as the victory was won, received a ball which fractured his leg, killing his horse. How noble and brilliant would have been his record, could it only have terminated here!

13. General Burgoyne, on the night of the 7th, changed his position to the heights on the west bank of the Hudson, near the present village of Wilbur's Basin. On the morning of the 8th the Americans took possession of his abandoned camp; and although a random fire of artillery and small-arms was kept up between the armies during the day, no further attack was made on either side. General Gates despatched a brigade under General Fellows to take post on the east side of the Hudson, opposite Saratoga, to cut off the enemy's retreat. Another detachment of two thousand men was sent to intercept him at Fort Edward, and a third, with a similar object, to the ford higher up.

14. Breaking up his command, and leaving behind him some three hundred of his sick and wounded in consequence of the bad state of the roads, Burgoyne, on the night of the 8th, retreated with great secrecy, with all his remaining baggage, to Saratoga (now Schuylerville), which he reached on the succeeding night. On the afternoon of the 10th he was overtaken by the Americans, and on the following morning an injudicious attempt on the part of Gates to bring on a general action, in ignorance of the position of the enemy, was only frustrated by the disobedience of his peremptory orders by the officers under his command.

15. On the 12th, no reliable information having been received either from Clinton or Howe, and the supply of provisions continuing inadequate, a council of officers decided upon the necessity and expediency of a retreat, if possible, by way of Fort Edward or Lake George. This having been found wholly impracticable, by the report of scouts, and three days' supply only remaining, a capitulation was determined upon on the next day. On the 16th the negotiations for this purpose were completed, and on the 17th the surrender effected in the presence of both armies, with all the usual formalities.

General Arnold wounded. — Movements of the two armies. — Burgoyne's retreat cut off. — Retreat to Saratoga. — Injudicious conduct of Gates. — Surrender of Burgoyne.

16. Twelve general officers, some thirty regimental officers, nearly nine hundred subalterns, and four thousand eight hundred and thirty-six privates, amounting in all to five thousand seven hundred and sixty-three, laid down their arms; and twenty-seven pieces of cannon, with implements and stores complete, five thousand stands of arms, and great quantities of ammunition, were captured.

17. The surrender of Burgoyne was followed by the evacuation of Ticonderoga and Crown Point, and the total prostration of the British power in the northern section of the State. Its effect upon the American army and the American people generally was electric. Following, as it did, upon the disastrous results of the campaign of the preceding year, and the recent defeats in Pennsylvania, it infused fresh spirit into the hearts of the desponding, encouraged and strengthened the timid, appalled the domestic traitors, and cheered the patriots throughout the country. It riveted the alliance of the French auxiliaries, and secured the respectful regards, if not the effective aid, of foreign States. Even in the British Parliament it called forth the indignant remonstrances of the ablest English statesmen, and enlisted the ardent sympathies of the friends of freedom throughout the world.

18. Sir Henry Clinton, with the view of co-operating with Burgoyne, had, early in October, ascended the Hudson with a strong force, and on the 6th a detachment under Lieutenant-Colonel Campbell gained possession of Forts Montgomery and Clinton, on the boundaries of Orange and Rockland County, after a severe contest, maintained, under the immediate direction of Governor Clinton, by Colonels Livingston, Bruyn, and McLoughry. Having also secured the occupation of Fort Constitution, opposite West Point, with the uninterrupted command of the river, they contented themselves with burning Kingston, and, intelligence of the defeat of Burgoyne rendering further advance unnecessary, returned to New York, while General Gates, with a thousand of his victorious troops, rejoined Washington's camp in Pennsylvania.

Effects of the surrender. — Capture of Forts Clinton, Montgomery, and Constitution, on the Hudson. — Burning of Kingston. — General Gates joins Washington's army in Pennsylvania.

CHAPTER IX.

INDIAN BARBARITIES. — MASSACRE AT CHERRY VALLEY. — SULLIVAN'S CAMPAIGN.

1. THE succeeding year was chiefly distinguished, in the annals of the State of New York, by an atrocious succession of Indian and Tory barbarities and massacres in the Mohawk Valley and among the interior settlements, under the auspices of Joseph Brant, the well-known chief of the Six Nations, and Walter Butler, the son of the fiendish miscreant John Butler, the chief agent in the famous massacre in Wyoming.

1778.

2. On the 1st of June, Captain Patrick, of Colonel Alden's Massachusetts regiment, with a small party of volunteers, was attacked at the little settlement of Cobleskill, on the Mohawk River, in Schoharie County, by a party of Indians and Tories commanded by Brant and one Service, numbering over three hundred and fifty. After a bloody and desperate contest, Patrick, with twenty of his men, was killed, and several others wounded and captured; and the enemy, having plundered and burnt the houses of the settlers, returned to Canada.

3. During the spring of this year, in apprehension of Indian hostilities, General Lafayette had directed a fort to be built at Cherry Valley, in Otsego County, then a part of Tryon County. Brant, with his savage warriors, hovered around the settlement while the work was in progress, destroying Springfield, and continuing his aggressions from time to time in the neighborhood, until they assumed so formidable a character that Colonel Ichabod Allen, with a regiment of Continental troops, was ordered to the village, and took possession of the church, surrounded by a heavy stockade, for the protection of the inhabitants.

4. At the approach of winter, however, the settlers returned to their deserted habitations, — further hostilities having apparently been abandoned, — and Brant retired with his forces

---

Indian and Tory atrocities. — Attack upon Cobleskill. — Destruction of the settlement.

to Niagara. On his journey he was met by Walter Butler at the head of a detachment of two hundred men known as "Butler's Rangers," — a band of Tories commanded by his father. Smarting under the indignities inflicted upon him by the patriots, who had a short time previous arrested and confined him as a Tory, and burning for revenge, he was on his way to destroy Cherry Valley, whither he was accompanied by Brant with five hundred of his party.

5. On the 6th of November, information of the intended attack was communicated to Colonel Alden by Colonel Gansevoort, the commander of Fort Schuyler; but the warning was contemptuously disregarded by the former, who refused to permit the return of the settlers to the fort, with their families and effects, and contented himself with sending out scouts, who fell victims to their wary and vigilant savage enemies, without having been able to apprise the garrison of the imminent danger hanging over it.

6. On the morning of the 11th of November, in the midst of a heavy storm of snow and rain, the enemy having on the previous night gained the outskirts of the town, and encamped upon a hill thickly covered with evergreens, about a mile from the fort, advanced upon the unsuspecting settlement by a path which had been left unprotected, and took possession of a swamp in its vicinity. Colonel Alden was again warned of their approach by a traveller, who had been shot at and wounded by two of their number on his way to the village, but still persisted with an inexplicable infatuation in discrediting the report.

7. The attack immediately commenced, Brant with his Indians leading the way, closely followed by Butler and his rangers. The house of Mr. Wells was first entered by a mixed party of Tories and Senecas, and his whole family, with one exception, — consisting of himself, wife, four children, mother, brother, sister, and three domestics, — ruthlessly massacred, one son, absent at school, only escaping. Colonel Alden, also an inmate of the house, was tomahawked and scalped in his attempted flight. The house of the aged pastor, Mr. Dunlap, was next attacked, his wife slain before his eyes, and his own life

---

Attack upon Cherry Valley. — Indiscriminate massacre of the inhabitants.

spared only through the interference of one of the Mohawk chiefs.

8. Colonel Campbell's house was then surrounded, and in his absence his wife and four children were taken prisoners. The indiscriminate slaughter of men, women, and children went on with relentless ferocity, until thirty-two of the inhabitants and eleven soldiers were slain; all the dwellings and out-houses, with their contents, burned; and forty prisoners, including the officers of the garrison, carried into captivity. On the next day, after securing all the sheep, cattle, and horses of the settlement, and discharging the captured women and children, the enemy retired.

9. It is but justice to Brant to state that the chief responsibility of this savage outbreak and wholesale massacre and robbery of innocent and defenceless women and children rested upon the head of the infamous Butler and his malignant band of traitors and Tories. Brant exerted himself throughout the fearful conflict to save the effusion of blood and arrest the indiscriminate slaughter going on around him. He succeeded in protecting and concealing several of the inhabitants, while Butler personally directed all the operations of the party.

10. Of the wretched survivors of this bloody massacre, nearly two hundred were deprived of house and home, and left almost entirely destitute of provision and clothing. Most of those killed were women and children, and many of the prisoners consisted of men suspected of Tory principles, and who consequently deemed themselves secure of protection from their captors. No distinction, however, seems to have been made between them and others by their infuriated enemies, and not even the influence of Brant was able to afford them any exemption from the general slaughter.

1779. 11. Early in June, 1779, General Clinton conducted an expedition up the Hudson, resulting in the capture of Stony Point, a rocky promontory at the head of Haverstraw Bay, on the west bank of the river, and Verplanck's Point, nearly opposite on the eastern side. On the 15th of July, however, General Wayne, acting under detailed and minute instruc-

---

Brant's complicity. — Wretched condition of the remaining inhabitants — Capture and recapture of Stony Point and Verplanck's Point.

tions from General Washington, recaptured the first-named fortress after a spirited and severe contest, with heavy loss of men and military stores on the part of the British. The fort on Verplanck's Point was immediately surrendered, and soon afterwards Major Lee surprised a British garrison at Paulus Hook, now Jersey City, on the west side of the Hudson, opposite New York, killing thirty men, and taking a large number of prisoners.

12. On the night of the 19th of July, Brant, at the head of sixty warriors of his tribe and twenty-seven Tories in Indian disguise, attacked the settlement at Minisink, in the western part of Orange County, lying on the Neversink River, at the foot of the Shawangunk Mountains. After setting fire to ten houses of the inhabitants, and destroying the church, barns, and mills in the neighborhood, they retired with their plunder, without attempting further violence.

13. Intelligence of this outrage having been forwarded to Colonel Tusten at Goshen, that officer at once proceeded with about a hundred and fifty men, many of them volunteers, to the settlement, where a council was held as to the best mode of avenging the injury. Colonel Tusten opposed pursuit until the arrival of reinforcements to his small band; but the majority, under the advice of Major Meeker, counselled an immediate march, which was accordingly directed. On the following morning, Colonel Hathorn arrived with a few recruits, and assumed command of the party as the senior officer.

14. Ascertaining the superiority of the enemy's force, of which the predatory band of the preceding day was only a portion, the officers of the detachment again counselled prudence, but were again overruled by their rash associates; nor did the death of Captain Tyler, who was soon afterwards shot down in a reconnoitring expedition by a party in ambush, induce greater caution. They soon came up with the main body of the enemy, moving towards the ford at the mouth of the Lackawaxen Creek, when Colonel Hathorn, with the view of intercepting their flight, turned to the right to escape observation until he could accomplish this object.

Surprise of British garrison at Paulus Hook. — Attack of Brant upon the settlement at Minisink.

15. Brant, having detected this movement, immediately threw his force into the rear of his opponent, and placed them advantageously in ambush, while he executed a series of skilful and successful manœuvres to draw off his attention. Upwards of fifty men were separated from the main body, leaving the remainder to sustain the shock of the enemy's attack. Occupying the summit of a hill, and drawn up in hollow squares, they maintained the unequal contest for several hours, when their sheltered position became exposed, and they were surrounded by their foes, and compelled to surrender at discretion or cut their way through their merciless enemies. The wounded—seventeen in number—were immediately butchered, forty-five were slaughtered in their efforts to retreat, and of the whole body thirty only escaped.

16. But the hour of fearful retribution was at hand. An expedition was organized under the direction of Washington, and placed under the command of General Sullivan, for the effectual extirpation of these savage and brutal marauders: the main body, under Sullivan in person, to operate in Pennsylvania and the neighborhood of the Wyoming Valley; and the other, under General James Clinton, brother of the Governor and father of De Witt Clinton, to move from Canajoharie by way of Otsego Lake and the Susquehanna River to unite with the main body at Tioga Point.

17. General Clinton, at the head of fifteen hundred men, reached Canajoharie on the 16th of June, and on the succeeding day commenced the transportation of his boats — two hundred and ten in number, with the necessary stores — to the head of Otsego Lake, a distance of twenty miles, over roads cut through the forests and over the hills. With the efficient assistance of Colonel Willett he accomplished this task in ten days, and on the 1st of July passed down the lake to its outlet, near the present village of Cooperstown, where he awaited orders from Sullivan, erecting, in the mean while, a dam across the outlet for facility of transportation, as well as for the destruction, by the overflow of its waters on removal, of the crops of the Indians on the banks of the Susquehanna, — both which objects were fully ac-

---

Battle at Minisink. — Generals Sullivan and Clinton's expedition against the Indians.

complished, to the astonishment and surprise of the savages, who were ignorant of the cause.

18. It was not, however, until late in August that the division joined General Sullivan at Tioga, and their united forces proceeded up the east bank of the Chemung River, destroying the crops of the Indians in their progress. On the 29th the enemy were discovered in force, occupying an advantageous position near the present site of Elmira. The brigades of Generals Clinton and Poor were advanced against the position occupied by the enemy's right, the possession of which was fiercely contested by Brant and his Indians, who, after a protracted and skilful defence, were at length driven back, and General Poor pressed to the attack of the left flank.

19. Rallying his warriors to a renewed effort, and supported by his Tory allies, Brant again sounded the terrible war-whoop, and the contest was resumed with desperate energy. The superiority of the invading force, however, and the presence of the artillery, soon compelled them to yield, and a precipitate retreat ensued. The fugitives were followed for two miles, leaving their dead and tomahawks and scalping-knives behind. During the ensuing two weeks their villages and crops were destroyed throughout the entire settlement, including the chief town, near Geneva, in which were some sixty houses surrounded by orchards and cornfields, and those on the present sites of Waterloo, Canandaigua, Honeyoye, Genesee, and Cuyler, and on the banks of Cayuga Lake.

20. On the 14th of September the army crossed the Genesee River, where, at the old town of Genesee, they found the mutilated remains of Lieutenant Boyd and Sergeant Parker, who had been cruelly put to death by torture, by command of Butler, notwithstanding the protection solemnly pledged them by Brant. Upwards of a hundred and twenty houses, seven hundred acres of growing corn, and vast quantities of other property belonging to the Indians, were here destroyed. Recrossing the river on the 16th, the troops commenced their homeward march, reaching

---

Progress of the expedition. — Defeat of the Indians, and destruction of their villages and crops. — Martyrdom of Lieutenant Boyd and Sergeant Parker. — Destruction of the old Genesee village. — Return of the expedition.

Wyoming on the 30th and Eastern Pennsylvania on the 15th of October.

21. This severe chastisement of the Indians, while it afforded a temporary check to their ravages and subjected them to great suffering and distress, failed, nevertheless, in reducing to any considerable extent their effective numerical force, or preventing their retaliation on the frontier settlements whenever a favorable opportunity was presented. The wholesale destruction of property by the invading army, and the disgraceful brutality of portions of the troops in emulating the worst barbarities of their savage foes, reflected no small discredit on the enterprise in the estimation of the friends of humanity at home and abroad.

CHAPTER X.

TREASON OF ARNOLD. — CAPTURE AND EXECUTION OF ANDRÉ. — CLOSE OF THE WAR.

1. On the 3d of February, 1780, five companies of Continental troops, consisting of about two hundred and fifty men, commanded by Lieutenant-Colonel Thompson, of Massachusetts, stationed at a place known as Young's house, on the Tarrytown Road, in Westchester County, a few miles north of the village, were attacked by a force of between five and six hundred royalists from Kingsbridge and Fort Washington, under the command of Colonel Norton. The little garrison, taken by surprise, were unprepared for defence; and after a gallant and severe conflict were compelled to retreat with the loss of one officer and thirteen men killed, thirty-seven wounded, and twenty prisoners. The Royal Grenadiers having forced a house in which a few of the fugitives had taken refuge, it was set on fire and burned to the ground, with five wounded men who were unable to effect their escape.

2. In the year 1778 a strong redoubt, called Fort Clinton in honor of George Clinton, then Governor of New York, had been

---

Results of the expedition. — Affair at Young's house, near Tarrytown.

erected on the extreme end of the promontory of West Point, on the west bank of the Hudson, which, with other defences, including an enormous iron chain, each ring of which weighed one hundred pounds, stretched across the river, were intended to strengthen this important position and prevent the access of the British.

3. BENEDICT ARNOLD, in an evil hour for his own fame, had been, in the fall of 1780, assigned to the command of this post. His previous splendid services in the French and Indian War and during Burgoyne's campaign had been somewhat obscured by subsequent events, while in temporary command at Philadelphia in 1778, and he had been reprimanded by Washington under sentence of a court-martial for alleged official malpractices and dishonesty. Still he possessed the full confidence of the Commander-in-Chief, and was believed to be entirely trustworthy.

4. Smarting under the disgrace of his sentence and the reprimand of the General, and oppressed by pecuniary embarrassments, he was induced, while in command of West Point, to enter into a treasonable correspondence with Sir Henry Clinton, the commander of the British army at New York, having for its ultimate object the betrayal of the fortress committed to his charge, with its dependencies, in consideration of fifty thousand dollars and a brigadier's commission in the English army.

5. On the 3d of August, Arnold took command of the fortress, establishing his head-quarters at a house on the opposite side of the river, formerly belonging to Colonel Beverly Robinson, but which, on account of his adhesion to the Royalists, had been confiscated by the Americans. West Point, occupying a position which commanded the communication between the Eastern and Southern States, and being considered impregnable to attack, was regarded as the strongest and most important military post in the Union. A treasonable correspondence had been carried on between Arnold and Major John André, Adjutant-General of the British army, in behalf of Sir Henry Clinton, for nearly eighteen months previous to the occupation of the fort, under the names of "Gustavus" and "John Anderson,"

Treason of Arnold. — Arnold's occupation of West Point. — His treasonable correspondence with André.

and a tempting opportunity was now afforded for the culmination of the negotiations.

6. Arnold was now desirous of a personal interview with André; and with a view to this object he informed Colonel Sheldon, the commander of a troop of horse at Salem, Westchester County, that he expected a person from New York with a flag of truce, directing him to meet him at Dobbs's Ferry and escort him to head-quarters. Sheldon, in ignorance of the purport of this communication, returned it, with a message that he would be unable to meet the flag, and expressing the hope that General Arnold would himself be able to do so. To this arrangement the latter assented.

7. On arriving at the ferry, however, neither André nor Beverly Robinson, who was cognizant of the whole affair, appeared. Arnold immediately wrote to Washington, who was at Tappan with the main body of the army, preparing for another attack on New York, informing him of his journey down the river for the examination of its defences and the arrangement of signals. Another meeting with André, in disguise, was appointed for the 20th of September. Clinton in the mean while had, on the 18th, sent the sloop-of-war Vulture up the river with Robinson, who despatched a note to Arnold at Verplanck's Point, requesting an interview, ostensibly with reference to the disposition of his property opposite West Point.

8. A few hours after the reception of this letter, Washington himself, accompanied by General Lafayette, arrived at Verplanck's Point, on his way to Hartford to meet Count Rochambeau. Arnold showed him Robinson's letter, and was cautioned by him to avoid all correspondence with the latter, as, in view of all the occurrences of the past year, calculated to implicate him unfavorably in the public estimation. The General with his suite crossed the river in Arnold's barge, where, from some chance observation of Lafayette's, and a suspicious scrutiny by Washington of the Vulture, which lay at anchor in the distance, he became seriously apprehensive of the discovery of his treason.

9. On the succeeding day he communicated with Robinson, apprising him of his intention to send a trusty messenger on the

---

Arrangements for an interview. — Arrival of Washington and Lafayette. — Apprehensions of Arnold.

next night to Dobbs's Ferry, or on board the Vulture, enclosing a copy of his letter to André, both which were transmitted by Robinson to Sir Henry Clinton, who, on the morning of the 20th, despatched André to Dobbs's Ferry, with positive instructions not to go within the American lines, to assume no disguise and receive no papers. Failing to meet any one at the ferry, André proceeded up the river to the Vulture, which he reached at seven o'clock, but found there no messenger from Arnold, as he had been led to expect.

10. A Mr. Joshua H. Smith, who resided near the village of Haverstraw and sustained a respectable character, having been frequently employed by Arnold and his predecessor in obtaining intelligence of the movements of the British, had been apprised by the former of the expected conference, and requested to bring "Mr. Anderson" on shore from the Vulture. Being unable to procure a boat for this purpose, he sent a message to that effect to head-quarters, and Arnold went himself to Verplanck's Point, and despatched a messenger to Continental Village for his own barge, with directions to forward it to the creek in Haverstraw near Smith's house.

11. On the night of the 21st, Smith, with muffled oars, descended the river to the Vulture, returning at a late hour with Major André, who, in spite of the remonstrances of Robinson, persisted in going on shore in his uniform, concealed, however, by a large blue surtout. Landing at the foot of Clove Mountain, six miles below Stony Point, he was conducted by Smith to the presence of Arnold, who awaited his arrival among the bushes in the vicinity. Their conference was prolonged until daybreak, when they rode together to the residence of Smith. The challenge of a sentinel, and the cannonade on the Vulture, compelling her to drop still farther down the river, were the first intimation to the unfortunate André of his presence within the American lines.

12. Everything having been satisfactorily arranged between the conspirators, Arnold returned at ten o'clock to his quarters; and André, exchanging his uniform for a disguise, and furnished with a pass from Arnold, with several important papers concealed

---

Progress of the negotiations between Arnold and André. — Interview between Arnold and André. — Consummation of the treason.

in his stockings containing full information of the condition and strength of the fort and the arrangements for the movements of the garrison in case of an alarm, proceeded on horseback, accompanied by Smith, to King's Ferry, which they crossed, and proceeded through the upper part of Westchester County on their route to the Vulture, Smith having refused, on pretence of fatigue and illness, to convey him thither by boat.

13. At about nine o'clock in the evening they were challenged by a sentinel eight miles from the ferry, and Captain Boyd, the commander of the post, made his appearance, inspected their passports, and demanded their business. Apparently satisfied with the explanation given by Smith, he informed him of the dangerous condition of the roads leading to White Plains, infested as they were by Cow-Boys and Skinners of both armies, and advised their remaining at the post until the next morning. Unwilling to excite increased suspicion, this arrangement was assented to, and they passed the night very uneasily at the house of Andreas Miller, who lived near by.

14. At dawn on the succeeding morning they resumed their journey, taking the route to Pine's Bridge, André being in unusually cheerful spirits, and conversing freely with his companion on literary and other topics. After partaking of a simple breakfast at a house about two miles north of the Bridge, Smith left André and returned to his family, then at Fishkill. The latter proceeded alone on his perilous journey through Tarrytown. Between eleven and twelve o'clock his progress was intercepted by three militia-men, — John Paulding, David Williams, and Isaac Van Wart, — while watching with their comrades for stragglers and stray cattle from the British lines, who, perceiving his approach, at once arrested him.

15. Losing his presence of mind at this unexpected obstacle, André, aware of the character of the region, and its common occupation by stragglers from both armies indiscriminately, immediately expressed to his captors his hope that they belonged to his own party. "Which party?" demanded Paulding. "The lower," replied André. "I do," observed the former; upon which André imprudently avowed himself a British officer,

---

André's retreat and capture at Tarrytown.

on particular business, and begged not to be detained for a moment. This sealed his doom.

16. On being informed of the truth by his captors, he produced Arnold's passport, and endeavored to excuse his previous statement by his apprehensions of falling in with a British party; but neither these nor his liberal offers of money and his gold watch were of any avail with these stern and incorruptible patriots. On discovering the important papers concealed on his person, he was conducted to the nearest military station at North Castle.

17. On the next day he was transferred, for greater security, to Colonel Sheldon's quarters at Salem, where he was recognized by Major Tallmadge, who urged Colonel Jameson, the commander of the post, not to return him to Arnold, and took charge of him himself. He was, however, very injudiciously permitted to communicate with Arnold, and thereby was the first to apprise him of the failure of their plans, and to enable him to make his escape, which he accordingly effected on the same day, in the Vulture, having taken a hurried leave of his wife, and manned his barge without a moment's delay.

18. Washington, in ignorance of all these events, arrived early in the morning at Arnold's head-quarters, and, having breakfasted, crossed over to West Point. Finding him absent, he spent some time in an examination of the defences of the post and returned in the afternoon, when he was informed by Colonel Hamilton of the whole conspiracy and its detection, but too late to prevent the escape of the traitor.

19. Meanwhile his unfortunate victim, Major André, was treated with great kindness and consideration by Major Tallmadge, who soon contracted a strong friendship and regard for him, and indulged him in every privilege of which his situation admitted, permitting him to communicate freely with Washington, which he did, informing him of his name and rank, the motives from which he acted, and his readiness to submit to such consequences as the stern laws of honorable warfare exacted.

20. On the 29th of September, Washington, after visiting

Washington's discovery of the treason. — Conduct of André.

West Point, and making every preparation for its defence, went to Tappan, where the army was encamped. André, in the mean time, had been taken from Sheldon's quarters to Robinson's house, thence to West Point, where he remained until the 28th, when he was conducted to Tappan. His behavior during this period, and his unaffected gratitude for all the indulgences permitted him, secured him the sincere sympathy and kindly regards of all with whom he came in contact.

21. A board of officers, consisting of six major-generals and eight brigadiers, was convened immediately on the arrival of Washington, before which André was tried, convicted, and sentenced to suffer death. Every effort was made by Sir Henry Clinton to avert his fate, and every opportunity afforded by Washington for his defence. His only request was that he might be shot, as became a soldier; but this mitigation of his sentence was deemed incompatible with the strict rules of the service. It was believed, however, that Washington would not have been unwilling to have exchanged him for the vile traitor whose dupe he had been.

22. Arnold, meanwhile, had taken up his abode in the city of New York, where a gallant effort was made for his capture by the chivalrous Champe, who feigned to desert to the British army, and met with a cordial reception from the traitor. Availing himself with promptitude of the facilities thus obtained, a plan for seizing and carrying him off was matured, but on the day preceding that fixed for its execution was unfortunately foiled by an order for the embarkation of Champe for the Chesapeake. He, however, embraced the earliest opportunity to desert from the British army and return to his comrades for the vindication of his honor and patriotism. Arnold remained in the service until the close of the war, when he repaired to England, where he died, several years afterwards, in obscurity and disgrace, thus closing in darkest infamy a career which might have been distinguished beyond most of his compeers for bravery and daring heroism.

23. The fatal day for his execution having arrived, André, at noon of the 2d of October, arrayed in the full dress of a British

---

Trial, conviction, and sentence of André by a military court. — Efforts for the capture of Arnold. — His subsequent career.

officer, with the exception of the sword, was conducted by a large detachment of troops, accompanied by an immense concourse of people, to the gallows, which was erected on the summit of a hill about a quarter of a mile west of Tappan Village. He manifested some surprise on becoming aware of the manner of his execution, of which he had not previously, as it would seem, been apprised; but soon recovering himself, adjusted the halter with his own hands, bandaged his eyes, called the spectators to witness that he died like a brave man, when the cart moved from beneath him, and in a few moments all was over.

24. Thus perished, in the twenty-ninth year of his age, the chivalrous and unfortunate Major André, around whose premature fate the sympathies of all Europe and America were clustered and still remain. Contrasting his treatment, the indulgent clemency extended to him by his judges, and the kind and tender respect which has been paid to his memory, with the brutal barbarities inflicted by the British upon the young American patriot Hale, under precisely similar circumstances, we may well be content to await the verdict of posterity!

25. On the 21st of November a party of Tory refugees from Rhode Island, occupying the St. George's Manor House on Smith's Point, Long Island, which they had fortified, were dislodged by Major Benjamin Tallmadge, under the direction of Washington, a severe chastisement inflicted upon a portion of the garrison, — who after its surrender fired upon the assailing party from one of the houses, — and a British vessel lying in the neighborhood secured with its crew. From thence Major Tallmadge, with Lieutenant Brewster and ten men, proceeded to Coram, where he destroyed a large quantity of forage collected for the use of the British army, and, having successfully accomplished the object of his expedition, returned to their quarters at Fairfield, Connecticut without the loss of a single man. Seven of the enemy were killed and wounded, and four officers and fifty soldiers taken prisoners. Major Tallmadge received the thanks of Congress and the warm approval of the Commander-in-Chief for his bravery and that of his men.

Execution of André. — General sympathy in his fate. — Contrast between André and Hale. — Capture of St. George's Manor House, Long Island. — Destruction of British supplies at Coram, Suffolk County.

1781–83.

26. The splendid victory at Yorktown on the 19th of October was virtually a close of the war. Public rejoicings pervaded every portion of the country, and the 13th of December was set apart as a day of general thanksgiving. Clinton was superseded in his command by Sir Guy Carleton, who soon afterwards arrived in New York; but all further hostilities were suspended. In March, 1782, Lord North retired from the British Cabinet, and Carleton was directed by his successor, Lord Rockingham, to open negotiations for a treaty of peace. The American Congress appointed John Jay, John Adams, Benjamin Franklin, Thomas Jefferson, and Henry Laurens, to act as commissioners for this purpose on the part of the United States. On the 30th of November the preliminaries were signed at Paris; and on the 3d of September, 1783, a definitive treaty, recognizing the independence of the United States, was concluded.

27. On the 3d of November the Continental army was disbanded by order of Congress, and on the 25th Washington entered the city of New York, and the British troops took their final departure. On the 4th of December, Washington took an affecting farewell of his old companions in arms, with whom he had been so long and so closely united in the struggle for national independence, and proceeded to Annapolis, where Congress was then in session. Having formally resigned his commission to that body as Commander-in-Chief, he returned to Mount Vernon as a private citizen, soon to be recalled from its quiet shades to preside over the destinies of the nation he had founded.

Close of the war. — General rejoicings. — Negotiations for peace. — Conclusion of treaty. — Disbandment of the army. — Evacuation of New York by the British. — Parting between Washington and his officers. — Resignation of his commission, and retirement to Mount Vernon.

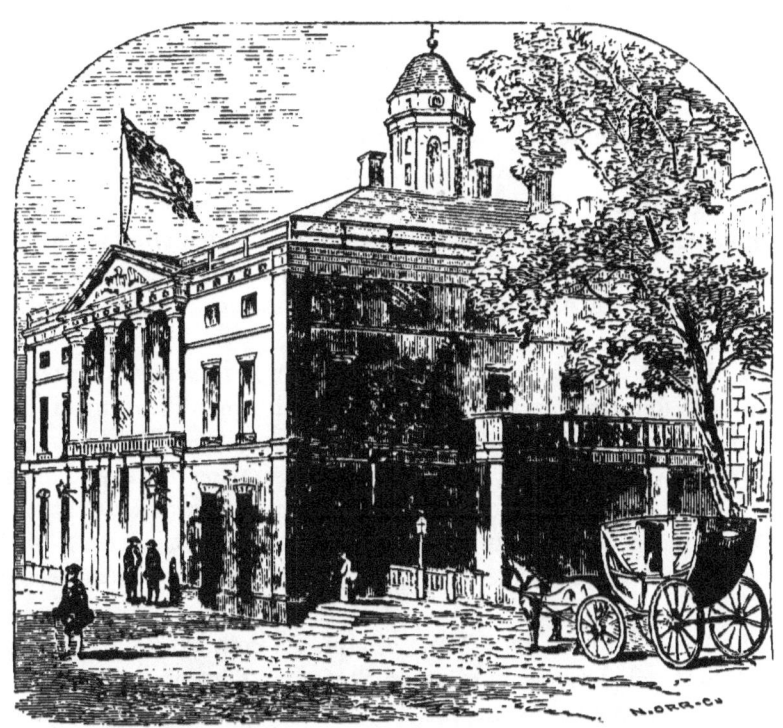

Old City Hall in Wall Street, New York, 1789.

SIXTH PERIOD.

THE STATE GOVERNMENT TO THE CONSTITUTION OF 1821.

CHAPTER I.

ADOPTION OF THE CONSTITUTION OF THE UNITED STATES.

1. THE war being now over, and the independent existence of the United States as a member of the family of nations having been officially recognized, it speedily became evident that the provisional constitution of government as established by the Articles of Confederation adopted by the Congress of 1777 was inadequate in many essential respects to the present exigencies of the public welfare.

1782.

Position of affairs at the close of the war.

2. By that instrument the several States of the Union were merely leagued together for the accomplishment of a specific purpose, retaining in all things their individual sovereignty, and only surrendering it in any case at the pleasure of their accredited representatives, acting under instructions from their own legislature. That purpose having now been accomplished, some more effective provision was deemed indispensable to the functions of a national government in its dealings with other nations, and its discharge of its obligations to its own constituent members.

3. Public attention in all the States was therefore turned to the consideration and discussion of such a modification of the existing system as should remedy its manifest defects, and, while providing for an efficient administration of the domestic and foreign affairs of the Union as a nation, should at the same time secure to its members respectively the rights and powers pertaining to them in their original capacity as sovereign States.

4. The State of New York occupied a commanding position, at this time, among her sister States. The prominent part taken by her citizens in the Revolutionary struggle; the fact that she alone of all the United Colonies had promptly met every demand and fulfilled every requisition of the Provisional Government, and even made advances on her own credit to supply the deficiencies of other States; her extensive commerce, and vast territory, and the ability and patriotism of her leading statesmen, — all entitled her to special consideration, and gave her a powerful influence in the national councils.

5. As early as 1783, immediately after the conclusion of the treaty of peace, a feeling of jealousy of the concentration of power in the hands of the central government was manifested by the repeal in the Legislature of an act passed in 1781, on the recommendation of Congress, granting to the United States the import duties collected in the port of New York, and directing their collection by officers appointed by Congress; and by substituting in its stead a similar appropriation of the duties, to be collected, however, by State officers. In the suc-

ceeding year an act was passed by the same body establishing a custom-house and a revenue system in place of the regulations previously adopted by Congress.

6. These acts were the natural result of the large increase of revenue accruing to the State by the revival of trade and commerce consequent on the return of peace and by the navigation laws of the other States, which rendered the city of New York the great commercial mart of the Union. Every effort to restore to Congress the disposition and control of this revenue proved futile. The collectors were appointed by, and made amenable exclusively to, the State authorities; and the Legislature, in 1786, went so far as to make the duties payable in the bills of credit issued by the State.

7. Congress, perceiving the dangerous consequences to the stability of the national credit of this enactment, — the inevitable effect of which would be the rapid depreciation of Government securities by the unlimited issue of an inconvertible paper currency, — requested Governor Clinton to convene the Legislature for its reconsideration. This, however, was declined by the Governor, upon the ground that no sufficient cause was shown for the exercise of this extraordinary power, the decision of the Legislature having been but recently made upon full consideration and mature deliberation.

8. In the mean time a convention of commissioners from the several States, held at Annapolis, in Maryland, in September, 1786, — New York being represented by General Hamilton, — for the purpose of taking into consideration the trade and commerce of the United States, and the necessity and expediency of a uniform system of commercial regulations, recommended the calling by Congress of a convention of delegates to meet at Philadelphia, in May of the ensuing year, for the sole and express purpose of revising the Articles of Confederation, and reporting to Congress and the several State legislatures such amendments and modifications as should, when confirmed by the former, and agreed to by the requisite number of States, be

1786.

Collection of revenue. — Proceedings of the State Legislature. — Proceedings of Congress. — Governor Clinton declines calling an extra session. — Convention of commissioners at Annapolis. — Recommendation for the call of a national convention at Philadelphia.

found adequate to the exigencies of the Government and the preservation of the Union.

9. Congress having adopted this recommendation, it became necessary for the Legislature of New York, at its regular session in the winter of 1787, to determine whether the State should be represented in that body, and if so, by whom. General Hamilton succeeded in procuring an election to the Legislature as a representative of the city of New York, and his father-in-law, General Philip Schuyler, was already a member of the Senate. In conjunction with Chief-Justice Jay, Chancellor Livingston, and the Van Rensselaers, these men were regarded as the leading champions of the Federal Government; while Governor Clinton, who had been successively re-elected to his present position from term to term, since the adoption of the State Constitution in 1777, with Justice Yates of the Supreme Court, John Lansing, subsequently Chancellor, and Melancthon Smith, were the prominent advocates of what were deemed States' rights.

1787.

10. The Legislature, on its assembling, after an animated debate, in which Hamilton took a leading part, approved, by a strong vote, the proceeding of the Governor in reference to the convocation of an extra session. Messrs. Yates, Lansing, and Hamilton were appointed delegates to the National Convention at Philadelphia; their powers being, however, specially restricted to the revision of the existing Articles of Confederation, in accordance with the call of the convention.

11. On the assembling, in May following, of the National Convention, presided over by General WASHINGTON, a great diversity of views prevailed among the delegates as to the proper course to be pursued. One portion of this number, including Messrs. Yates and Lansing of New York, insisted upon confining their deliberations to such an amendment of the Articles of Confederation as should enlarge the powers of the national government, and give it greater efficiency. Another, under the lead of Hamilton, advocated the formation of an entirely new Constitution, with ample provisions for the concentration of the

---

Proceedings of the Legislature in its session of 1787. — Approval of the Governor's course. — Appointment of delegates to the National Convention. — Their instructions. — State of parties in the convention.

executive power in a president and senate, to hold office during good behavior, with the power to appoint State governors and control State legislation, a House of Representatives elected triennially, and a permanent judiciary.

12. A third, whose views ultimately predominated, headed by Randolph of Virginia, in accordance with the views of James Madison, a leading statesman of that Commonwealth, contended for the establishment of a government representing in its Constitution both the national and State sovereignty and the people collectively, — through the President and House of Representatives, chosen virtually by the people, and a Senate, the members of which should be elected by the State legislatures respectively.

13. On the final prevalence of this plan, the delegation from New York, with the exception of General Hamilton, withdrew from the convention, regarding its determination in this respect as at variance with their instructions and with the explicit object to which the convention itself was restricted. The Constitution — having, however, been completed in accordance with the views of the majority — was, on the 17th of September, adopted and submitted for approval to the several States, through conventions to be called for that purpose, the assent of nine of the thirteen States being required for its ratification.

14. Immediately on its publication in New York, a violent and spirited contest ensued between its advocates and opponents, who, in accordance with their previous proclivities, ranged themselves into two distinct and well-organized parties, the former known as Federalists, and the latter as Anti-Federalists. Hamilton, in conjunction with Madison and Jay, commenced and continued in the public papers the admirable series of articles entitled, "THE FEDERALIST," which exerted a powerful influence upon the public mind, and essentially contributed to the final adoption of the Constitution. Its opponents, however, under the lead of Governor Clinton and his associates, backed by the popular majorities which had hitherto sustained them, rallied with great enthusiasm and ability to the defence of State rights.

Submission of the Constitution to the States. — Organization of parties. — "The Federalist."

15. On the one hand it was urged by the assailants of the proposed Constitution, that by its adoption a fatal blow would be struck at the independent sovereignty of the States, by the gradual absorption of the principal functions of government by the central power; that the wealth and immense resources, of New York especially, instead of being devoted to the expansion, development, and cultivation of its vast territory, and the prosperity and welfare of its own citizens, would be largely diverted to the national coffers; that its preponderance of population would be sacrificed, through the agency of the Senate, to the interests of the smaller States, and the popular element swallowed up by an aristocratic concentration of the executive and legislative departments; that the inevitable tendency of such a state of things would be to the establishment of a virtually monarchical government; and that the framers of the instrument submitted for ratification clearly and palpably exceeded the powers conferred upon them, which embraced only a revision and modification, instead of a repeal, of the existing Articles of Confederation.

16. To these arguments it was replied by the Federalists, that the distribution of the powers of the new government was so carefully arranged, that, so far from enabling it to trench upon the jurisdiction and sovereignty of the States, it was itself liable to constant and serious encroachments on their part, thereby weakening instead of strengthening the executive and even the legislative department; that the existing confederacy, consisting as it did of a mere league of independent States, held together only by the common interest of all its members, and subject to disintegration at the pleasure of any, was wholly inadequate to the purposes of government, and unsusceptible of any alteration not radically affecting the fundamental principle of its Constitution; that in view of the probable assent of the requisite number of States for the ratification of the new Constitution, independently of the vote of New York, that State would occupy the unenviable and untenable position of a neutral sovereign, surrounded by a great nation, bound together by a federative union; and that ample provision was made by the instrument submitted for adoption, by which the rights and interests of all classes of citizens and all State organizations were effectually secured.

17. Governor CLINTON, in his annual message to the Legislature of 1788, avoided all allusion to the proposed submission of the Constitution to the approval of the State. The subject was, however, brought before the Legislature on the 17th of January, by a resolution proposing the call of a convention for that purpose, which, after some opposition, was passed; and in the ensuing spring sixty-seven delegates were elected to the convention at Poughkeepsie, of whom a clear majority were opposed to the Constitution. Alexander Hamilton, John Jay, Chancellor Livingston, Chief-Justice Richard Morris, and James Duane were returned from the city of New York; and Messrs. Yates and Lansing, Governor Clinton and his brother James Clinton, and Melancthon Smith, were among the delegates from the other counties.

1788.

18. The convention organized on the 17th of June by the appointment of GEORGE CLINTON as President. A majority of its members strongly urged the calling of a new national convention, for the purpose of making additional amendments specified by them, or at the least giving their assent to the proposed Constitution *on condition* of the adoption of such amendments; but on the receipt of intelligence of the ratification of the Constitution by the requisite number of States, contented themselves with its adoption on the 26th of July, by a vote of thirty to twenty-seven, with the *recommendation* merely of the proposed amendments.

19. On the 13th of September the new Constitution was officially proclaimed; and on the 8th of December the Legislature, specially convened by Governor CLINTON, proceeded to the choice of five delegates to represent the State in the concluding session of the Continental Congress. Provision was also made, on a subsequent day, for the choice of presidential electors, and the State divided into congressional districts, in pursuance of which, EGBERT BENSON, WILLIAM FLOYD, JOHN HATHORN, JEREMIAH VAN RENSSELAER, and PETER SYLVESTER were elected representatives in the First Congress of the United States.

Election of delegates to State Convention at Poughkeepsie. — Ratification of the Constitution. — Official proclamation of the Constitution. — Special session of the Legislature. — Choice of presidential electors and representatives in Congress.

20. The two Houses not being able to agree upon the mode of choosing senators, the State remained unrepresented in the Senate during the first session. An address to Congress was adopted, requesting the call of another convention at the earliest practicable period, for the purpose of proposing amendments to the national Constitution. Important improvements in legal jurisprudence, chiefly prepared by Samuel Jones, an eminent lawyer, were also ingrafted upon the statute-book of the State.

CHAPTER II.

ORGANIZATION OF THE NATIONAL GOVERNMENT. — INAUGURATION OF WASHINGTON AND ADAMS. — INTERNAL IMPROVEMENTS. — PUBLIC LANDS.

1. EARLY in February, 1789, the presidential electors of the several States assembled at their respective capitals, and unanimously made choice of GEORGE WASHINGTON of Virginia as President, and JOHN ADAMS of Massachusetts as Vice-President, of the United States. The city of New York having been selected by Congress as the seat of the national government, the City Hall, in which the Continental Congress was accustomed to hold its sessions, was remodelled and repaired for the accommodation of its successors. On the 4th of March, the day appointed for the organization of the new government, the hall was thrown open amid the firing of cannon and ringing of bells. A few only of the members of Congress, however, made their appearance; and in their absence the residue, owing to the state of the roads and the deficiency of public conveyances, awaited for upwards of a month the arrival of their colleagues. On the 6th of April a sufficient number had arrived to constitute a quorum; and the Senate and House of Representatives effected an organization, and proceeded to count the votes for President and Vice-President and declare the result.

1789.

Recommendation for new convention to propose amendments to the Constitution. — Improvement of the law. — Election of President and Vice-President. — Organization of the new government. — First meeting of Congress at New York.

2. On the 21st, Vice-President ADAMS arrived in the city, having been conducted with a military escort from the boundary of the State to Kingsbridge by Governor Clinton, where he was received by both branches of Congress, and accompanied by them to the City Hall. Two days afterwards, President WASHINGTON arrived from Mount Vernon, whence his journey to the capital had been a continuous triumphal procession. At Alexandria, Georgetown, Philadelphia, and Trenton his progress was greeted with the most enthusiastic demonstrations.

3. At Elizabethtown, New Jersey, he was taken in charge by a committee of Congress, and embarking in a barge, splendidly decorated, was conducted to the foot of Wall Street, where he was received by the Governor and the municipal authorities and a large procession of citizens, and escorted to his residence in Cherry Street. In the evening the city was brilliantly illuminated, and a splendid display of fireworks closed the festivities of the day.

4. At noon on the 30th of April, after the performance of religious services in all the churches of the city, the inauguration ceremonies were commenced by the formation of a procession from the house of the President elect, headed by the city cavalry, and consisting of the members of Congress and heads of departments in carriages, followed by WASHINGTON in a separate carriage, and his military family and resident foreign ministers in others.

5. On reaching the Senate Chamber he was received by the Vice-President and conducted to the balcony fronting on Broad Street, where, in the presence of an immense crowd, the oath of office was administered by Chancellor LIVINGSTON. Returning to the Senate Chamber, the President delivered the inaugural address, after which the whole assembly proceeded on foot to St. Paul's Church in Broadway, where prayers were read by the chaplain to the Senate, and at their conclusion the President was escorted to his residence. A display of fireworks in the evening concluded the ceremonies.

6. The triumph of the Federalists in the adoption of the Constitution, and the prevailing popular sentiment in favor of the

---

Arrival of the President and Vice-President. — Triumphal progress of Washington. — Inauguration ceremonies.

new administration of the general government, gave rise to a strong feeling of opposition to the re-election of Governor Clinton, whose official term would expire in July. Vigorous efforts were accordingly made, preparatory to the April elections, to replace him by Associate-Justice ROBERT YATES, of the Supreme Court, who although a leading opponent of the new Constitution, had since its ratification uniformly given it, officially and otherwise, his support, and who, from his popularity with the Anti-Federalists, might, it was supposed, detach a sufficient number of his friends from the support of Governor Clinton to insure his defeat.

7. The contest, however, after an animated canvass, resulted in the re-election of Governor CLINTON by a reduced majority. Notwithstanding the general success of the Federalists in both branches of the Legislature, Pierre Van Cortlandt was elected Lieutenant-Governor. Both General Hamilton and Colonel Burr actively participated in the contest as supporters of Justice Yates, as did most of the prominent and leading men of the Federal party.

8. On the 6th of July the Legislature convened in special session under the proclamation of the Governor; and on the 19th, General PHILIP SCHUYLER and RUFUS KING were appointed senators of the United States. The latter gentleman had been a representative from Massachusetts in the Continental Congress, where he had distinguished himself for his abilities and practical talents, and had but recently become a citizen of New York. No other business of general importance was transacted during the session.

1790.
9. During the second session of the first Congress, which convened on the 8th of January, 1790, the Secretary of the Treasury, General HAMILTON, proposed the assumption of the foreign and domestic public debt, amounting to fifty-four millions of dollars, together with the debts of the respective States contracted during the war, estimated at about half that amount. So acrimonious were the debates and discussions on

---

Opposition to the re-election of Governor Clinton. — Nomination of Chief-Justice Yates. — His support by the Federalists. — Re-election of Clinton. — General success of the Federalists. — Appointment of United States senators. — Hamilton's plan for the assumption of the public debt.

the latter part of this proposition, that serious apprehensions were entertained of the dissolution of the Union. Through the joint exertions of Hamilton and Jefferson, however, the measure was finally adopted by the vote of the Southern delegates, in return for which the North consented to the permanent location of the national capital on the banks of the Potomac after the expiration of ten years, during which its seat should be at Philadelphia. The State election in April resulted in a Federal majority in both Houses.

10. The Legislature assembled in the city of New York on the 3d of January, 1791. By the census of the preceding year the population of the State amounted to 324,127, showing an increase chiefly in the northern and western counties of upwards of 85,000 during the past five years. A new apportionment of representatives and senators became, therefore, necessary, and was recommended by the Governor in his annual message; and a communication between the Hudson and Lake Champlain on the north and Wood Creek on the west, by clearing out the obstructions in the Mohawk, and cutting a canal, were suggested for the purpose of affording greater facilities to the settlers in that region.

1791.

11. The term of office of General Schuyler as United States Senator having expired, AARON BURR was appointed as his successor. A new apportionment of senatorial districts was made, the State being divided into four great districts, — Eastern, Western, Southern, and Middle; the Eastern and Western each electing five, the Middle six, and the Southern eight senators. Three new counties — Herkimer, Otsego, and Tioga — were formed out of Montgomery, formerly a portion of Tryon County. The Assembly under the new apportionment consisted of seventy-three and the Senate of twenty-four members. The State elections in April exhibited no material change in the state of parties.

12. At the termination of the war the State found itself the owner of more than seven millions of acres of wild, unculti-

---

Removal of the capital. — State election. — Meeting of the Legislature. — Population of the State. — Recommendations of the Governor — Internal improvement. — Election of Aaron Burr as United States' Senator. — Reapportionment of the State.

vated, and unimproved lands, situated chiefly in the northern and western portions of its territory. Prior to the present year few sales of this vast possession had been made; and an act was accordingly passed authorizing the Commissioners of the Land Office, consisting of the Governor, Secretary of State, Attorney-General, Treasurer, and Auditor, to dispose of these lands in such manner as they should judge most conducive to the public interests.

13. Under this act, upwards of five millions of acres were sold during the year for about one million of dollars, — more than one half of the whole to a single individual, — Alexander McComb, — for eightpence per acre, on a long credit without interest. Large parcels were also sold for a trifling consideration to other purchasers. Such an indiscriminate and wholesale disposition of this vast inheritance was, to say the least, injudicious in the extreme, and wholly indefensible on any sound principles of political economy, and could scarcely fail to subject its agents to severe condemnation.

1792. 14. During the session ensuing, commencing on the 5th of January, 1792, an act was passed, in accordance with the recommendation of the Governor, incorporating the "Western Inland Lock Navigation Company," of which General Philip Schuyler was President, for the improvement of the navigation of the Mohawk River and the construction of a canal from thence to Seneca Lake and Lake Ontario. The "Northern Inland Lock Navigation Company" was soon afterwards organized under the same auspices, for the purpose of opening a communication between the Hudson River and Lake Champlain, and the route carefully surveyed by Mr. Weston, a civil engineer, and Thomas Eddy; thereby laying a foundation for those magnificent works of internal improvement, destined hereafter to exert so great an influence on the prosperity of the State.

15. The Governor, in his speech at the opening of the session, recommended the application of the proceeds from the sale of unappropriated lands to the payment of the State debt and the current expenses of the government. This opened the

---

The public lands. — Act providing for their sale. — Disposition of them. — Western and Northern Inland Lock Navigation Companies. — Proceedings of the Legislature.

whole question of the disposition of the public lands, and gave rise to an animated debate in the House on a resolution censuring, in strong terms, the commissioners for the course pursued by them, resulting, however, in the rejection of the resolution, and the adoption of a substitute, approving their proceedings.

16. The April elections, after a spirited canvass, resulted in the re-election, by a close vote, of Governor CLINTON and Lieutenant-Governor VAN CORTLANDT, over Chief-Justice Jay and Stephen Van Rensselaer, the candidates of the Federalists. On the 6th of November the Legislature again assembled in New York, and proceeded to the choice of presidential electors. The presidential canvass resulted in the unanimous re-election of General WASHINGTON and Vice-President ADAMS.

17. The arrival of Citizen GENET, in the spring of 1793, as the envoy of the new French Republic, a few days after the declaration of war between that country and England, was the harbinger of new political complications. The obvious policy of the American Government was that of strict neutrality, while all the sympathies of the people were with their late chivalrous allies in the Revolutionary struggle. The Federalists ranged themselves, as a party, in support of the Government, and their opponents in favor of active interference in behalf of the French. Genet, secure of the popular support, proceeded to fit out privateers for the destruction of British commerce on the high seas, while Washington sternly declared his determination of enforcing the proclamation of neutrality.

1793.

18. The reception of the French minister in the city of New York in the summer of this year was enthusiastic in the extreme, and his hostility to England was so warmly seconded throughout the country, that nearly fifty British vessels were captured during the year by privateers from the various ports manned by American seamen. Genet still further strengthened his interest and increased his popularity by a marriage with the daughter of Governor Clinton, the leader of the republican party. He

---

Debate on the public lands. — Approval of the commissioners. — Re-election of Governor Clinton. — Meeting of the Legislature. — Choice of presidential electors. — Re-election of President Washington and Vice-President Adams. — Diplomatic mission of Citizen Genet.

was, however, soon afterwards recalled, on the demand of the President, by the French Government; but, although deprived of all official authority, still remained in the country, of which he became a permanent citizen.

CHAPTER III.

Foundation of the Common-School System. — Administration of Governor Jay. — Internal Improvements.

1795. 1. The Legislature met at Poughkeepsie on the 6th of January, 1795. Governor CLINTON communicated his annual message, in which, after renewing his recommendation for the revision of the criminal code, he reminded the Legislature, that, while liberal provisions had been made for the endowment of colleges and other higher seminaries of learning, no legislative aid had yet been afforded to the Common Schools. Deeply impressed with the paramount importance of these agencies for the diffusion of knowledge among the people, he earnestly recommended a suitable provision for their encouragement and support.

2. An act was accordingly, at an early period of the session, introduced and passed into a law, appropriating an annual sum of fifty thousand dollars for five years to this object, the interest of which was directed to be paid over to the several county treasurers in amounts proportioned to the population of the respective counties and towns, the latter of which were also required to raise by tax an amount equal to one half of the apportionment made to them respectively, — the whole to be applied, under the direction of proper officers in each school-district, to the payment of the wages of teachers duly employed and properly qualified. This was the origin of the present Common-School system of the State, now so important and flourishing a branch of its government.

3. On the 27th of January, RUFUS KING was re-elected a Senator in Congress for the ensuing term of six years. Governor

---

Session of 1795. — Governor's message. — Original foundation of the Common-School system — Re-election of Rufus King as United States Senator.

Clinton's official term having nearly expired, he declined being considered as a candidate for re-election. A continuous service of nearly thirty years in the colonial assemblies and executive department had undermined his health, and entitled him, in his judgment, to a retirement from the public service. Lieutenant-Governor Van Cortlandt also declined a re-election on account of his advanced age. JOHN JAY was again placed in nomination by the Federalists as Governor, with STEPHEN VAN RENSSELAER for Lieutenant-Governor, while the Republicans nominated Chief-Justice Yates and William Floyd as their candidates.

4. At the ensuing spring election, Messrs. JAY and VAN RENSSELAER were duly elected, with a decided Federal majority in both Houses of the Legislature. Mr. Jay, at the time of his election, was absent from the country, having been despatched to England by the United States Government to negotiate a treaty with Great Britain. He arrived at New York on the 26th of May, where he was received with the greatest enthusiasm. The treaty with England concluded by him was exceedingly unpopular with the Republican party throughout the country, which sympathized almost universally with the French revolutionists, and were equally hostile to British influence.

5. Governor JAY, in his speech at the opening of the session of 1796, after expressing his acknowledgments for the confidence reposed in him by the electors, urged the adoption of efficient measures for the military defence of the State in the event of invasion. Provision was made by the Legislature for the improvement of the criminal jurisprudence, and for a reapportionment of representatives and senators under the census of the preceding year. A bill was introduced early in the session, in accordance with the views of Governor Jay, providing for the gradual abolition of slavery in the State, which, however, after a prolonged and exciting debate, was virtually defeated by a close vote, in committee of the whole, by the adoption of a resolution providing for compensation to the holders of that species of property.

1796.

Governor Clinton declines a re-election. — John Jay elected Governor. — Jay's treaty. — Meeting of the Legislature. — Bill for the abolition of slavery.

6. Through the violent and revolutionary excesses of the French republic, and the rash and indiscreet conduct of their agent, M. Genet, in this country, the popular excitement against the treaty concluded by Governor Jay with Great Britain had to a very great extent subsided. The universal confidence reposed in the administration of General Washington, whose second term approached its close, and who declined a re-election, and the high character of Jay in connection with his unexceptionable discharge of the official duties intrusted to him, had strengthened the hold which the Federal party had already obtained upon the public confidence and support. The spring elections, therefore, exhibited the usual preponderance of that party in both branches of the Legislature.

7. This body assembled in the city of New York on the 1st of November for the choice of presidential electors, and appointed electors, who cast the twelve votes of the State in favor of JOHN ADAMS of Massachusetts for President, and Thomas Pinckney of South Carolina for Vice-President. JOHN LAWRENCE, of the city of New York, was chosen United States Senator in place of Rufus King, who had recently been appointed Minister to England. The Legislature then adjourned to meet at Albany on the 3d of January ensuing. The congressional election in December terminated in the election of the Republican candidates, — Edward Livingston of New York, Philip Van Cortlandt of West Chester, J. N. Havens of Suffolk, and Lucas Elmendorff of Ulster.

1797. 8. On the reassembling of the Legislature, an act was passed creating the office of Comptroller, which was bestowed upon SAMUEL JONES, of New York. The county of Delaware was erected from portions of Albany and Ulster; and the seat of government was permanently located at Albany, and provision made for the erection of a capitol and suitable government offices. Colonel Burr's term of office as United States Senator having expired, PHILIP SCHUYLER, of Albany, was chosen in his place.

9. In the mean time, JOHN ADAMS, of Massachusetts, had been

Spring elections. — Meeting of the Legislature. — Presidential electors. — Congressional elections. — United States senators. — Appointment of Comptroller. — Location of the capital at Albany.

elected President, and THOMAS JEFFERSON, of Virginia, Vice-President of the United States, and duly inaugurated at Philadelphia on the 4th of March. The State elections in April indicated a decided gain in favor of the Republicans, especially in the city of New York, where their representatives in the Legislature, including Aaron Burr, Dr. Samuel L. Mitchell, and De Witt Clinton, were returned by a heavy majority.

10. Governor JAY and Lieutenant-Governor VAN RENSSELAER, were re-elected, the latter unanimously, and the former by a decided majority over Chancellor Livingston, the candidate of the Republicans. This party, however, obtained a decided preponderance in the Legislature. DE WITT CLINTON and AMBROSE SPENCER were elected to the Senate; and among the leading Republican representatives in the Assembly were Aaron Burr and John Swartwout of New York, David Thomas of Washington, Erastus Root of Delaware, Obadiah German of Chenango, and Jedediah Peck of Otsego. 1798.

11. At this period the line of demarcation between the Federalists and Republicans was strongly marked, and party dissensions ran high. The administration of the general government, under the elder Adams, supported by General Hamilton and Governor Jay, was characterized by a series of high-handed and despotic measures, altogether at variance with the democratic principles which were beginning to prevail. Governor Jay, ten years previously, in a communication to General Washington, had expressed opinions decidedly averse to the sovereignty of the States, and in favor of a concentration of power in the general government; and the recognized leaders of the Federal party were despondent as to the issue of the experiment of republican institutions.

12. In the mean time these men were the dispensers of Federal and State patronage, increased by a system of internal taxation adopted by the United States Government; a standing army had been organized, unlimited authority to borrow money conferred upon the President, and arbitrary authority to prosecute and imprison all aliens or citizens venturing to arraign the

---

Election of Adams and Jefferson as President and Vice-President. — State elections. — Spring elections. — Re-election of Governor Jay and Lieutenant-Governor Van Rensselaer. — State of parties.

proceeding or policy of the administration exercised without restraint. All these circumstances combined to create an intense feeling of hostility to the party in power, both in the State and nation.

13. A special session of the Legislature was convened at Albany, by Governor Jay, in August. A war with France being imminent, as the result of the special mission to France of Messrs. Pinckney, Gerry, and Marshall and the nefarious practices of the French Republic, the Governor called the attention of the Legislature to the necessity of efficient preparations, on the part of the State, for defence, to which that body responded with energy and vigor.

14. The first practical suggestion for the improvement of the facilities for internal communication between the Atlantic Ocean and the northern lakes was made by General WASHINGTON in 1784. Having, during that year, personally explored the region between the Hudson River and Lakes Erie and Ontario, by the route of the Mohawk River, Wood Creek, Oneida Lake, and the Oswego River, and made a tour through Lakes George and Champlain to Crown Point, he communicated to Mr. Jefferson, the Secretary of State, and others of his correspondents, his views of the importance of opening and improving those channels of communication.

15. At about the same period, CHRISTOPHER COLLES, a resident of the city of New York, who some twelve years previous had delivered a course of public lectures in Philadelphia on the subject of Lock Navigation, submitted a proposition to the State Legislature for the improvement of the navigation of the Mohawk. That body, deeming the enterprise too expensive for State adoption, offered to secure to him and his associates all profits which might accrue from its prosecution by private means, and in 1785 made him a grant of one hundred and twenty-five dollars for its encouragement.

16. During that year, Mr. Colles issued proposals for the establishment of a company for the improvement of the inland

---

Legislative proceedings. — Apprehensions of war with France. — Origin of the system of internal improvements. — General Washington's explorations and views. — Proposition of Christopher Colles. — Legislative encouragement.

navigation between Albany and Oswego, setting forth, with great ability and comprehensiveness, the advantages which would accrue from such an enterprise, and the facilities for its accomplishment. In the succeeding year the Legislature, on the renewal of his application, evinced their approbation and a sense of its importance, but no effectual measures were taken for its prosecution, and it was abandoned by its enterprising projector, who long afterwards died in obscurity in the city which his genius, if properly encouraged, would have enriched. Others were destined to reap the abundant harvest of the fertile seeds sown by him.

17. At the opening of the session of the Legislature in 1791, Governor GEORGE CLINTON adverted to the importance of providing facilities of communication between the seaboard and the frontiers of the State; and an act was passed directing the exploration and survey of the route between the Mohawk and Hudson Rivers and Wood Creek with the view to the construction of a canal. At the succeeding session the report of the commissioners appointed for that purpose was favorable, and Governor Clinton renewed his recommendation for its earnest consideration.

18. In the mean time, General PHILIP SCHUYLER and ELKANAH WATSON, in ignorance of the plans and views of Mr. Colles, had exerted themselves with great energy and spirit in the prosecution of the same idea. In 1791, Mr. Watson made a journey through the western portion of the State, discovered its facilities for internal navigation, and published a series of able essays, which essentially contributed to the adoption of initiatory measures for carrying out this important project.

19. During the session of the Legislature in 1792, as already stated, acts had been passed incorporating the Western and the Northern Inland Lock Navigation Companies, the harbingers of the Erie and Champlain Canals. General Schuyler was elected President of the joint company; and among its most efficient members were Thomas Eddy, Jeremiah Van Rensselaer, Barent

---

Unsuccessful efforts of Mr. Colles. — Governor Clinton's messages. — Survey of the route. — Favorable report. — Efforts of General Schuyler and Elkanah Watson. — Incorporation of the Western and Northern Inland Lock Navigation Company. — Its principal directors.

Bleecker, Elkanah Watson, and Robert Bowne. Its objects were the improvement of the navigation of the Mohawk River, and the opening of canals and lock navigation between that river to Seneca Lake and Lake Ontario, and between the Hudson and Lake Champlain.

20. In the year 1796 the Western Company had completed a canal at the Little Falls of about three miles in length, with five locks, and another of a mile and a quarter at German Flats; and, in 1797, one from the Mohawk to Wood Creek, nearly two miles in length, — making in all about seven miles, with nine locks. Between the Hudson and Lake Champlain the Northern Company had accomplished nothing of importance. The expenses of construction, reconstruction, and repairs of the canal between Schenectady and the Oneida Lake, when finally completed, were found to be so great that the tolls required for its navigation rendered it virtually useless.

21. In 1798 an act was passed incorporating a company for the construction of a canal from Lake Ontario to Lake Erie, with sufficient lockage, passing around the cataract of Niagara. Up to this period no distinct conception of a canal, with lock navigation, from the Hudson to Lake Erie, seems to have been entertained in any quarter; and no further efforts were made for carrying into effect the partial enterprises which were already commenced. All that had been accomplished was the removal of obstructions from the channel of the Mohawk and its tributary streams, and the construction, at an enormous expense, of a small canal connecting it with the adjacent waters.

1799. 22. An act "for supplying the city of New York with pure and wholesome water" was passed during the session of the Legislature of 1799, which was afterwards found to confer very important banking powers, under a clause authorizing the establishment of the Manhattan Bank, and gave rise to very serious political complications, resulting in the defeat of many of the leading Republican candidates at the spring election, especially in the city of New York, and the triumph of the Federal party throughout the State. These successes were, however,

---

Objects of the Western and Northern Inland Lock Navigation Company. — Canal at Little Falls. — German Flats and Wood Creek. — Proposed canal from Lake Ontario to Lake Erie. — The Manhattan Bank Charter.

neutralized by the intolerant enforcement of the unpopular seditious laws of the general government by the executive officers of the State and nation.

23. The death of General WASHINGTON, on the 14th of December, cast a deep gloom over the whole country. The most imposing funeral honors were paid to his memory in all the principal towns and cities of the Union; and in the city of New York especially, all parties vied in the expression of their sympathy for the general loss.

24. The Legislature met at Albany on the 28th of January, 1800. The Governor, after pronouncing a brief and feeling eulogy upon General Washington, submitted various recommendations for amendment of the existing laws, and concluded by earnestly urging upon the Legislature an adequate provision for the support of common schools. GOUVERNEUR MORRIS was chosen United States Senator in place of James Watson, resigned.

1800.

25. The April elections resulted in a complete triumph of the Republican (now known as the Democratic) party. De Witt Clinton, Brockholst Livingston, Mr. Swartwout, General Gates, John Broome, Henry Rutgers, and Samuel Osgood were elected to the Legislature from the city of New York, Aaron Burr from Orange, and Smith Thompson from Dutchess. THOMAS JEFFERSON, of Virginia, was nominated by the National Republican Convention at Philadelphia, held in May, for President, and AARON BURR for Vice-President. Messrs. Adams and Pinckney were renominated for these positions by the Federalists.

26. On the first Tuesday in November the Legislature convened, and the Republican candidates for electors of President and Vice-President were elected by a large majority. JOHN ARMSTRONG was elected United States Senator in place of John Lawrence resigned, after which the Legislature adjourned until the last Tuesday in January. GEORGE CLINTON was placed in nomination by the Republican member for Governor, and

---

Intolerant proceedings of the Federalists. — Death of Washington. — Legislature of 1800. — Result of April elections. — The Democracy triumphant. — Nominations for President and Vice-President. — Choice of presidential electors. — Election of United States Senator. — Nomination of candidates for Governor and Lieutenant-Governor.

JEREMIAH VAN RENSSELAER for Lieutenant-Governor; and Stephen Van Rensselaer and James Watson were the candidates of the Federalists.

CHAPTER IV.

ORGANIZATION OF THE COMMON-SCHOOL SYSTEM. — RE-ELECTION OF GOVERNOR GEORGE CLINTON. — DUEL BETWEEN HAMILTON AND BURR. — DEATH OF HAMILTON.

1. DURING the session of the Legislature of the ensuing year, the first of the century, a bill for the organization of the Common Schools of the State was introduced by Judge PECK, of Otsego, and an act passed directing the raising by lottery, under the control of managers appointed by the State, of the sum of one hundred thousand dollars, twelve thousand five hundred of which were to be apportioned by the regents of the University among the colleges and academies, and the residue, including the avails of the fund previously appropriated in 1795, among the Common Schools in such manner as the Legislature should prescribe. An act was also passed, recommending a convention of delegates to be held at Albany in the ensuing October, for the amendment of the existing Constitution of the State in reference to the apportionment of members of the Legislature and the appointing power.

[margin: 1801.]

2. On counting the votes for President and Vice-President by Congress in February, it was ascertained that THOMAS JEFFERSON and AARON BURR had each received seventy-three votes for their respective offices, and John Adams and Mr. Pinckney each sixty-five votes. Under the then existing provisions of the Constitution, requiring the election of the highest candidates voted for as President, and the next highest as Vice-President, no choice had been effected, and the election was thrown into the House of Representatives. The ballotings by States in this body continued, amid intense excitement, during four days and nights;

Organization of the Common-School system. — Recommendation of a convention for the amendment of the Constitution. — Contest between Jefferson and Burr for the Presidency.

and it was not until the thirty-sixth ballot that Mr. JEFFERSON was finally declared elected President, and Mr. BURR Vice-President.

3. Whatever may have been his private intrigues, it does not appear that Colonel Burr had in any way openly participated in this contest. During its prevalence he remained at Albany, in the discharge of his legislative duties; and although it is scarcely to be supposed that he was devoid of interest in the result, there is nothing to show that any efforts were made on his part to defeat Mr. Jefferson, the candidate of his party. His previous high standing, however, as a Republican leader was seriously impaired.

4. The spring elections resulted in the choice of Governor GEORGE CLINTON, and Lieutenant-Governor JEREMIAH VAN RENSSELAER, with a Republican majority in both branches of the Legislature. Both the national and State governments were now in the hands of the Republican or Democratic party. At the special election, in August, for delegates to the State Constitutional Convention, a similar preponderance of Republicans appeared. John V. Henry was chosen from Albany, De Witt Clinton from Kings, Aaron Burr from Orange, William P. Van Ness and Daniel D. Tompkins from New York, and Smith Thompson from Dutchess.

5. The convention assembled at Albany on the 13th of October, and organized its deliberations by the election of Colonel Burr as President. After transacting the special business for which they were convened, an adjournment was effected at an early day. JOHN LANSING, Jr., was appointed Chancellor in place of Mr. Livingston, who was soon afterwards made, by the President, Minister to France, where he succeeded in negotiating the celebrated treaty for the purchase of Louisiana.

6. The Legislature met at Albany on the 26th of January, 1802, and AMBROSE SPENCER was appointed, by the Council, Attorney-General in place of Josiah Ogden Hoffman, resigned. An apportionment of the members of assembly, now

1802.

Agency of Burr in the contest. — Re-election of Governor Clinton and Lieutenant-Governor Van Rensselaer. — State elections. — Proceedings of the Convention. — Appointment of Chancellor. — Meeting of the Legislature. — Ambrose Spencer appointed Attorney-General.

fixed by the amended Constitution at one hundred, was made, and a resolution adopted on motion of Mr. Clinton, proposing an amendment to the United States Constitution, providing for the choice of electors of President and Vice-President by single electoral districts, and requiring such electors to designate on their ballots the person voted for by them for each office.

7. On the 9th of February, DE WITT CLINTON was elected United States Senator in place of General Armstrong, resigned. The spring elections resulted in another Democratic triumph, including every member of the Senate and a large majority in the House. Soon after this period an imbittered personal and political warfare sprang up between the friends of Colonel Burr and those of De Witt Clinton, carried on through the columns of the American Citizen, edited by James Cheetham, in the interest of the latter, and the Morning Chronicle, edited by Dr. Irving, in that of the former, and resulting in a duel between Mr. Clinton and Mr. Swartwout.

8. When the Legislature convened in January of the succeeding year, it speedily became apparent that a large majority of its members disapproved of the conduct of Colonel Burr, and that he and his friends no longer possessed the confidence of the Republican party. The latter obtained a signal and decisive triumph at the April elections. DE WITT CLINTON was appointed Mayor of the city of New York in place of Edward Livingston, who had been appointed, by the President, United States District Attorney; and AMBROSE SPENCER was appointed a Judge of the Supreme Court in place of Jacob Radcliff, resigned.

1804. 9. On the 31st of January, 1804, the Legislature again assembled. The Governor communicated to both Houses the amendment of the Constitution recently adopted, requiring the presidential electors to designate the candidates voted for respectively as President and Vice-President. Governor GEORGE CLINTON was placed in nomination by the democracy of the na-

---

De Witt Clinton appointed United States Senator. — Proposed amendment to the national Constitution. — Controversy between the friends of Clinton and Burr. — Duel between Clinton and Swartwout. — Parties in the Legislature. — Triumph of the democracy. — Appointments and removals. — Proceedings of the Legislature. — Amendment of the United States Constitution in reference to presidential electors.

tion as a candidate for Vice-President at the ensuing presidential election in place of Colonel Burr, who had forfeited their confidence. The latter was, however, placed in nomination by his friends for the office of Governor.

10. At the February term of the Supreme Court, Chief-Justice Lewis presiding, Harry Croswell, editor of a leading Federal paper published at Hudson, was indicted and convicted, under the provisions of the English common law, for a libel against the President, notwithstanding the offer on his part to prove the truth of the allegations. His counsel, General Hamilton, made an eloquent defence in his behalf; and in the succeeding year the law in this respect was changed, and the truth of any alleged libel was thenceforth permitted to be given in evidence. This was the last and most brilliant forensic effort of Hamilton.

11. MORGAN LEWIS and JOHN BROOME were respectively elected Governor and Lieutenant-Governor by a large majority at the April elections, together with a majority of Democrats in both branches of the Legislature. Mr. Tompkins was elected to Congress from the city and county of New York. The defeat of Burr rendered him desperate, and in his mortification and chagrin, in view of the disappointment of all his political prospects, he seems to have availed himself of every opportunity of revenging himself against those whose influence he had reason to suspect had contributed to the result.

12. Of these individuals he had chosen to regard HAMILTON as the most prominent. His opposition had been felt in the contest for the presidency against Jefferson; and in his recent struggle for political ascendency, Burr had reason to suspect his active hostility. Burning for revenge, he had determined to call his great and powerful adversary to a stern and severe account; and for this purpose had watched for an opportunity when he could safely accomplish his nefarious purpose.

13. During the February term of the Supreme Court at Albany, some expressions of political hostility towards Burr had fallen from Hamilton, in a social conversation with one of his friends, with whom he was dining. The report of this coming to the ear

---

Election of Governor and Lieutenant-Governor. — Trial of Croswell for libel. — Election of Governor Lewis and Lieutenant-Governor Broome. — Democratic triumph. — Hostility between Burr and Hamilton.

of Burr in a distorted form, was construed by him as involving a personal charge, and a prompt acknowledgment or denial of the offensive terms demanded on the 18th of June. On the 20th Hamilton declined complying with this demand on account of the vagueness and indefiniteness of the charge, at the same time expressing his willingness to do so whenever it should be made more explicit, or to abide the consequences of his present refusal. In a subsequent note, through his friend, Mr. Pendleton, in reply to an offensive answer from Burr, Hamilton repeated in distinct terms his willingness, in response to any specific inquiry, to disclaim having at any time cast an imputation upon the private character or personal conduct of the former.

14. Burr, notwithstanding this candid and explicit disclaimer, persisted in regarding it as a mere evasion, and demanded immediate satisfaction. A hostile meeting was arranged on the 27th, which took place at Weehawken, on the Jersey shore, on the morning of the 11th of July. Hamilton was mortally wounded on the first exchange of shots, discharging his pistol in the air. He was conveyed from the field to the house of a friend on the opposite shore, where he expired on the afternoon of the next day. On the 14th his remains were conveyed to Trinity Church, when, after an eloquent discourse pronounced by his friend Gouverneur Morris, they were deposited, with military honors, in the adjoining churchyard.

15. The death of Hamilton, and the unfortunate circumstances which led to the melancholy catastrophe, cast a deep shade of gloom over the whole community. His military services, splendid talents, the high positions occupied by him in the civil departments of government, and his unexceptionable character in all the relations of life, had secured for him the warm affections and regard of his fellow-citizens generally; and his premature death by violence, in the maturity of his powers and the fulness of his fame, was universally lamented.

16. By the election of Governor Lewis a vacancy had occurred in the office of Chief-Justice of the Supreme Court, which was soon afterwards filled by the appointment of JAMES KENT and the promotion of DANIEL D. TOMPKINS to the position of Asso-

ciate Justice. The Legislature assembled in November for the choice of presidential electors, and after the transaction of the special business for which they were convened, and the election of Dr. SAMUEL L. MITCHELL as United States Senator in place of General Armstrong, appointed Minister to France, an adjournment to the ensuing January took place. At the meeting of the several electoral colleges in December, Mr. JEFFERSON was re-elected President, and GEORGE CLINTON, of New York, chosen Vice-President by a majority of one hundred and sixty electoral votes.

CHAPTER V.

ADMINISTRATION OF GOVERNOR LEWIS. — COMMON-SCHOOL FUND. — FREE-SCHOOL SOCIETY OF NEW YORK. — ELECTION OF GOVERNOR TOMPKINS. — BURR'S CONSPIRACY. — STEAM NAVIGATION. — ERIE CANAL.

1. THE State Legislature reassembled on the 22d of January, and a special message was received from Governor LEWIS strongly urging the importance of encouraging popular education by the elevation and improvement of the common schools of the State, and recommending the exclusive appropriation of the avails of the public lands, now consisting of a million and a half acres, to this end.   1805.

2. In accordance with this recommendation an act was introduced and passed, appropriating the net proceeds of five hundred thousand acres of the public lands to the support of common schools, the interest, when amounting to fifty thousand dollars, to be annually apportioned to these institutions for the payment of teachers' wages. The foundations of a permanent school fund were thus judiciously provided. The FREE-SCHOOL SOCIETY of the city of New York for the education of destitute children was also incorporated, with DE WITT CLINTON as its

---

Choice of presidential electors. — Appointment of United States Senator. — Re-election of President Jefferson, and election of Vice-President Clinton. — Meeting of the Legislature. — Special message of the Governor relative to common-school education. — Common-school fund. — Free-School Society of New York.

President, chiefly through his exertions and those of the Society of Friends; and the first school was opened on Tryon Row in December, 1809.

3. At this time WILLIAM W. VAN NESS, of Columbia, in the Senate, and OBADIAH GERMAN, of Chenango, in the House, were the recognized leaders of the Federal and Democratic parties respectively. The preponderance of public sentiment throughout the State was strongly in favor of the Democrats, and the result of the spring elections of this year only served to confirm this result. Manifest indications, however, had recently appeared, of irreconcilable dissensions among the majority, which threatened for a period seriously to disturb their harmony, if not to interrupt their predominance. Mr. Clinton and his friends, in connection with the late political adherents of Colonel Burr, ranged themselves in opposition to the administration of Governor Lewis, and a deadly political feud seemed imminent.

1806. 4. At the succeeding session of the Legislature in 1806, the sentence of death against Stephen Arnold, a teacher of Otsego County, for causing the death of a child by whipping for a venial offence, was, on the recommendation of the Governor, commuted to imprisonment for life, — a proceeding which created great popular indignation throughout the State. A recommendation was also submitted for the improvement of the discipline of the militia; the Governor, in his capacity of commander-in-chief, having, during the preceding autumn, made an official tour of inspection and review. Preparations for an apprehended war with Great Britain were also strongly urged. During this session, ARCHIBALD McINTYRE of Montgomery was appointed Comptroller. The Federalists, as a body, transferred their support to Governor Lewis in the approaching contest between his friends and those of Mr. Clinton; and, aided by this coalition, a majority of the members of the Legislature in favor of the administration were returned at the ensuing spring elections.

1807. 5. In April of the ensuing year, the regular Republican ticket, headed by DANIEL D. TOMPKINS as Governor and

---

State of parties. — Political feud between the friends of Mr. Clinton and Governor Lewis. — Proceedings of the Legislature. — Stephen Arnold. — Appointment of Comptroller. — Coalition of Federalists and Republicans. — Results of the election.

John Broome as Lieutenant-Governor, was successful by a majority of about four thousand votes, carrying with it a majority of both branches of the Legislature. WILLIAM W. VAN NESS was promoted to the bench of the Supreme Court, by the Council chosen during Governor Lewis's administration, in place of Brockholst Livingston, appointed an Associate Justice of the United States Supreme Court.

6. Colonel Burr was, in May, placed on his trial for treason, before Chief-Justice Marshall of the United States Supreme Court at Richmond, Virginia, charged with an attempt to procure a severance of the States west of the Alleghany Mountains, and with them, in conjunction with Mexico, to establish an independent government. He had been driven from New York by the public indignation created by the death of Hamilton, and since that occurrence had traversed the Southern and Western States and territories, engaging in treasonable intrigues with the disaffected, and other suspicious undertakings which had excited the vigilance of the government and produced his arrest as a criminal. No sufficient proof, however, of his complicity having been presented, he was acquitted and discharged.

7. On the 7th of August the first STEAMBOAT, the Clermont, was completed by ROBERT FULTON, of New York, and launched from Jersey City, on its trial trip up the Hudson for Albany, where it arrived on the next day, after a successful voyage of thirty-two hours. Chancellor Robert R. Livingston had, in 1798, obtained from the Legislature the exclusive right of steam navigation in the waters of the State for twenty years, on condition of building a boat, within one year, of an average speed of four miles per hour. Failing in the accomplishment of this object, and having made the acquaintance of Fulton in France, he obtained a renewal of the grant in 1803, when the former joined him in New York, and in four years thereafter their joint efforts were crowned with a brilliant success.

8. In November of the preceding year the British Government, now engaged in a war with the French Empire under Napoleon

---

Election of Daniel D. Tompkins as Governor, and Lieutenant-Governor Broome. — Trial and acquittal of Burr at Richmond for treason. — Launch and successful trip of the first steamboat on the Hudson by Fulton. — History of the enterprise.

Bonaparte, had issued a series of "Orders in Council" prohibiting all trade with France or her allies by the vessels of neutral nations. In retaliation, the Emperor proclaimed the celebrated Milan decree, forbidding all trade with England and her colonies, thereby effectually cutting off all American commerce, in neutral ships, with either of the belligerents. On the 23d of September, 1807, Congress laid an embargo on all vessels in the harbors of the United States, the results of which were exceedingly disastrous to the entire mercantile interest of the country.

9. The Federalists, as a body, together with that section of the Democrats heretofore acting in concert with Mr. Clinton, ranged themselves in determined opposition to this measure of the government; while Mr. Clinton himself, and the great majority of the Democratic party, were its advocates. The leaders of the former contended that the British Orders in Council were rendered necessary by the supplies constantly furnished to the French by American vessels, and which were not needed by the English; while the latter justified the Milan and Berlin decrees as a necessary measure of retaliation on the part of the French, and the embargo as the sole means of procuring a repeal of both ordinances.

10. The practicability of the construction of a canal from Lake Erie to the Hudson River had, to a greater or less extent, occupied the attention of reflecting and scientific minds since the failure of the efforts towards the close of the preceding century to improve the navigation of the Mohawk, and connect its waters, by means of small canals and lockage, with Lake Ontario. GOUVERNEUR MORRIS, JESSE HAWLEY, and JAMES GEDDES had recently directed public attention to this subject through the press and other channels, and the time seemed auspicious for its more mature consideration.

1808. 11. During the session of the Legislature of the succeeding year, Mr. JOSHUA FORMAN, of Onondaga, proposed in the Assembly a concurrent resolution, which was subsequently adopted by the Senate on motion of Mr. GOULD, directing the Surveyor-General to cause a survey to be made "of the most

---

British Orders in Council. — Berlin and Milan decrees. — State of parties. — Proposed canal from Lake Erie to the Hudson. — Survey of the route.

eligible and direct route of a canal to open a communication between the tide-waters of the Hudson River and Lake Erie." The sum of six hundred dollars was appropriated for this purpose, and JAMES GEDDES, of Onondaga, employed to make the survey. His report in favor of the practicability of the undertaking was submitted to the Surveyor-General, and communicated by him to the Legislature at its ensuing session.

12. The strength of the Federalists in the Legislature was somewhat increased by the result of the spring elections, although the Democrats still retained a decided preponderance in both branches. During the summer, Colonel Burr sailed for Europe, where he remained for several years engaged in fruitless efforts to secure the co-operation of the English and French Governments in an expedition against Mexico.

13. On the 1st of November the Legislature reassembled for the choice of presidential electors. The electors appointed were uncommitted to any candidates, but, on their meeting, cast the vote of the State for JAMES MADISON as President and GEORGE CLINTON as Vice-President, who were subsequently elected by a large majority.

14. The Legislature reassembled on the 27th of January, 1809. Resolutions were introduced in the Senate by Mr. Clinton, and adopted, after an exciting debate, by a large majority of both Houses, approving of the measures of the general government and pledging the State to their support. General OBADIAH GERMAN, of Chenango, was elected United States Senator as the successor of Dr. Samuel L. Mitchell, whose term had expired. The representative of the English Government at Washington, in pursuance of an understanding with the French Emperor, had consented in April to a repeal of the obnoxious Orders in Council, which was to be followed by a similar abrogation of the Milan and Berlin decrees on the part of the French, and of the embargo and other restrictive regulations on the part of the American Government.

15. In the mean time, however, the Federalists, strengthened

Report of Mr. Geddes. — Results of the spring elections. — Departure of Colonel Burr for Europe. — Election of President Madison and Vice-President Clinton. — Proceedings of the Legislature. — Negotiations for a repeal of the English and French decrees.

by the popular discontent induced by the pressure of the embargo upon the mercantile and agricultural interests of the country, had again, after an interval of ten years, obtained the ascendency at the spring elections. The 10th of June, the day on which the repeal of the embargo was to take effect, was celebrated by public rejoicings throughout the State; but these festivities were speedily damped by the disavowal of the treaty by the English Government, and its peremptory refusal to repeal the Orders in Council. These proceedings created a feeling of intense indignation against the British authorities which the Federalists were powerless to assuage.

1810. 16. On the 13th of March of the ensuing year, the subject of the construction of a canal from the Western lakes to the Hudson River was brought up in the Senate by the report of JAMES GEDDES, of Onondaga, the surveyor of the proposed route. Through the influence of Mr. CLINTON and JONAS PLATT, of Oneida, the project was favorably received, and a Board of Commissioners, consisting of GOUVERNEUR MORRIS, STEPHEN VAN RENSSELAER, WILLIAM NORTH, THOMAS EDDY, and PETER B. PORTER, appointed to make an additional exploration of the entire route, and report the results to the Legislature at its next session.

17. At the April elections, Governor TOMPKINS and Lieutenant-Governor BROOME were re-elected by a large majority, together with a decided Democratic Legislature. This result was due in a great measure to the effect of public sentiment produced by the refusal of Great Britain to sanction the treaty for the repeal of the Orders of Council, by the growing feeling of hostility towards that nation, the substitution of the non-intercourse system by the general government for that of the embargo, and the increasing popularity both of the general and State administrations. The country was rapidly drifting into another war with its ancient enemy, and the people of the State of New York especially were with great unanimity preparing for the impending contest.

Triumph of the Democrats at the spring elections. — Refusal of the English Government. — Erie and Champlain Canal. — Report of surveyor. — Appointment of commissioners. — Re-election of Governor Tompkins and Lieutenant-Governor Broome. — Preparations for war with England.

Lewiston Landing in 1840.

CHAPTER VI.

ADMINISTRATION OF GOVERNOR TOMPKINS. — COMMON SCHOOLS. — SECOND WAR WITH GREAT BRITAIN. — COLONEL BURR. — BATTLE OF QUEENSTOWN HEIGHTS.

1. THE right of searching American vessels for British soldiers or sailors, claimed and exercised by England in addition to her other encroachments on our national rights, had at this period become so obnoxious as to demand from the United States Government the most decided measures for their repression. So strong was this feeling throughout the country, that a very large party in New York and other States, distrusting the energy of President Madison, presented the name of DE WITT CLINTON as a candidate for that office at the ensuing election. 1811.

2. During the session of the Legislature of this year, a bill was passed for the appointment of five commissioners to report

---

Condition of national affairs. — Nomination of Mr. Clinton for the presidency.

a system for the establishment and organization of Common Schools; and under this act, JEDEDIAH PECK, of Otsego; John Murray, Jr., of New York; Samuel Russell, Roger Skinner, and Samuel Macomb, — were appointed.

3. GOUVERNEUR MORRIS, in behalf of the commissioners appointed for the exploration and survey of the proposed canal from the Hudson to Lake Erie, submitted a report, accompanied by a finely executed map of the entire route; and an act was passed on the 8th of April, drawn up by Mr. CLINTON, adding the names of ROBERT R. LIVINGSTON and ROBERT FULTON to the commission, and giving full authority to the Board for the construction of this great work.

4. The commissioners were also empowered to make application to Congress, to the legislatures of the several States, and to individuals, for pecuniary aid in the prosecution of the enterprise; but beyond these appeals, which were strongly urged by Mr. CLINTON and Mr. MORRIS in person, no further progress was made until after the close of the pending war.

5. The general results of the spring elections were favorable to the Democratic party; in consequence of the death of Lieutenant-Governor Broome, a new election was ordered to fill the vacancy, which resulted in the choice of NICHOLAS FISH, of New York, the Federal candidate, over Mr. CLINTON, the candidate of the Democrats. Both branches of the Legislature were, however, strongly Democratic.

1812. 6. Governor TOMPKINS, in his speech to the Legislature at the opening of the session of 1812, took occasion to protest in strong terms against the increase of a paper currency, through the growing tendency to the multiplication of banks of issue. On the 14th of February the commissioners appointed for the organization of a common-school system made an elaborate and able report, accompanied by a bill for that purpose, which was subsequently passed into a law.

7. Early in the session a bill was introduced for the charter

---

Appointment of commissioners for the establishment of common schools. — Bill for the construction of the canal. — Application to Congress and State legislatures. — Spring elections. — Democratic triumphs. — Death of Lieutenant-Governor Broome, and election of Nicholas Fish. — Organization of the common-school system.

of the BANK OF AMERICA in the city of New York, with a capital of six millions of dollars, — four hundred thousand to be paid over for the benefit of the common-school fund; one hundred thousand to the literature fund, for the support of colleges and academies; another hundred thousand to the State treasury, at the expiration of twenty years, provided no other bank should during that period receive a charter; one million of dollars to be loaned to the State for the construction of the canals; and another million to farmers and others throughout the State, for the promotion of agriculture and manufactures.

8. This bill passed the House by a strong majority; but during its pendency in the Senate, and when its passage by that body was certain, the Governor, on the 27th of March, prorogued the Legislature until the 21st of May ensuing, on the allegation that sufficient proof existed of corrupt practices on the part of the friends of the measure for the procurement of the charter.

9. On the 20th of April the venerable GEORGE CLINTON, Vice-President of the United States, died at Washington, in the seventy-fourth year of his age, after a long career of official honors and patriotic services. On the 21st of May the Legislature reassembled, when the pending bill for the charter of the Bank of America was immediately taken up and passed by both Houses. On the 28th, DE WITT CLINTON was formally nominated by the Democratic members of the Legislature as a candidate for the presidency, in opposition to Mr. Madison.

10. On the 8th of June, after an absence of four years in Europe, Colonel Burr returned to the city of New York, broken in spirit, disappointed in all his expectations of foreign aid in his ambitious aspirations for empire and power, deserted by his former friends, destitute in his circumstances, and heavily encumbered by debts. The death of his only and accomplished daughter, Theodosia Burr Alston, who went down, with every other passenger on board, during the voyage in a schooner from her residence in Charleston to New York a few days after her

---

Charter of the Bank of America. — Prorogation of the Legislature. — Death of George Clinton. — Reassembling of the Legislature. — Passage of the charter of the Bank of America. — Return of Colonel Burr. — Death of Theodosia Burr Alston.

father's arrival, added a still deeper shade of melancholy to his declining years and blasted prospects. He resumed the practice of his profession, and, struggling under the heavy burden of the calamities which weighed down his energies, spent the remaining twenty years of his life in comparative obscurity. He died in New York on the 14th of December, 1836, in the eighty-first year of his age.

11. Colonel Burr was a man of marked ability and brilliant talents. Destitute of all high principles, either of religion or morality, his master passion was personal and political ambition. To that insatiable spirit he sacrificed reputation, friendship, honor, patriotism, and happiness. The terrible retribution which speedily overtook him followed him in his gloomy retirement, and left him only at the portals of the grave. His career furnishes another sad example of the miserable results of unchastened ambition combined with the absence of moral integrity.

12. On the 20th of June, war was declared by Congress against Great Britain, the Democratic members and senators from New York generally voting against it, not because sufficient reason in their judgment did not exist for the measure, but because the country was, as they believed, unprepared for the commencement of hostilities. The Federalists, as a body, were opposed to the war, not only for this reason, but because they conceived no adequate provocation had been given by England which did not equally exist against France. The great mass of Democrats in both branches of Congress (with the exception of the New York delegation) sustained the declaration. Congress immediately passed a bill for the enlistment of twenty-five thousand regular troops and fifty thousand volunteers, and organized the West Point Military Academy for the instruction of cadets for the army.

13. At the September term of the Circuit Court, held in Chenango County, General David Thomas, State Treasurer, was indicted and tried before Judge William W. Van Ness for attempting to bribe Casper M. Rouse, a Senator from that county, during the pendency of the bill for the charter of the Bank of

---

Subsequent career and death of Burr. — Declaration of war against Great Britain. — State of parties. — Organization of the West Point Military Academy.

America. No sufficient proof of the charge having been produced, General Thomas was acquitted. Solomon Southwick, then editor of the Albany Register, was also tried and acquitted during the same month before Chief-Justice Kent at the Montgomery circuit, for an attempted bribery of Alexander Sheldon, Speaker of the Assembly. Thomas Addis Emmett, of New York, recently appointed Attorney-General in place of Matthias B. Hildreth, deceased, conducted these prosecutions on the part of the State.

14. In the mean time, General Hull, who had been appointed to the command of the forces in the territory of Michigan, with orders to invade Canada, had in August yielded to a slightly superior force of British and Indians, commanded by General Sir Isaac Brock and the Indian chief Tecumseh, and surrendered at Detroit his army of eight hundred men, thirty-three pieces of artillery, and a vast quantity of naval and military stores to the enemy. For this act he was, two years later, tried by court-martial, convicted of cowardice, and sentenced to be shot, but in consideration of his Revolutionary services received a pardon from the President.

15. The naval engagements of this year were notable. Captain Isaac Hull, of the frigate Constitution, a vessel better known as Old Ironsides, had, on the 19th of August, captured, after a brilliant engagement, the British frigate Guerrière, commanded by Captain Dacres, off the mouth of the St. Lawrence; Captain Decatur, of the United States, had, off the Azores, in October, compelled the British frigate Macedonian to strike her flag; and Captain Jones, of the Wasp, after capturing the British brig Frolic, was himself, with his prize, forced to yield to the Poictiers, a seventy-four gun frigate. Soon afterwards Captain Bainbridge, who had succeeded to the command of the Constitution, took and burned the British frigate Java off the coast of Brazil.

16. Captain CHAUNCEY, of the New York Navy-yard, had been assigned to the command of Lakes Ontario and Erie; and, with a small sloop-of-war of sixteen guns, and a fleet of merchant-vessels fitted out with guns and other naval equipments,

---

Trial and acquittal of David Thomas and Solomon Southwick for bribery. — Surrender of Detroit by Hull. — Naval successes on the ocean. — Fleets on Lakes Erie and Ontario.

and brought from Albany at an immense expense of labor, soon succeeded in clearing Lake Ontario of British ships and driving them into Kingston Harbor on the Canada shores. Lieutenant Elliott, having equipped a fleet on Lake Erie, by a bold and daring movement, under the guns of the British fort on the opposite shore, captured two British armed vessels which had come down the lake from Detroit.

17. On the 19th of July an unsuccessful attack was made upon Sackett's Harbor, on the eastern shore of Lake Ontario, by a squadron of five British vessels from the Canada shore. The Harbor was defended by the United States brig Oneida, of sixteen guns, commanded by Lieutenant M. T. Woolsey, having in charge a British schooner which had been seized for a violation of the revenue laws, and by a military force of about three thousand regulars and volunteers. Lieutenant Woolsey, failing in his attempt to engage the British commodore, took command of a battery on the shore, whence, after two hours' firing, he crippled and dispersed the hostile fleet, without the loss of a man on the American side. An attack upon Ogdensburg, on the 4th of October, by a British fleet of twenty-five boats, with seven hundred and fifty men, was also gallantly repulsed by General Jacob Brown after a severe and protracted contest.

18. Early in September a large body of militia had been concentrated in the vicinity of Lewiston, on the Niagara River, under the command of Major-General Stephen Van Rensselaer. An attack upon the village and heights of Queenstown, on the western bank of the Niagara, a few miles below the Falls, was soon afterwards planned, and the requisite arrangements made for transportation of the troops, on the morning of the 11th of October, to the opposite shore. Through some deficiency or treachery on the part of Lieutenant Sims, the officer employed for this service, the boats failed to reach their destination, and the expedition was postponed.

19. On the morning of the 13th, however, ten boats, under the direction of Lieutenant-Colonels Chrystie and Solomon Van Rensselaer, with about two hundred and twenty-five men, crossed over to Queenstown, and, having landed the troops, immediately

---

Attack on Sackett's Harbor and Ogdensburg.— Concentration of troops at Lewiston.

returned for additional reinforcements. In the absence of Colonels Chrystie and Van Rensselaer, who remained on the opposite shore to superintend the embarkation of the residue of the troops, the command of the small force at Queenstown devolved on Captain JOHN E. WOOL, the senior officer present.

20. The landing of this force was resisted with great spirit and energy by Captain Dennis, the British commandant of the post, who had become aware of the movement; and Lieutenant Rathbone was mortally wounded, and other severe injuries sustained by the detachment, before their purpose could be accomplished, and a line formed on the plateau near the foot of the heights above the village, by the companies of Captains Wool, Malcolm, and Armstrong.

21. Orders from head-quarters were immediately transmitted to Captain Wool to storm the heights, but before the ascent was commenced these orders were countermanded, and a vigorous attack was made on the right flank and front of Wool's line by Captain Dennis, who had been strongly reinforced by two additional companies of regular troops, stationed on the heights. After a short but severe engagement, in which two officers were killed, and Captains Wool, Malcolm, and Armstrong wounded, the enemy's force on the plains was repulsed. Lieutenant-Colonel Solomon Van Rensselaer was so severely wounded as to be unable longer to remain in command of the expedition.

22. The attack from the heights on the left flank of the detachment was still continued, until orders were received for its retreat to the beach, out of range of the enemy's fire. Still suffering from annoyance in this quarter, Captain Wool obtained permission to attempt the capture of the heights; and, reinforced by a fresh company under command of Captain Ogilvie, though suffering from his wounds, at once commenced the ascent, and by an unfrequented path accomplished his daring object without the loss of a single man.

23. With the rising of the sun the American flag was planted on the British works. General Sir Isaac Brock, who had now arrived on the ground, rallied the retreating forces of the English, and, having repulsed a portion of Captain Wool's command

---

Attack upon Queenstown. — Battle of Queenstown Heights.

sent to occupy the heights above the battery, concentrated his forces against the remainder, who were driven back, in considerable confusion, upon the precipitous bank of the river.

24. In this critical position, Captain Ogilvie was seen to raise a white handkerchief on a bayonet, as a token of submission. Captain Wool with his own hands indignantly tore down the craven emblem, reanimated his troops by a spirited appeal to their bravery and courage, and renewed the doubtful and desperate contest with the superior force arrayed against him, led by the ablest general in the British service. Having exhausted their ammunition, a bayonet charge was made, and the enemy forced to retreat.

25. While engaged in an effort to rally his flying troops, General Brock received a mortal wound, and Captain Wool and his gallant band again took possession of the heights of Queenstown. General Wadsworth and Lieutenant-Colonel WINFIELD SCOTT soon afterwards joined the detachment, now consisting of about six hundred regulars and militia, the command having been assigned to the latter. A brisk onslaught was immediately made upon the force by a band of Mohawk Indians, armed with tomahawks and knives, led by John Brant and Captain Jacobs, who, after a severe contest, were repulsed and driven from the heights, under the lead of Colonel Scott.

26. Meantime a strong reinforcement from Fort George, under the command of General Sheaffe, was seen approaching the heights; and General Van Rensselaer, who was on the field, immediately returned to Lewiston, to expedite the passage of the remaining militia reserves. In spite of all his efforts, not one of their number could be induced to cross the river in support of their exhausted comrades. The failure of several boats which had previously been sent over, and the capture or loss of their passengers, had effectually discouraged any subsequent attempt.

27. Intelligence of this disaster was conveyed to Lieutenant-Colonel Scott, who, nevertheless determined, single-handed and worn down by the fatigues of the day, to encounter the overpowering force brought to bear against him. At four in the afternoon the action again commenced; and so severe and well supported was the onslaught, and so superior were the numbers

of the enemy, that the Americans were forced to retreat and finally to surrender. About a thousand prisoners were taken, less than one third of whom had participated in the action, the residue having either deserted or concealed themselves among the surrounding rocks and bushes. The British force numbered thirteen hundred and fifty. The Americans lost ninety men killed, and one hundred wounded; the British about one hundred and fifty of both, exclusive of Indians.

28. Thus terminated the well-fought field of QUEENSTOWN HEIGHTS, — deeds of heroism and valor having been displayed by officers and men never before exposed to fire, which would compare favorably with those of veterans inured to the service. The field in which Lieutenant-General WINFIELD SCOTT and Major-General JOHN E. WOOL first "won their spurs" was nobly illustrated by the chivalrous minute-guns, which, by direction of General VAN RENSSELAER, were fired from the American batteries at the conclusion of the funeral ceremonies of the British commander, General Sir ISAAC BROCK!

29. On the 23d of October, a detachment of militia, chiefly from the city of Troy, commanded by Major Guilford D. Young of that place, occupying French Mills on the St. Regis River, attacked and captured a company of Canadian "Voyageurs," which, in contravention of a stipulation for neutrality, had occupied the Indian village of St. Regis, situated on the northeastern borders of St. Lawrence County, and were endeavoring to induce the inhabitants to join the British standard. On this occasion the first British flag taken in the war was captured by Lieutenant WILLIAM L. MARCY, afterwards honorably distinguished in the highest executive and legislative departments of the State and Union.

30. On the 2d of November the Legislature convened for the choice of presidential electors. MARTIN VAN BUREN, of Columbia, made his first appearance in a legislative capacity, at this session, as a Senator from the Middle District, and at once assumed the leadership of the Democratic party. Electors in favor of Mr. Clinton were duly chosen on joint ballot, a portion

---

Capture of British troops at St. Regis. — First appearance in public life of Martin Van Buren. — Presidential electors in favor of Mr. Clinton chosen.

of the Federalists voting with the majority of Democrats. Mr. MADISON was, however, re-elected, by a majority of thirty-nine electoral votes, over Mr. Clinton, and ELBRIDGE GERRY, of Massachusetts, Vice-President, by a majority of forty-five votes, over Jared Ingersoll, of Pennsylvania.

CHAPTER VII.

ADMINISTRATION OF GOVERNOR TOMPKINS. — SECOND WAR WITH GREAT BRITAIN. — COMMON SCHOOLS. — CAMPAIGN OF 1813. — NAVAL VICTORY ON LAKE ERIE. — CAPTURE OF YORK. — SIEGE OF FORT GEORGE. — DEFENCE OF SACKETT'S HARBOR. — BLACK ROCK AND BUFFALO.

1. THE State Legislature reassembled on the 12th of January, 1813. RUFUS KING, of New York, was elected United States Senator in place of General John Smith, whose term had expired. GIDEON HAWLEY, of Albany, was appointed by the Council Superintendent of Common Schools, under the provisions of an act passed the preceding year for their better organization. DE WITT CLINTON was reappointed Mayor of New York. On the 28th of January, Chancellor ROBERT R. LIVINGSTON died, in the sixty-sixth year of his age. His eminent talents, long service in public life, and timely benefactions to his friend ROBERT FULTON in his great enterprise, endeared his memory to his fellow-citizens of all parties.

2. The spring elections resulted in the re-election of Governor TOMPKINS and the election of JOHN TAYLER as Lieutenant-Governor, with a strong Democratic majority in the Senate, and a small Federal majority in the other branch of the legislature. Stephen Van Rensselaer of Albany and George Huntington of Oneida were the Federal candidates for Governor and Lieutenant-Governor. In view of the bitter opposition of the New England States to the pending war with England and the administration of the general government, the triumph of the Democratic party in New York, in the re-election of Governor

Tompkins, was hailed with the highest gratification by its members throughout the Union.

3. Meantime General JOHN ARMSTRONG, of New York, had been appointed Secretary of War by the President. The surrender of Detroit, the heroic episode of Queenstown Heights, and the brilliant victories of our infant navy, had infused a new spirit into the West, and volunteers from every quarter flocked to the patriotic standard. The army of the West, stationed at the head of Lake Erie, was placed under the command of General WILLIAM HENRY HARRISON, of Ohio; that of the centre, between Lakes Erie and Ontario, under General HENRY DEARBORN, of Massachusetts; and that of the North, in the vicinity of Lake Champlain, under General WADE HAMPTON, of Virginia. Frenchtown, on the Raisin, had been occupied by Winchester, under the directions of General Harrison, and retaken by Proctor, the British commander, under circumstances of barbarous cruelty to his prisoners, who were left to the tender mercies of his Indian allies, notwithstanding the most solemn assurances of safety and security, and Forts Meigs and Stephenson gallantly defended by General Clay and Major Croghan, a youth of twenty-one, against Proctor and the Indian chief TECUMSEH.

4. On the ocean, Captain JAMES LAWRENCE, in command of the Hornet, had, in February, captured the British frigate Peacock off the South American coast, and in the ensuing June, having been transferred to the command of the frigate Chesapeake in Boston harbor, had, with his accustomed impetuosity, engaged the British frigate Shannon, Captain Broke. At the commencement of the action he was mortally wounded, his ship boarded, and after a severe hand-to-hand conflict her flag was struck, notwithstanding the dying command of her brave commander, "Don't give up the ship!"

5. On the 7th of February, Major Benjamin Forsyth, of the United States Rifles, stationed at Ogdensburg with a party of two hundred men, organized a successful expedition for the rescue of several prisoners arrested in St. Lawrence County by the British authorities as deserters, and confined in the jail at Elizabethtown, in Upper Canada. For this exploit he received

a brevet commission from the American Government as Lieutenant-Colonel.

6. A retaliatory expedition was, on the 22d, organized against Ogdensburg under the direction of Lieutenant-Colonel McDonnell, with eight hundred men. Colonel Forsyth's garrison at the time consisted only of a single company of riflemen, a few volunteers from Albany, and the inhabitants of the village. With two iron twelve-pounders and six iron and brass six-pounders, trophies of the Revolutionary field of Saratoga, mounted on rude wooden breastworks, and manned chiefly by the citizens, he made a gallant defence, killing six and wounding forty-eight, including Lieutenant-Colonel McDonnell and six officers.

7. After a severe contest, however, he was forced to surrender the town, the public property and military stores in which were removed to Canada. Two armed schooners and two gunboats were burned; fourteen hundred stands of arms and accoutrements, twelve pieces of artillery, together with a vast quantity of ammunition, tents, and camp equipage, fell into the possession of the enemy, and a considerable amount of damage was inflicted upon the private property of the inhabitants.

8. On the 25th of April, General Dearborn embarked a force of seventeen hundred men on board Commodore Chauncey's fleet at Sackett's Harbor for the capture of York, the capital of Upper Canada, the chief military depot of the British army. On their landing on the 27th they were met by a galling fire from the British and Indians, whom they speedily drove back to their fortifications; and General ZEBULON MONTGOMERY PIKE, pressing forward to the attack, was mortally wounded by the blowing up of the magazine of the fort. The assailants were, however, successful, and the American flag soon floated in triumph over the fort.

9. On the 27th of May the squadron, after having returned for supplies and relief to the wounded, again weighed anchor for the Canadian shore, and in conjunction with Captain Oliver H. Perry of the navy, Colonel Winfield Scott and Major Forsyth of the Rifles, Colonel Porter and Colonel Alexander Macomb of the artillery, and Generals Boyd, Winder, and Chandler, pro-

---

Capture of Ogdensburg. — Capture of York. — Death of Zebulon Montgomery Pike.

ceeded to an attack upon Fort George, on the western shore of the Niagara River. The troops, under the personal direction of Captain Perry, effected a landing, and in the face of a formidable force of eight hundred men well posted on the summit of a precipitous bank, Colonel Scott, after a desperate conflict, and after having three times been compelled to fall back, succeeded in carrying the position with a loss to the enemy of their brave commander, Myers, eleven officers, and nearly four hundred men.

10. Colonel Scott pursued the enemy as far as the village of Niagara, and, having sent a detachment to cut off their retreat to Burlington Heights, returned to Fort George, where a small party of the British, under the command of Brigadier-General Vincent, still remained. This officer, after directing the evacuation of Fort Erie, and the abandonment of Chippewa, ordered the magazine of the fort to be fired and the party left in charge to rejoin the main body at the Beaver Dams. The explosion of the magazine threw Colonel Scott from his horse; but, in the absence of any serious injury, he immediately took possession of the fort, and, after hoisting with his own hand the American flag, pressed forward in pursuit of the retreating garrison, until, recalled by his commanding officer, General Boyd, he reluctantly returned to the main body. The entire loss of the Americans in this enterprise was seventeen killed and forty-five wounded. Three hundred and sixty-six British regulars and five hundred militia were captured.

11. On the 29th of May an unsuccessful attempt was made by General Sir George Prevost and Commodore Sir James L. Yeo for the capture of Sackett's Harbor, the principal forces for the defence of which had been withdrawn for the expeditions against the enemy's posts on the Niagara frontier. Lieutenant-Colonel Backus, of the Light Dragoons, having been left in command of the garrison with about eight hundred men, in conjunction with Brigadier-General Jacob Brown, who resided in the vicinity, so effectually resisted the attack of the British troops, numbering in the aggregate about a thousand men, with a strong party of Indians, that a retreat was ordered after an

---

Capture of Fort George. — Attempted capture of Sackett's Harbor. — Successful resistance of the garrison.

hour's severe conflict, with the loss of forty-eight men killed and about two hundred wounded. The Americans had fifty men killed and eighty-four wounded.

12. The capture of this important post would have inflicted a heavy disaster upon the American cause. Large quantities of naval and military stores had been collected and deposited there; several vessels were in process of construction, and a prize vessel, previously captured from the enemy, and two United States schooners, lying in the harbor; and the arsenal, various batteries, cantonments, and other public buildings required for the service of the troops, were of the most valuable nature. The bravery and intrepidity of its defenders against a greatly superior force deserved and received the highest appreciation of the national authorities.

13. The failure of the expeditions against Stoney Creek, and the Beaver Dam Meadows, organized by Major-General Dearborn, and the prevalence of a general public feeling of his inefficiency and incompetency, about this time led to the removal of that officer from the command of the central division, and the substitution of Major-General WILKINSON, Secretary of War of the United States.

14. An attack upon the village of Black Rock, on the eastern bank of the Niagara River, on the 11th of July, by Lieutenant-Colonel Bishopp, of the British army, was gallantly repulsed by the American General PETER B. PORTER, — Colonel Bishopp having been mortally wounded, and a large number of his men killed, wounded, or captured, while the Americans, though greatly outnumbered, sustained a very trifling loss.

15. On the 14th of August the brig-of-war Argus, commanded by Lieutenant William H. Allen, of Rhode Island, having on board the American minister to France, the Hon. William H. Crawford, was captured on her return voyage, after having destroyed twenty English vessels, by the British brig Pelican. Lieutenant Allen was mortally wounded. On the 5th of September the British brig Boxer, Captain Blyth, was captured off the coast of Maine by the Enterprise, Lieutenant William Burrows, who was killed in the action.

Importance of the post. — Removal of General Dearborn. — Attack upon Black Rock. — Capture of the Argus by the Pelican. — The Boxer.

16. The most brilliant and important naval victory of the campaign and of the war, however, was that of Commodore OLIVER HAZARD PERRY on Lake Erie, on the morning of the 10th of September, over the British squadron commanded by Commodore Barclay, consisting of six vessels mounting sixty-three guns. The American fleet consisted of the flag-ship Lawrence, the Niagara, — of twenty guns each, — and eight smaller vessels with thirteen guns in all.

17. At sunrise, the enemy's fleet having been discovered in motion, the line of battle was formed under the direction of Commodore Perry, and in perfect order slowly approached the opposing squadron. At noon the signal for action — the blue flag of the Lawrence with the inspiring motto " DON'T GIVE UP THE SHIP !" — was displayed, and the action commenced.

18. The Lawrence closed with the enemy at canister-shot distance, and for half an hour, assisted by the Ariel and Scorpion, sustained a heavy and destructive fire from their long guns. Commodore Perry, advancing his ship to close quarters with the Detroit, the British flag-ship, and leaving behind him his whole force, with the exception of the Ariel and Scorpion, for two hours maintained the unequal contest, until nearly every gun of the Lawrence was disabled, her sails torn to pieces, her bulwarks beaten in, and of one hundred efficient men upwards of eighty killed or wounded.

19. At this crisis, Commander ELLIOTT, of the Niagara, perceiving the crippled and unmanageable condition of the Lawrence, and the imminent danger of her capture and the defeat of the fleet, ventured, without orders, to leave the line and go to her relief. While passing her to the windward in the midst of a heavy and raking fire from four of the enemy's vessels, Commodore Perry sprang aboard his cutter, with his brother, Midshipman J. Alexander Perry, and the flag of the Lawrence, and succeeded in reaching the Niagara.

20. The contest was again renewed with the utmost alacrity and spirit ; the entire fleet, with the exception of the Lawrence, brought into action, through the exertions of Commander Elliott ; a continuous shower of broadsides poured right and left

---

The Enterprise. — Battle of Lake Erie.

into the enemy's vessels, and in half an hour the entire fleet surrendered. Returning to the deck of the shattered Lawrence, Commodore Perry received the swords of the several hostile commanders, and indited and forwarded to General Harrison the laconic and memorable despatch, "WE HAVE MET THE ENEMY, — AND THEY ARE OURS!"

21. This brilliant victory was followed on the 5th of October by the defeat of the British General Proctor and his entire army by General Harrison at the battle of the Thames, in which Tecumseh was slain, the territory of Michigan, ingloriously surrendered at the commencement of the war by Hull, regained, and hostilities on the northwestern frontier terminated.

22. In the latter part of October an ineffectual movement was made, under the direction of General Wilkinson, by General Izard, for a descent upon Canada, and the capture of Montreal and Kingston. At Chateaugay, in Franklin County, near the confluence of the Chateaugay and Oudarde Rivers, within a few miles of the St. Lawrence, a force of about four thousand men, led by Generals Izard and Hampton, was repulsed by the British under Lieutenant-Colonel De Salaberry, and compelled to retreat with considerable loss, and the expedition against Montreal was temporarily abandoned.

23. Early in November, however, another expedition organized under the command of Generals Brown and Macomb, with about seventeen hundred men, proceeded from the vicinity of Lake Champlain down the St. Lawrence in a flotilla of three hundred boats extending over a distance of five miles, under the immediate direction of General Wilkinson in person. At Chrystler's Farm, near the Canadian village of Williamsburg, they were encountered by a heavy British force under Lieutenant-Colonels Morrison and Pearson, in which Colonel E. P. GAINES, Lieutenant-Colonel Aspinwall, and Lieutenant W. J. WORTH distinguished themselves, and after a severe contest of two hours, and with no material advantage on either side, a retreat to the boats was ordered by General Wilkinson, and the expedition again abandoned.

Battle of the Thames. — Defeat of the British army. — Death of Tecumseh. — Recovery of Michigan Territory. — Abortive expeditions against Canada. — Action at Chateaugay. — Battle of Chrystler's Farm.

24. The transfer of the principal part of the American forces from the Niagara frontier to the vicinity of Sackett's Harbor and Lake Champlain, and the arrival of heavy reinforcements of the enemy under Lieutenant-General Drummond to the former position, compelled General McClure to abandon Fort George. Accordingly, after having deposited his military stores in Fort Niagara, and burned the village of Newark, he opened a fire upon Queenstown and inflicted great and unnecessary distress upon the defenceless and unoffending citizens of those villages.

25. On the 18th of December a fearful series of retaliatory barbarities was commenced by a detachment of the Royal Artillery under Colonel Murray, numbering about five hundred and fifty men. On the morning of the 19th, Fort Niagara was entered, and the entire garrison, with a few exceptions, including a large number of hospital patients, bayoneted without mercy, in revenge for the burning of Newark and Queenstown.

26. Another party, led by General Rial and Lieutenant-Colonel Gordon, consisting of detachments from the Royal Scots and a body of five hundred Indians, crossed over from Queenstown to Lewiston, which was burned and plundered, and the inhabitants subjected to the most atrocious cruelties. Similar vindictive retaliation was extended to the villages of Youngstown, Manchester, Fort Schlosser, and the Indian settlement at Tuscarora, and for several miles the entire frontier was desolated and ravaged.

27. On the 26th, General Hall, of the New York militia, took command of a large body of undisciplined troops at Buffalo, and Lieutenant-General Drummond, after having reconnoitred these forces, despatched General Rial on the 29th with a large body of regulars, Canadians, and Indians to the vicinity of the village of Black Rock, near Buffalo. On the next day a sanguinary engagement occurred between the two armies, resulting in the retreat of the Americans, and the abandonment of both the villages of Buffalo and Black Rock to the same fate which had swept over the neighboring settlements.

Evacuation of Fort George. — Burning of Newark and Queenstown. — Retaliatory descent upon Fort Niagara, Lewiston, Youngstown, and other villages. — Capture and destruction of Buffalo and Black Rock.

28. This savage and merciless warfare, originally provoked by the unjustifiable and wanton aggression of General McClure, reflected the deepest disgrace upon both nations, and elicited from all quarters, both in England and America, the strongest feeling of indignation and mutual recrimination. Its unavoidable tendency was fearfully to imbitter the sanguinary contest in which the two countries were engaged, and to defer the period of reconciliation.

CHAPTER VIII.

ADMINISTRATION OF GOVERNOR TOMPKINS. — SECOND WAR WITH GREAT BRITAIN. — BATTLES OF CHIPPEWA AND LUNDY'S LANE.

1. THE Legislature convened on the 25th of January, 1814. Governor TOMPKINS, in his address to the Legislature, recommended the assumption by the State of its quota of the direct tax imposed by Congress for the support of the war. This proposition was favorably entertained by the Senate, but rejected by the Assembly by a strict party vote. General Root, Nathan Sandford, and Mr. Van Buren were the Democratic leaders in the Senate; and the Federalists in the Assembly were marshalled by David B. Ogden, Samuel Jones, Jr., and Charles King of New York, and Jacob Rutsen Van Rensselaer of Dutchess. Chief-Justice KENT was appointed Chancellor in place of Mr. Lansing; Smith Thompson succeeded him as Chief-Justice of the Supreme Court; and Jonas Platt, of Oneida, was appointed Associate Justice in his place.

2. Liberal appropriations of money, to be raised by State lotteries, were made, during the session, to Union, Columbia, and Hamilton Colleges, and to various medical colleges. The common-school law of 1812 was remodelled, in accordance with the views of the superintendent, Mr. Hawley. The April elections terminated in the complete success of the Republican

---

Proceedings of the Legislature. — Appointments and removals. — Appropriations to colleges. — Common-school law. — April elections. — Triumph of the Republicans.

party in both branches of the Legislature, and the congressional representation.

3. In February, General Wilkinson moved from French Mills to Plattsburg, and General Brown, with two thousand men, occupied Sackett's Harbor. In the ensuing March, Wilkinson, in an attack upon the British near Rouse's Point, was repulsed, and replaced by General Izard. On the 5th of May a British squadron, with three thousand men, under the command of Lieutenant-General Drummond, appeared before Oswego, with the view of capturing the naval and military stores deposited at Oswego Falls, but met with so spirited a resistance from Colonel Mitchell, and a small flotilla under Captain Woolsey, that they withdrew with a heavy loss.

4. These stores, thus preserved from destruction, were transferred, under the direction of Captain Woolsey, aided by a corps of riflemen commanded by Major Appling, to Sackett's Harbor. On reaching Sandy Creek, within eight miles of their destination, through the treachery of the crew of one of the boats sent as a convoy, the British admiral, Sir James Yeo, was apprised of their destination, and immediately despatched a force to intercept them. Major Appling, on being apprised of this movement, placed his riflemen, artillery, dragoons, and a body of Indians in ambush; and on the approach of the unsuspecting detachment gave them so sudden and unwelcome a reception that they were driven back in confusion, and the convoy proceeded to its destination.

5. Major-General JACOB BROWN, with Brigadier-Generals SCOTT and RIPLEY, were at this period in command on the Niagara frontier; and instructions from the War Department having been received for the capture of Fort Erie, Chippewa, Fort George, and Burlington Heights, on the Canada shore, active preparations were immediately made for the accomplishment of these results. On the morning of the 3d of July, General Scott, with four regiments, crossed the Niagara River, landing below Fort Erie, and was followed by General Ripley, with four additional

---

Movements of General Wilkinson and General Brown.—Unsuccessful attack upon Rouse's Point. — Removal of Wilkinson and appointment of General Izard. — Repulse of the British at Oswego — Transportation of military stores to Sackett's Harbor. — Action at Sandy Creek.

regiments, occupying a position above the fort, which, with its garrison, was immediately surrendered to them.

6. The next morning, General Scott, with his brigade and a corps of artillery under Captain Towson, driving before him the British advance under the command of Lieutenant-Colonel Pearson, took position behind Street's Creek, a small stream entering the Niagara River about a mile and a half above Chippewa. On the same evening, General Ripley's brigade, the field and battery train, and Major Hindman's artillery corps, encamped in the rear of General Scott's position; and on the morning of the 5th, General Peter B. Porter, with a part of the New York and Pennsylvania volunteers and a small party of Indians, occupied a position in rear of General Ripley.

7. General Rial, with a force of about twenty-five hundred men, consisting of the flower of the British army, was posted behind a heavy line of intrenchments below the CHIPPEWA Creek, at the distance of about a mile and a half north of the American encampment, and separated from it by a large plain of about a mile in width, lying between the two creeks, bounded on the east by the Niagara River, and on the west by a heavy wood, with occasional openings of low ground.

8. Towards the middle of the day this wood was found to be occupied by strong bodies of the enemy's light troops and Indians; and General Porter was despatched with his brigade for their dispersion, which was soon accomplished with considerable slaughter. On emerging from the wood, the enemy were discovered drawn up in battle array on the plain; and the detachment, panic-stricken, dispersed in all directions, notwithstanding the efforts of their gallant commander to rally them.

9. General Scott, in the mean time, ignorant of these movements of the enemy, had conducted his brigade across the creek into the plain, for martial exercise, at the same moment that the British line were entering it from the north. Displaying his force near its southern extremity, General Rial was confronted by the brigade of General Scott drawn up in line with military precision, and fully prepared, at all points, for the approaching combat.

10. The battle instantly commenced with the utmost spirit and vigor on both sides, but with a numerical superiority of nearly two to one in favor of the British, — General Porter's command having become entirely demoralized, and General Ripley's forces not having been able to reach the position assigned them. The destructive effect of the American fire on his exposed lines soon compelled the British General to order a concentrated charge on his opponent's front, which was so gallantly received that a retreat was immediately ordered. General Scott at once charged upon the whole line and triumphantly drove them from the field in uncontrollable disorder to their camp on the Chippewa.

11. The enemy's loss in this battle was six officers and two hundred and thirty men, including eighty-seven Indians killed, and twenty-six officers and about three hundred men wounded; while that of the Americans, during the action and the preceding skirmishes, was sixty men killed without the loss of a single officer, and nine officers and two hundred and thirty-eight men wounded.

12. General Rial soon afterwards broke up his encampment at Chippewa and fell back on Queenstown, and, having thrown part of his forces into Fort George and Mississaga, took post on Twenty Mile Creek. General Brown, on the 10th, advanced to Queenstown, where he encamped with his army; and General Rial, having effected a junction with his reinforcements, occupied a new position at the Fifteen Mile Creek, about thirteen miles from Queenstown.

13. On the morning of the 20th, General Brown, in accordance with the decision of a council of war, advanced from Queenstown to Fort George, with the design — in conjunction with the fleet of Commodore Chauncey on Lake Ontario — of investing and recapturing that fortress. Failing, however, in his efforts to secure the co-operation of the fleet, he withdrew his forces on the 24th to Chippewa, where he encamped on the south side of the Niagara River. On the morning of the 25th the advance of the British army, under Lieutenant-Colonel Pearson, took position near LUNDY'S LANE, — a road entering

---

Movements of the two armies. — Battle of Lundy's Lane.

the main road below the Falls, — at a distance of about three miles from the American camp.

14. In ignorance of this movement of the enemy, General Brown ordered the First Brigade, Captain Towson's artillery, and the cavalry and mounted men, under the direction of General Scott, to move towards Queenstown, with the view of checking the progress of General Rial, in case he should have determined to cross the river and execute a flank movement up the eastern bank. In compliance with these orders, General Scott, between five and six o'clock in the afternoon, proceeded with his brigade down the road towards the Falls.

15. Overtaking a small detachment of British cavalry in the neighborhood of the Falls, information was immediately sent by Scott to the main body of the presence of the enemy in force, and of his intention to engage them. The column again moved forward in the direction of Lundy's Lane, in its march to Queenstown, and, passing a narrow strip of woods, suddenly emerged in front of General Rial's entire army, strengthened by a heavy reinforcement just arrived under Lieutenant-General Drummond, strongly posted on a commanding elevation, on the summit of which frowned a battery of seven formidable pieces of artillery.

16. Against this overwhelming force, consisting of upwards of three thousand five hundred regulars, militia, and Indians, with its artillery in the centre and its wings thrown forward, ready to infold and crush all opposition, General Scott advanced at sunset with his single brigade, numbering not more than thirteen hundred men in all, separated into two divisions, and with only two small field-pieces. A brisk fire was immediately opened upon the enemy's line by this small park of artillery; and so vigorous was the attack of Major Jesup's regiment on the extreme right, that the British left, on its front, was partially forced back for some distance, and General Rial and his staff captured while on a reconnoissance, by Captain Ketchum.

17. In the mean time, General Brown had promptly despatched General Ripley with the Second Brigade, and General

---

General Scott's advance. — He encounters the entire British force. — He attacks with a single brigade.

Porter with the volunteers, to the support of General Scott, and proceeded himself to the field. Before the arrival of this reinforcement the night had closed in, and the battle continued to rage in its darkness. The incessant and deadly fire of the enemy's battery in the centre shattered the advancing columns as they approached, and the complete destruction of the gallant band seemed inevitable.

18. At this crisis, General Ripley inquired of Colonel MILLER and Captain McDonald whether it might not be possible, notwithstanding the great disparity of force, to capture and silence this formidable battery. The reply of Colonel Miller — "I'LL TRY, SIR!" — has passed into history. Preparations were immediately made for carrying this daring resolution into effect.

19. Colonel Miller's regiment was moved forward silently and cautiously, but in perfect order, to a fence on the slope of the hill in rear of the battery, where it drew up in line; and, after pouring in a well-directed volley, the men rushed forward with their bayonets, and, driving before them the artillerists, took possession of the guns, and occupied the summit of the hill, surrounded by a legion of infuriated foes.

20. The First Brigade, under General Scott, continued in the face of a galling fire to maintain its position, although regiment after regiment of its brave defenders was decimated, and one alone remained to sustain, with a spirit and bravery bordering on desperation, the impetuous charge of the enemy. Major Jesup still held the ground he had wrested from the enemy on the Queenstown road. Not a ray of light, except the occasional flashes of the artillery or muskets of the combatants, illuminated the darkness of the night; and at half past ten the enemy's whole line, discomfited and defeated, had fallen back, and again attempted to rally their broken forces in rear of their former position.

21. During the ensuing two hours a series of bold and desperate efforts were made by the British, reinforced by two companies of artillery, to regain the captured battery, and with it the ground they had lost. Charge after charge, in the deep obscurity of midnight, was made with the bayonet, and resisted

with unflagging pertinacity by the same deadly weapon; and after a hand-to-hand contest of two hours, waged with a bravery and determination unparalleled in the annals of modern warfare, the enemy were again driven from the well-contested field.

22. Generals Brown and Scott having both been severely wounded, the command now devolved on General Ripley; and, after maintaining their position for an hour after the retreat of the enemy, the American force retired, under orders received from General Brown, to their encampment at Chippewa, leaving the captured battery, which they had no means of removing, to fall into the possession of its original owners.

23. The loss of the Americans in this battle was ten officers, and one hundred and sixty-one men killed, and forty-eight officers and five hundred and seventy-one men wounded; while that of the British was five officers and seventy-nine men killed, Lieutenant-General Drummond, General Rial, thirty-seven officers, and five hundred and eighteen men wounded or captured.

CHAPTER IX.

ADMINISTRATION OF GOVERNOR TOMPKINS. — SECOND WAR WITH GREAT BRITAIN (*concluded*). — SIEGE OF FORT ERIE. — NAVAL VICTORY ON LAKE CHAMPLAIN. — ATTACK ON PLATTSBURG.

1. ON the 26th of July the American army, under General Brown, fell back on Fort Erie, without being in any manner harassed or disturbed by the enemy. In this new position strong intrenchments and additional defences were thrown up, when, on the 3d of August, the British, again reinforced, appeared in strength before the fort, and, after having opened fire upon it, employed themselves for several days in vigorous preparations for a siege.

1814.

2. At sunrise on the 7th of August the enemy's first battery was unmasked; and from five pieces of artillery a volley was poured upon the American lines, from which the national flag

---

Retirement of the Americans. — Losses. — Siege of Fort Erie. — First attack.

was proudly displayed, amid the inspiriting strains of the various regimental bands. For an entire week the siege was prosecuted with great vigor, the fire was unremitting and severe, and the defence, under the immediate direction of General Gaines, spirited and persistent.

3. At about two o'clock in the morning of the 15th, a combined assault was commenced on the extreme left of the American lines by the enemy, under Lieutenant-Colonel Fischer, with from fifteen hundred to two thousand men. After having been repulsed four times, with great spirit and energy, and with a heavy loss, by the Twenty-First Regiment, under Major Wood of the Engineers, Captain Towson's artillerists, and the Twenty-Third Regiment, the attack in that quarter was abandoned.

4. In the centre, however, General Porter's brigade, two regiments of the rifle corps, and a detachment of artillery under Major Hindman, were confronted by a force of about five hundred men under Lieutenant-General Drummond. The garrison, under the lead of Captain Williams and Lieutenants McDonough and Watmough, gave them a spirited reception, hurled back their scaling-ladders, and drove them from the bastions with a heavy loss. A second and third assault followed, with the same results; the garrison being now strengthened by General Ripley's brigade of regulars.

5. Soon afterwards, taking advantage of the darkness of the morning and the heavy columns of smoke, Lieutenant-General Drummond moved his troops silently round the ditch, repeated his charge, and reascended his ladders with such celerity as to obtain a footing on the parapet before any effectual opposition could be made. Orders were given to show no mercy to the garrison. The conflict was desperate; Captain Williams and Lieutenants McDonough and Watmough fell, the former mortally wounded; charge followed charge in rapid succession until daybreak, when the enemy, in spite of every effort, retained possession of the bastion.

6. On the extreme right, defended by the remnant of the First (Scott's) Brigade, under the command of Lieutenant-Colonel Aspinwall, the Douglass Battery, Colonel McRee, and Cap-

---

Combined assault and its repulse. — Drummond's attack, repulse, second attack and repulse.

tains Boughton and Harding of the Volunteers, an ineffectual assault was also repeatedly made by the enemy under Lieutenant-Colonel Scott. The resistance in this quarter was so spirited and persistent that at daybreak the British troops were withdrawn.

7. The struggle for the possession of the fort was now concentrated in the central bastion, which, at the moment of the advance of the British reserve to support the successful advance, burst with a terrific explosion, and a jet of flame, mingled with fragments of timber, earth, stone, and human bodies, rose to the height of more than a hundred feet in the air, and fell in a shower of ruins in every direction. The reserves immediately fell back; and soon afterwards the conflict ended in the entire defeat of the enemy, whose shattered columns returned to their encampment with the loss of two hundred and twenty killed, one hundred and seventy-four wounded, and nearly two hundred prisoners.

8. During the ensuing month the American army were busily engaged in repairing the ruined bastion, and strengthening and increasing the works. Both armies in the interval had received reinforcements, and the siege was prosecuted and the defence sustained with skill and spirit on both sides. General Gaines had left the encampment and returned to Buffalo, and General Brown, who had recovered from his wounds, resumed the command of the army.

9. On the morning of the 17th of September, in the midst of a heavy fog with occasional showers of rain, a sortie was made from the fort, in two divisions, commanded respectively by Generals Porter and Miller, supported by Colonel Miller's regiment under General Ripley as a reserve. At noon, General Porter's division, accompanied by Colonel Gibson and Major Wood, moved from the encampment, and, marching through the woods, at three o'clock rushed upon the enemy's lines and carried them by assault.

10. Simultaneously with this movement, General Miller, with the right division, attacked the centre of the British lines, and compelled its defenders to a precipitate flight, after capturing their batteries and fortifications. In this gallant and success-

---

Central bastion. — Defeat of the British. — Reinforcements. — Sally from the fort.

ful achievement the Americans suffered severely, Major-General Davis, Lieutenant-Colonel Wood, Colonel Gibson, with seven other officers and seventy men, having been killed, and Generals Porter and Ripley, Lieutenant-Colonel Aspinwall, twenty-two other officers, and one hundred and ninety men wounded. The British loss was equally severe; and, after collecting his scattered forces, General Drummond broke up his encampment, and resumed his former position on the Chippewa.

11. The British having, in August, captured the city of Washington, and burned and destroyed the principal public buildings, and the entire coast being blockaded by the English fleet, energetic measures for the defence of the city of New York were adopted by the inhabitants. An enthusiastic public meeting was held, and the citizens, without distinction of party, pledged themselves to a vigorous co-operation with the national and State authorities in the prosecution of the war. The various fortifications in and around the city were strengthened and supplied with effective garrisons, twenty thousand troops were raised and stationed in the city under the command of Major-Generals Morgan Lewis and Ebenezer Stevens, and Commodore Decatur placed in charge of the fleet lying in the harbor. The city and its suburbs became one vast camp, animated by a firm determination to uphold the national honor, and preserve at all hazards their beautiful metropolis.

12. On the refusal of the banks to advance the requisite funds for the organization and support of this immense force on the security of the United States Treasury notes alone, Governor Tompkins patriotically came forward and pledged his own personal and official security as indorser on the part of the State for a loan of half a million of dollars, which were thereupon promptly advanced.

13. In the mean time, General Sir George Prevost, with fifteen thousand men from the Duke of Wellington's successful army, aided by a strong naval squadron under Sir James L. Yeo, prepared for an invasion of the State by way of Lake Champlain. The greater part of the American forces stationed at Plattsburg, under the command of General Izard, having been transferred

---

Preparations for defence of the city of New York. — Indorsement of the credit of the government by Governor Tompkins. — Invasion of New York.

to the Niagara frontier, Sir George at once put his command in motion without waiting for the co-operation of the squadron, and early in September advanced through Clinton County to a point within eight miles of Plattsburg on Lake Champlain.

14. While these movements were in progress, General Macomb gathered together at Champlain the fragments of the American army, numbering not more than fifteen hundred effective men, and, retiring before the British general, fell back on Plattsburg and completed the defences which had been commenced on the southern bank of the Saranac, a small stream which enters the lake at that place.

15. Against this small force, General Sir George Prevost moved his army in two columns on the two parallel roads leading to Plattsburg. On the upper, or Beekmantown road, Brigadier-General Mooers with seven hundred militia, and Major John E. Wool with two hundred and fifty regular troops and two pieces of artillery, disputed and considerably checked his progress, while the defence of the lower or lake-shore road was intrusted to Lieutenant-Colonel Appling and Captain Sproul.

16. General Prevost, however, succeeded, with considerable loss, in reaching Plattsburg; and both divisions of the American force, slowly retiring before him, and destroying the bridges over the Saranac, entered their works, whence they poured a storm of hot shot into the buildings of the town occupied by the British. The latter contented themselves for the ensuing week in the preparation of batteries for assaulting their position, and in the mean time awaiting the arrival of the naval squadron.

17. During this period, Commodore THOMAS McDONOUGH, with a fleet consisting of four large vessels — the Saratoga, Eagle, Ticonderoga, and Preble — and ten small galleys, mounting in all about seventy guns, lay at anchor in the bay off Plattsburg, adjoining Lake Champlain. The enemy's squadron, under Captain George Downie of the Royal Navy, made its appearance, entering the bay around Cumberland Head on the morning of the 11th of September, consisting of the sloop Finch, the flag-ship Confiance, the brig Linnet, and the sloop Chubb, with twelve

gunboats, mounting in all ninety-five guns, including an eighteen-pound Columbiad.

18. As this imposing squadron came into line around Cumberland Head, — the Chubb moving against the Eagle, the Finch towards the Preble and Ticonderoga, and the Confiance against the Saratoga, — the several small vessels prepared for action. After solemn prayers on board the flag-ship, and without waiting the signal for attack, the Eagle opened fire for some time without effect, followed, as soon as her guns began to tell, by the Saratoga and the remainder of the vessels.

19. The Linnet, then anchored in a favorable position forward of the Eagle's beam, poured a well-directed broadside into the Saratoga; while the Chubb, seeking a position from which to rake the American line, received a broadside from the Eagle, which carried away her cables, bowsprit, and boom, and inflicted so severe an injury that she drifted down between the two opposing lines, until, after receiving another shot from the Saratoga, she was compelled to surrender, and was towed to the shore by one of the Saratoga's boats.

20. Extraordinary efforts were made during the action, by the Finch, to disable the Ticonderoga and Preble; and the Confiance opened fire upon the Saratoga with terrible effect, killing or wounding about forty of her crew. But in the course of an hour the Finch, badly disabled, was driven from her position near the Ticonderoga, and, running upon Crab Island, was there captured, while on the American side the Preble was compelled to fall back out of range of the enemy's guns.

21. The contest had now narrowed down to the Confiance and Linnet, on the right of the line, against the Eagle, the Saratoga, and the galleys, and on the left the British gunboats against the Ticonderoga. The Linnet had secured an admirable position at the head of the enemy's line, and gallantly sustained and returned the fire of the Eagle; the Confiance was pouring in her broadsides on both the Eagle and the Saratoga, and the gunboats were struggling for supremacy with the Ticonderoga.

22. The Eagle having lost her springs, and being prevented from bringing her guns to bear, her commander ran her down

---

Progress of the fight. — Disabling of the British vessels Chubb and Finch, and of the American vessel Saratoga.

between the Saratoga and Ticonderoga, where he again opened fire on the Confiance and Linnet, the former in the mean time raking the Saratoga on her bows. The Saratoga in turn having become disabled, Commodore McDonough brought her around, in the face of a galling fire from the Linnet, in a position enabling her to bring her batteries to bear on the Confiance, and, after a gallant contest of upwards of two hours, compelled that vessel to strike her colors.

23. Within fifteen minutes afterwards the Linnet surrendered to the Saratoga, and the gunboats, withdrawing from their attack on the Ticonderoga, escaped from the harbor. The commanders of the several remaining vessels surrendered their swords to Commodore McDonough, on the Saratoga, who courteously returned them to their brave owners, with the remark that they " were worthy to wear them." The prisoners were ordered to Crab Island, with the strictest directions to treat them kindly, and speak to them encouragingly.

24. After the completion of this signal victory the troops were withdrawn by Sir George Prevost from the town, the batteries dismantled, the artillery and stores removed, and during the succeeding night he followed with his entire army, leaving behind him the sick and wounded, together with immense quantities of provisions, camp equipage, and other stores, as trophies of his signal discomfiture.

25. The loss of the British on this occasion was three officers and thirty-four men killed, and eight officers and one hundred and forty-two men wounded, on shore; Captain Downie, four officers, and fifty-two men killed, and three officers and sixty-nine men wounded, on the lake. The Americans lost one officer and thirty-six men killed, and two officers and sixty men wounded, on land; and four officers and forty-eight men killed, and four officers and fifty-four men wounded, on the lake.

26. Governor TOMPKINS, in consequence of the exposed situation of the country, and the imminent danger of invasion of the State, convened the Legislature, by proclamation, on the 26th of September. SAMUEL YOUNG, of Saratoga, was chosen Speaker, and Aaron Clark, of New York, Clerk of the Assembly.

Surrender of the Linnet. — Complete victory of McDonough. — Special session of the Legislature.

Acts were passed for the increase of the pay of the militia in the service of the United States, providing for the raising of troops for the defence of the State and city of New York, including two regiments of colored soldiers, and authorizing the formation of associations for the encouragement of privateering. Provision was also made for indemnifying Governor Tompkins for all expenditures and responsibilities incurred by him in the defence of the State, not provided for by existing laws.

27. These energetic and spirited proceedings of the New York Legislature, combined with the prompt measures for the defence of the city of New York by its inhabitants, gave great satisfaction to the government at Washington; and so highly were the patriotic efforts and sacrifices of Governor Tompkins at this crisis appreciated, that President Madison tendered him the position of Secretary of State of the United States, Mr. Monroe having now the charge of the War Department. The Governor, however, conceiving that, in his present position, he could be of greater service to the country, declined the flattering offer.

CHAPTER X.

ADMINISTRATION OF GOVERNOR TOMPKINS. — TREATY OF PEACE WITH GREAT BRITAIN. — ELECTION OF GOVERNOR DE WITT CLINTON. — ERIE AND CHAMPLAIN CANAL. — COMMON SCHOOLS. — STATE OF PARTIES.

1. AT the meeting of the Legislature in January, 1815, NATHAN SANFORD, of New York, was elected United States Senator in place of Obadiah German, whose term had expired, and MARTIN VAN BUREN Attorney-General, in place of Abraham Van Vechten, removed. On the 12th of February, information was received of the conclusion of a treaty of peace between Great Britain and the United States at Ghent, on the 24th of December previous, and of the splendid victory of General JACK-

1815.

Spirited proceedings for the public defence. — Their reception at Washington. — Governor Tompkins declines the State Department. — United States Senator. — Attorney-General. — Treaty of peace with Great Britain. — Battle of New Orleans.

son at New Orleans on the 8th of January. This intelligence created a general feeling of joy and satisfaction throughout the country, and was appropriately celebrated in the several towns and cities of the State.

2. In December of this year a large public meeting was held in the city of New York in reference to the construction of the Erie and Champlain Canal, spirited resolutions in its favor adopted, and a strong memorial to the Legislature, drawn up by Mr. CLINTON, directed to be forwarded to that body. Governor TOMPKINS, in his speech at the opening of the session of 1816, expatiated upon the importance of this great enterprise, not only to the State of New York, but to the Western and Eastern States, and anticipated the zealous co-operation of those States in the proposed work. The citizens of Albany also held a large meeting and passed strong resolutions in favor of the measure.

1816.

3. The difficulties to be surmounted in the further prosecution of this great undertaking were formidable in the extreme, and nothing but the indomitable energy and perseverance of Mr. CLINTON and his associates in the canal commission could have succeeded in overcoming them. The funds of the State had been wellnigh exhausted by the efforts rendered necessary in the prosecution of the war; all aid from the general government or the adjacent States had been pertinaciously withheld; the resources of private enterprise crippled and paralyzed by the financial embarrassments of the crisis, and the project itself was almost universally regarded as visionary and chimerical. The preliminary measures put in operation for the commencement of the work, under previous acts of the Legislature, however ably devised and faithfully executed, had been necessarily attended by great expense to the State, and the current of public sentiment ran strongly against any additional legislation in behalf of an enterprise so vast in its conception and inexhaustible in its demands upon the public treasury.

4. On the 17th of April the Legislature was induced, principally through the exertions of Mr. CLINTON, powerfully sup-

---

General rejoicings. — Canal meetings in New York and Albany. — Governor's speech. — Difficulties and embarrassments of the undertaking. — Energy and perseverance of Mr. Clinton in its prosecution.

ported by Mr. Van Buren and Colonel Young, to pass an "Act to provide for the improvement of the internal navigation of the State" repealing the previous statutes on the subject, and appointing Stephen Van Rensselaer, De Witt Clinton, Samuel Young, Joseph Ellicott, and Myron Holley Canal Commissioners, with authority to prosecute all necessary surveys for the route of the proposed canal, and report to the Legislature at its next session. Twenty thousand dollars were appropriated for this purpose from the State treasury.

5. The April elections resulted, by a large majority, in favor of the Republicans. Governor Tompkins and Lieutenant-Governor Tayler were re-elected, over Rufus King and George Tibbetts, with a Republican majority in both branches of the Legislature. This body met on the 5th of November for the choice of presidential electors. Electors were appointed favorable to James Monroe of Virginia for President, and Daniel D. Tompkins of New York for Vice-President, who were subsequently elected by a nearly unanimous vote; Massachusetts, Connecticut, and Delaware casting thirty-four votes only for Rufus King for President, and twenty-two for John E. Howard, of Maryland, for Vice-President.

6. At the opening of the session on the 28th of January, 1817, Governor Tompkins sent a message to the Legislature recommending the entire Abolition of Slavery in the State from and after the 4th of July, 1827. By a previous act, all males born of slave parents subsequent to the year 1799 were to become free at the age of twenty-eight, and females at twenty-five. The recommendation of the Governor was unanimously concurred in by the Legislature. Thus through the philanthropic exertions of the Society of Friends in the city of New York and elsewhere, and the energetic aid of Cadwallader D. Colden, Peter A. Jay, William Jay, Governor Tompkins, and other friends of humanity throughout the State, the dark blot of slavery was destined to be forever erased from our escutcheon. 1817.

7. A few days previous to the 4th of March, Vice-President Tompkins resigned his office as Governor, the duties of which

---

Act for appointment of Canal Commissioners, and survey of canal. — Election of President Monroe and Vice-President Tompkins. — Abolition of Slavery. — Resignation of Governor Tompkins.

were devolved upon Lieutenant-Governor Tayler. An act was passed providing for the election of a successor at the ensuing spring elections, at which term DE WITT CLINTON, by a nearly unanimous vote, was elected Governor, and JOHN TAYLER Lieutenant-Governor, with a decided Republican majority in both branches of the Legislature.

8. On the 10th of March the Canal Commissioners presented to the Legislature an elaborate report of their proceedings; and on the 17th of April, after the most strenuous opposition, an act was passed, prepared by Mr. CLINTON, authorizing the construction of the proposed canal from the Hudson to Lakes Champlain and Erie, — three hundred and sixty-three miles in length, with a surface of forty feet in breadth, declining to eighteen at the bottom, with a depth of four feet of water, sufficient for the conveyance of vessels of one hundred tons' burden.

9. On the 4th of July succeeding, this great enterprise was commenced at Rome, in the presence of Governor CLINTON and the commissioners, by James Richardson, and the first steps were taken for the construction of a magnificent public work, hitherto unequalled in importance and extent in the civilized world, and destined in the future to exert an immense influence upon the agricultural, commercial, and mechanical interests of the entire Union.

1818. 10. On the 27th of January, 1818, the Legislature again assembled. Governor CLINTON, in his first address to that body, after presenting a clear view of the financial affairs of the State, and recapitulating the progress made in the construction of the canal, submitted various recommendations for the improvement of the civil and criminal laws of the State. A formidable political opposition to his administration, headed by Mr. Van Buren, Colonel Young, Roger Skinner, Walter Bowne, General Root, and other leading Republicans, soon developed itself, and gave origin to the formation of two new and distinctly marked parties, known as the Bucktail, or Democratic, and the Clintonian. JOHN VAN NESS YATES was ap-

---

Election of Governor Clinton and Lieutenant-Governor Tayler. — Passage of the act for the construction of the canal. — Commencement of the work. — New organization of parties.

pointed Secretary of State by the Council, in place of Dr. Cooper, removed.

11. On the 16th of March, GIDEON HAWLEY, the Superintendent of Common Schools, transmitted to the Legislature his fifth annual Report, from which it appeared that there were in the State upwards of five thousand schools properly organized, in which more than two hundred thousand children were annually taught during an average period of from four to six months. The Lancasterian system of instruction was fully indorsed, and its advantages were pointed out at great length. This system, however, after a brief experiment, failed in accomplishing the favorable results which were expected, and was finally abandoned.

12. During the session an able report on the subject of domestic manufactures was presented by PEREZ RANDALL of Chenango, chairman of the committee on that subject, recommending, in view of the high price of foreign fabrics and the depressed condition of the country generally, consequent on the exhaustion produced by the war, the development and cultivation of our own industrial and mechanical resources, and the reliance, as far as practicable, upon domestic manufacture, especially in the article of clothing.

13. The results of the spring elections were generally favorable to the Clintonians, a majority in both branches of the Legislature and of the popular vote having been secured in their favor. Most of the prominent Federalists of the State were among the leading supporters of the administration of Governor Clinton, although that party, as a distinctive political organization, had ceased to exist.

14. The Legislature convened on the 5th of January, 1819. General OBADIAH GERMAN, of Chenango, was chosen Speaker of the Assembly, after a violent political contest, lasting for two days. Governor Clinton, in his address, again adverted to the canal policy of the State, reminding the Legislature, that, under the act of 1817, the commissioners were only authorized to contract for the construction of canals between

---

Report of the Superintendent of Common Schools. — The Lancasterian system of instruction. — Report on domestic manufactures. — Spring elections. — Triumph of the Clintonians. — Meeting of the Legislature. — Recommendations of the Governor.

the Mohawk and Seneca Rivers and the Hudson and Lake Champlain, and strongly urging the opening of the entire line from Lake Erie to the tide-waters of the Hudson, and from Fort Edward to the head of sloop navigation on that river. These views were concurred in by the Legislature, and an act was passed for carrying them into effect. HENRY SEYMOUR, of Oneida, was appointed Canal Commissioner in place of Mr. Ellicott, resigned.

15. The appointment of Chief-Justice THOMPSON as Secretary of the Navy under the United States Government produced another vacancy on the bench of the Supreme Court of the State, which was filled by the promotion of AMBROSE SPENCER as Chief-Justice, and the appointment of JOHN WOODWORTH as Associate Justice. An act was passed requiring the Comptroller to liquidate and settle the outstanding accounts — as between Vice-President Tompkins and the State, and also between the State and the general government — growing out of the late war.

16. The annual report of the Superintendent of Common Schools exhibited a gratifying increase in the number of schools and of children taught. On his recommendation the general school law was revised and consolidated, and its provisions were, with necessary forms and instructions, published and distributed among the several school districts of the State.

17. The April elections terminated favorably to the friends of Governor Clinton in both branches of the Legislature. Mr. Van Buren was soon afterwards removed from the office of Attorney-General, and THOMAS J. OAKLEY, of Dutchess, appointed in his place. During the summer an animated controversy was maintained between the State Comptroller, ARCHIBALD McINTYRE, and Vice-President TOMPKINS, in reference to the settlement of the accounts of the latter under the act passed by the late Legislature. The deficiency of these accounts amounted to about $120,000 out of an expenditure of several millions, and were chiefly explainable by the unmethodical manner in which they were kept, and the urgency of the crisis in which the funds

---

Amendment of the canal law. — Appointment of Henry Seymour as Commissioner. — Judicial appointments. — Settlement of Vice-President Tompkins's accounts. — Report of the Superintendent of Common Schools. — Revision of the school law. — Result of the spring elections. — Attorney-Generals. — Controversy between the Vice-President and the Comptroller.

were expended. No moral delinquency was attributable to or charged upon the Vice-President. On the 22d of October the first boat on the Erie Canal sailed from Rome to Utica with Governor Clinton, Chancellor Livingston, General Van Rensselaer, and other distinguished citizens on board.

18. The Legislature reassembled early in January, 1820. Rufus King was unanimously re-elected United States Senator, and joint resolutions were unanimously adopted in opposition to the admission of Missouri as a State, with a constitution permitting the existence of slavery. Several ineffectual efforts were made in the two Houses for the adjustment of the pending controversy between the Vice-President and the Comptroller, but no definitive result was reached. *1820.*

19. An exciting political contest now ensued between the candidates of the rival parties for Governor and Lieutenant-Governor at the approaching spring election. The Democrats placed in nomination Vice-President TOMPKINS for the former, and General BENJAMIN MOOERS, of Clinton, for the latter office. Governor CLINTON and Lieutenant-Governor TAYLER were re-nominated by the Clintonians, and, after a spirited canvass on both sides, re-elected by about fourteen hundred majority. The Democrats succeeded, however, in carrying a majority of both Houses of the Legislature.

20. The success of Governor Clinton at this time was due in a very great measure to his popularity as the leading champion of the canal interest. During the progress of that great work a decided revolution had taken place in the public mind as to its practicability and prospective value, and the agricultural and mercantile interests of the State especially looked forward to its completion with the highest expectations of success. To the merely local issues of the canvass they were comparatively indifferent; but on this absorbing question they were determined to sustain the able and far-seeing statesman who had identified himself and his administration with the splendid system of internal improvement now in progress.

First boat on the Erie Canal. — Proceedings of the Legislature. — Re-election of Rufus King as United States Senator. — Exciting political campaign. — Re-election of Governor Clinton and Lieutenant-Governor Tayler. — Republican triumph in the Legislature. — The canal policy.

21. The Legislature reassembled in November for the appointment of presidential electors. Governor CLINTON, in his address, recommended the passage of a law for the choice of presidential electors by the people, and for the calling of a convention for the amendment of the State Constitution. He also entered a solemn protest against the interference of the officers of the United States Government with the State elections.

22. After the choice of presidential electors, General Root, of Delaware County, introduced a bill declaring the incompatibility of the existence of slavery in this State with its constitution and laws. No action was, however, taken upon the proposition, although it was ably supported by its mover. On the 10th of November a bill was introduced and passed accepting a release, on the part of Vice-President Tompkins, of all claims against the State, and directing the Comptroller, on filing the same, to balance all accounts between the respective parties.

23. The bill for the call of a Constitutional Convention passed both Houses on the 18th, but was rejected by the casting vote of Governor Clinton in the Council of Revision. After calling upon the Governor for proof of his charges of interference on the part of the officers of the general government with the State elections, and the interchange of a few brief but spicy messages between the Senate and Governor, the Legislature adjourned. Messrs. MONROE and TOMPKINS were re-elected President and Vice-President without serious opposition.

Choice of presidential electors. — Governor's message. — Proceedings of the Legislature. — Settlement of the controversy between the Vice-President and Comptroller. — Re-election of President Monroe and Vice-President Tompkins.

CHAPTER XI.

SECOND ADMINISTRATION OF GOVERNOR CLINTON. — CONSTITUTIONAL CONVENTION OF 1821. — ADOPTION OF THE NEW CONSTITUTION.

1. On the 9th of January, 1821, the Legislature again assembled, and on the 17th the Governor transmitted a special message, containing specific and voluminous proofs of his allegations in reference to the interference of the general government in State elections. A new and amended bill was introduced, and passed both Houses, providing for the call of a Constitutional Convention, subject to the approval of the people at the ensuing spring election. MARTIN VAN BUREN was elected United States Senator to fill the vacancy occasioned by the expiration of the official term of Nathan Sanford and WILLIAM C. BOUCK, of Schoharie, appointed an additional Canal Commissioner.

2. GIDEON HAWLEY, of Albany, was at this time removed by the Council of Appointment from the office of Superintendent of Common Schools, — a position which he had occupied for eight years to the universal acceptance of all parties, and with the greatest ability and fidelity to the important interests confided to his charge. His successor was Welcome Esleeck, a young lawyer of Albany, so utterly incompetent for the position that the Legislature abolished the office, devolving its duties upon the Secretary of State.

3. The joint committee of both Houses, to whom was referred the special message of the Governor, presented their report on the 15th of March, commenting with great asperity on the language of the message, submitting counter-evidence to its charges, and concluding by expressing the opinion that no extraneous influences had been shown to exist in any State election. The Legislature finally adjourned in the latter part of March.

Proceedings of the Legislature. — Governor's special message. — Bill for Constitutional Convention. — Election of United States Senator. — Appointment of Canal Commissioner. — Proceedings of the Council of Appointment. — Abolition of the office of Superintendent of Common Schools, and devolvement of its duties on the Secretary of State. — Report of the joint committee on the Governor's special message.

4. The April elections resulted in a decided Democratic triumph in both branches of the Legislature, and a majority of nearly seventy-five thousand for the proposed convention for the amendment of the Constitution. On the third Tuesday of June an election was accordingly held throughout the State for the appointment of delegates from the several counties.

5. Although a large majority of these delegates were members of the Democratic party, political distinctions and local residence were, in many parts of the State, set aside for intellectual ability and high moral worth. Mr. VAN BUREN, though a resident of Columbia, was returned from Otsego; and Vice-President TOMPKINS, Chancellor KENT, Judges SPENCER, VAN NESS, and PLATT, NATHAN SANFORD, of New York, JOHN DUER, from Orange, Colonel YOUNG, of Saratoga, General ROOT, of Delaware, SAMUEL NELSON, of Cortland, RUFUS KING, ABRAHAM VAN VECHTEN, and STEPHEN VAN RENSSELAER, of Albany, ELISHA WILLIAMS, of Columbia, and several others of the most distinguished citizens of the State, were elected to this body.

6. The convention assembled at the capitol, in the city of Albany, on the 28th of August, presenting an array of talent, political ability, public experience, and weight of personal character unsurpassed by any similar body of men heretofore convened in the Union. One hundred and ten delegates were present; and after having been called to order by General Root, DANIEL D. TOMPKINS of Richmond, Vice-President of the United States, was, with almost entire unanimity, elected President, and John F. Bacon and Samuel L. Gardner, Secretaries. William L. Stone, editor of the New York Commercial Advertiser; Nathaniel H. Carter, of the Statesman; Moses I. Cantine, of the Albany Argus; Marcus T. C. Gould and Levi H. Clarke, stenographers, — were formally admitted within the bar as reporters.

7. The Convention remained in session for two months and a half, during which period the debates and discussions were of the highest interest, and conducted with the most signal ability. The right of suffrage was extended to every male citizen of the

---

Spring elections. — Triumph of the Democracy. — Delegates to the Constitutional Convention. — Meeting and organization of the Convention. — Proceedings of the Convention. — Character of the debates. — Extension of the right of suffrage.

age of twenty-one years and upwards, with no other restriction than that of residence and exemption from criminal conviction, and the requisition of a freehold qualification of two hundred and fifty dollars in the case of colored voters. The councils of appointment and revision were abolished, the functions of the former being devolved upon the Governor and Senate, and of the latter upon the Governor, who was vested with the veto power.

8. The judiciary system was remodelled by the substitution of circuit courts in eight judicial districts, into which the State was divided, in place of the previous system of trials of important issues before one of the judges of the Supreme Court; the reduction of the Supreme Court to a Chief-Justice and two Assistant Justices, with the right of appeal to the Senate, Chancellor, and Judges of the Supreme Court, sitting as a Court for the Correction of Errors, the several judges to hold office until the age of sixty years, unless previously removed for cause; and the appointment of a chancellor, for the determination, subject to the same right of appeal, of all cases of equity jurisdiction. The various county courts of Common Pleas and General Sessions, and Justices of the Peace in the several towns, were retained, the judges and justices to be appointed by the Governor and Senate.

9. The legislative department was declared to consist of a Senate, composed of thirty-two members, distributed equally over eight Senate districts, elected for four years, one fourth of this number going out each year, presided over by the Lieutenant-Governor, with a casting vote; and an Assembly consisting of one hundred and twenty-eight members, apportioned among the several counties according to population, and annually elected. A Governor and Lieutenant-Governor were to be biennially elected, and the several State officers, with the exception of the Adjutant-General, chosen by joint ballot of the Senate and Assembly once in every three years. Sheriffs, county clerks, and coroners were to be elected by the people of the several counties for a term of three years.

10. After adopting these various provisions, and also a sec-

Judicial system. — Legislative and executive departments. — County and State officers.

tion requiring the call of future conventions for the amendment of the Constitution on the expiration of each period of twenty years thereafter, and authorizing the Legislature, in the mean time, by a two-thirds vote, to submit any amendment deemed requisite to a popular vote for its ratification, the Convention finally adjourned on the 10th of November; and at a special election, held in the ensuing February, the new Constitution was approved and adopted by a majority of thirty-four thousand votes.

Provisions for future amendments. — Adjournment of the Convention. — Ratification of the Constitution by the people.

Aqueduct Bridge on the Erie Canal at Little Falls.

SEVENTH PERIOD.

FROM THE CONSTITUTION OF 1821 TO THE CONSTITUTION OF 1846.

CHAPTER I.

ADMINISTRATION OF GOVERNOR YATES. — THIRD ADMINISTRATION OF GOVERNOR CLINTON. — THE ELECTORAL LAW. — PEOPLE'S PARTY. REMOVAL OF GOVERNOR CLINTON AS CANAL COMMISSIONER. — RE-ELECTION AS GOVERNOR. — VISIT OF GENERAL LAFAYETTE. — STATE ROAD. — COMPLETION OF THE CANAL. — GRAND CELEBRATION.

1. THE Legislature assembled on the 2d of January, 1822. Governor CLINTON, in his address, after adverting to the importance of protection to the domestic manufactures of the State, congratulated the Legislature on the rapid progress of the canals, and the probability of their early completion, 1822.

and recommended various modifications of the civil and criminal laws. The two Houses then proceeded to apportion the members of the Assembly among the respective counties, prescribe the time and manner of appointing State and county officers, and divide the State into thirty congressional districts.

2. The new Constitution having provided that no lottery should hereafter be authorized in the State, and directed that the sale of tickets, except in lotteries already established by law, should be prohibited, John B. Yates and Archibald McIntyre were appointed managers of the existing State lottery for the provision of funds for the several colleges and academies theretofore authorized by various legislative acts. This trust was faithfully executed by these gentlemen, in accordance with the spirit of the endowment; and at its termination, within a short time afterwards, this objectionable system of supporting the literary institutions of the State, was abandoned.

3. The time for holding the general State elections having been changed by the new Constitution from April to the first week in November, JOSEPH C. YATES, of Schenectady, one of the judges of the late Supreme Court, was elected Governor, and General ERASTUS ROOT, of Delaware, Lieutenant-Governor, with no other opposition than that of SOLOMON SOUTHWICK, a self-nominated candidate for Governor, who received a few scattering votes in different sections of the State. Both branches of the Legislature were overwhelmingly Democratic.

1823. 4. This body met and organized on the 7th of January of the ensuing year. Governor YATES transmitted a brief message to the two Houses, recommending the early passage of the various laws necessary to carry into effect the provisions of the new Constitution, and suggesting improvements in the penitentiary system of the State, and a general revision of the statute laws. The new Supreme Court was organized by the appointment of JOHN SAVAGE of Washington as Chief-Justice, and JACOB SUTHERLAND of Schoharie, and JOHN WOODWORTH

Abolition of lotteries. — State literature lottery. — Election of Joseph C. Yates as Governor, and Erastus Root, Lieutenant-Governor. — Democratic majority in both Houses. — Meeting of the Legislature. — Appointment of Chancellor, judges of the Supreme Court, and circuit judges.

of Albany, Justices. NATHAN SANFORD, of New York, was appointed Chancellor, with circuit judges in the several judicial districts.

5. On the 13th of February the Legislature, by joint ballot, made choice of JOHN VAN NESS YATES, of Albany, as Secretary of State and *ex-officio* Superintendent of Common Schools; WILLIAM L. MARCY, of Rensselaer, Comptroller; SAMUEL A. TALCOTT, of Oneida, Attorney-General; and SIMEON DE WITT, of Albany, Surveyor-General.

6. At the fall elections the Democratic organization throughout the State was divided upon the question of the choice of presidential electors by the people; and a new party sprang up, known as the "People's Party," which received a considerable accession of strength at the polls, and succeeded in carrying several of the largest and most Democratic counties in the State.

7. On the 6th of January, 1824, the Legislature again convened, and Governor YATES, in his message, repeated his recommendation for a general revision of the statutes of the State, urged the importance of encouraging domestic manufactures by an increase of duties on foreign importations, and called the attention of the Legislature to the subject of such a change in the electoral law as would give to the people the choice of presidential electors. A bill was accordingly introduced at an early period in the Assembly, in accordance with these views, but requiring that the persons so elected should have received a majority of all the votes cast; and in this shape it passed the House by nearly a unanimous vote. In the Senate, however, it was indefinitely postponed by a vote of seventeen to fourteen.

1824.

8. On the last day of the session, and a short time previous to its final adjournment, the Senate, on motion of Mr. Bowman, of Monroe, passed a resolution for the removal of DE WITT CLINTON from the office of Canal Commissioner, which was immediately concurred in by the House by a large majority.

Election of State officers. — Fall elections. — The "People's Party." — Legislative proceedings. — Message of the Governor. — Choice of presidential electors. — Defeat of the electoral law. — Removal of Governor Clinton as Canal Commissioner.

This unjustifiable procedure created an intense feeling of popular indignation throughout the State, and, in conjunction with the rejection of the electoral law, gave a powerful impetus to the People's party. Large and enthusiastic public meetings were held in the principal cities of the State, denouncing the action of the Legislature, and warmly approving the high public services and character of Governor Clinton.

9. On the second day of June, Governor Yates issued a proclamation convening an extra session of the Legislature on the 2d of August for the reconsideration of the subject of the electoral law. A full attendance of the members of both Houses was obtained; and, after listening to the Governor's message, reciting his reasons for the call, Mr. Flagg, of Clinton, offered a resolution for an immediate adjournment, on the ground that no necessity for special legislation at this time existed. The House, after adopting a resolution in favor of the passage of the electoral law, concurred in Mr. Flagg's motion, and, with the assent of the Senate on the 6th, an adjournment to the first Monday in November was carried.

10. At the November election, DE WITT CLINTON, previously nominated by a State Convention at Utica, was re-elected Governor, over Samuel Young, by a majority of nearly seventeen thousand votes; and General JAMES TALLMADGE, of Dutchess, Lieutenant-Governor, over General Root, by a majority of upwards of thirty-two thousand, he having received the undivided support of both the Democratic and People's party. The latter party secured a majority of three fourths of the Assembly, and elected six of the eight senators. Mr. Bowman, the mover of the resolution for Governor Clinton's removal as Canal Commissioner, was defeated by an overwhelming majority in the seventh district by Mr. John C. Spencer.

11. On the 2d of November the two Houses assembled for the choice of presidential electors. At this period five prominent candidates for the Presidency were in the field, and public opinion throughout the Union was divided on their respective

---

Intense public indignation. — Extra session of the Legislature. — Election of Governor Clinton and Lieutenant-Governor Tallmadge. — Triumph of the People's party in the Legislature. — Defeat of Mr. Bowman in the seventh district. — Choice of presidential electors. — Candidates for the Presidency.

claims to support. WILLIAM H. CRAWFORD, of Georgia, was the Democratic candidate, placed in nomination by the congressional caucus. JOHN QUINCY ADAMS, of Massachusetts, Secretary of State of the United States, was the candidate of the national administration. HENRY CLAY, of Kentucky, late Speaker of the House of Representatives; General ANDREW JACKSON, of Tennessee; and JOHN C. CALHOUN, of South Carolina, Secretary of War, — were respectively nominated by their personal and political friends and admirers in different sections of the Union. Mr. CALHOUN's name was subsequently withdrawn, and he became a candidate for Vice-President. On joint ballot of the Senate and Assembly thirty-two electors in favor of Mr. Adams and four in favor of Mr. Crawford were chosen.

12. On the 15th of August of this year, the illustrious LAFAYETTE, the companion-in-arms of WASHINGTON during the Revolutionary struggle, arrived on our shores, in the ship Cadmus, by invitation of the United States Government, on a visit to the country of his adoption, after an absence of forty years and a brilliant but diversified career. He landed at Staten Island, and remained as the guest of Vice-President TOMPKINS until the next day, when he was escorted to the city of New York by a large naval fleet. Landing at Castle Garden on the Battery, amid the ringing of bells, the salutes of artillery, and the shouts of the multitude, he was welcomed by the Corporation, conducted to the City Hall, and became the guest of the city for several days, visiting the public institutions and holding crowded levees of the citizens.

13. From New York he made a tour through the principal cities and villages of the Union, everywhere receiving magnificent ovations from a grateful people, welcomed by the President and Congress, by governors and State legislatures, and civic municipalities, and attended by vast crowds of citizens, until September of the ensuing year, when he took his final departure from New York, at the conclusion of a brilliant ovation at Castle Garden, with the blessings of millions indebted to him, in great part, for the rich inheritance of freedom bequeathed to them by the Revolution.

Visit of General Lafayette to the United States. — His reception in New York.

14. The new Legislature convened on the 4th of January, 1825, and Governor CLINTON, in his message, recommended the passage of a law for the choice of presidential electors by the people by a plurality of votes on a general ticket, and the creation of a board of internal improvements, for the completion and extension of the canal system and the construction of a State road from the Hudson River to Lake Erie, through the southern tier of counties. No choice of President having been made by the electoral colleges, General JACKSON, Mr. ADAMS, and Mr. CRAWFORD, the three candidates who received the highest vote, were balloted for by the House of Representatives, in pursuance of the provisions of the Constitution. JOHN QUINCY ADAMS, of Massachusetts, was duly elected President; and JOHN C. CALHOUN, of South Carolina, having received a majority of electoral votes, was declared elected Vice-President.

1825.

15. In accordance with the recommendation of the Governor, and the memorial of a convention of prominent citizens of the southern and western portions of the State, the Legislature at this session passed an act for the appointment of three commissioners to explore and cause to be surveyed a route for a State road from the Hudson River to Lake Erie, through the southern tier of counties. NATHANIEL PITCHER of Washington, and JABEZ D. HAMMOND and GEORGE MORELL of Otsego, were appointed Commissioners under this act.

16. One of the earliest acts of President ADAMS, after his inauguration on the 4th of March, was to offer Governor Clinton the post of Minister of the United States to Great Britain. This offer was, however, respectfully declined, and Rufus King appointed to that station. During the summer, Governor Clinton visited Philadelphia, where he met with a cordial and most gratifying reception; and soon afterwards, in company with Judge Alfred Conkling, of Cayuga, and several other distinguished

---

Meeting of the Legislature. — Governor's message. — Election by the House of Representatives of John Quincy Adams as President, and of John C. Calhoun as Vice-President, by the electors. — Appointment of commissioners for survey of State road through the southern tier of counties. — Appointment of Minister to England. — Tour of Governor Clinton through Pennsylvania, Ohio, and Kentucky.

gentlemen, visited Ohio and Kentucky for the purpose of inspecting the public works in progress in those States. He was everywhere received on his route with the highest demonstrations of respect.

17. The ERIE AND CHAMPLAIN CANAL having, after eight years' incessant labor, been completed, a grand and imposing celebration of the great event took place at the city of New York in the fall of this year. On the morning of the 26th of October the first flotilla of canal-boats left Buffalo, on Lake Erie, for New York, where intelligence of its departure was, in an hour and twenty minutes thereafter, received by the discharge of cannon posted at intervals on the entire route, and again communicated to Buffalo by the same signals.

18. On the arrival of the fleet at Albany, with the Governor, Canal Commissioners, State officers, and distinguished citizens from every part of the State, they were received by a vast crowd and, amid the acclamations of the multitude, the roar of artillery, and, the ringing of the bells of the city, escorted to the Capitol, where they were cordially welcomed by Philip Hone, Mayor of the city of New York, in behalf of its citizens.

19. At five o'clock in the morning of the 4th of November, the fleet, consisting of the Chancellor Livingston,—in which were Governor Clinton and his party, — the Seneca Chief, the Young Lion of the West, and a long line of canal packets, arrived at New York, where they were met by the steamship Washington, with a deputation from the Common Council, and conducted around the Battery and up the East River to the Navy-Yard opposite Brooklyn. Here, amid the ringing of bells and the continued discharge of cannon, they were met by a grand naval procession, consisting of nearly all the vessels in the harbor, gayly festooned with the flags of all nations, and escorted to the schooner Dolphin, moored at Sandy Hook.

20. Arrived at their destination, the Governor, the State and city officers, and distinguished guests, entered the Dolphin; and, the convoy of vessels having formed an immense circle around the schooner, Governor CLINTON poured a keg of fresh water from Lake Erie into the waves, thus signalizing the marriage of

---

Celebration at Albany and New York of the completion of the canal. — Imposing ceremonies on the ocean.

the inland seas with the Atlantic Ocean. Dr. Samuel L. Mitchell then made an oblation into the same element of the waters of the Ganges, the Indus, the Gambia, the Nile, the Thames, the Seine, the Rhine, the Danube, the Mississippi, Columbia, Orinoco, La Plata, and the Amazon, gathered by him from every quarter of the civilized world, in token of that commercial reciprocity prefigured by this great and successful enterprise.

21. On their return to the city, they were met at the Battery by an immense procession of four and a half miles in length, numbering nearly seven thousand persons, which paraded the principal streets with banners and music until a late hour, when the city was brilliantly illuminated, and the festivities were closed with a magnificent display of fireworks. Thus terminated, without an accident to mar its success, the most gorgeous and splendid celebration ever witnessed in the city.

22. The November elections terminated adversely to the friends of Governor Clinton, by a small majority in the Assembly, although a majority in the Senate still consisted of supporters of his administration. The People's party were virtually disbanded, and the lines appeared to have been again drawn between the Clintonians and the Democracy.

CHAPTER II.

THIRD ADMINISTRATION OF GOVERNOR CLINTON.—COMMON SCHOOLS. —ABDUCTION OF MORGAN.—ANTI-MASONIC EXCITEMENT.—POLITICAL ORGANIZATIONS.—PROSCRIPTION OF MASONS.

1. THE Legislature again met on the third day of January, 1826. Governor CLINTON, in his message, urged the importance of an improvement of the Common-School System of the State by the establishment of seminaries for the special preparation of teachers, and repeated his recommendation for

1826.

Grand procession, illumination, and fireworks in New York.—The November elections.—Extinction of the People's party.—Meeting of the Legislature.—Message of the Governor.—The Common-School System.—Seminaries for the education of teachers.—State road.

the construction of a State road through the southern tier of counties. NATHAN SANFORD was elected United States Senator in the place of Rufus King, and Samuel Jones appointed Chancellor in place of Mr. Sanford. AZARIAH C. FLAGG, of Clinton, was appointed Secretary of State and Superintendent of Common Schools.

2. On the 4th of February, Mr. JOHN C. SPENCER, from the Literature Committee of the Senate, to whom was referred that portion of the Governor's message relating to the improvement of the Common-School System, submitted an able report, suggesting the expediency of a plan of county supervision, concurring with the recommendations of the Governor for the establishment of institutions for the training of teachers, and directing the attention of the Legislature to the propriety of employing the various academies of the State for that purpose, and appropriating a specific portion of the public funds to the performance of this duty.

3. Resolutions recommending an amendment of the Constitution, extending the right of suffrage and providing for the election of Justices of the Peace by the people, in accordance with the recommendations of the Governor, were introduced during this session and passed both Houses. The bill for the construction of the State road through the southern counties, in accordance with the report of the commissioners appointed for its exploration and survey, was defeated by a close vote in the Assembly.

4. During the summer of this year, WILLIAM MORGAN, a Royal Arch Freemason, and a printer of Batavia, Genesee Co., had determined on publishing a pamphlet purporting to reveal the secrets of Masonry. His intentions having become known to the society, on the 11th of September, a Mr. Cheesebrough, Master of a Masonic lodge at Canandaigua, procured a warrant at Batavia for his arrest for some petty theft, and conveyed him to Canandaigua, where he was discharged for want of proof of the alleged offence. He was then immediately rearrested for a

---

Election of United States Senator, and appointment of Chancellor and Secretary of State. — Report of John C. Spencer on the Common-School System. — Resolutions for amendment of the Constitution. — Defeat of the State Road Bill.

debt of two dollars to one Ashley, which had been assigned to Cheesebrough, judgment rendered, and execution instantly sworn out by the latter, and Morgan committed to close confinement in the Canandaigua jail.

5. On the night of the 12th he was clandestinely taken from the jail by a number of members of the Masonic fraternity, thrown into a covered carriage, gagged, and conveyed, on the evening of the 14th, to the Canada side of the Niagara River, thence returned to the American shore, and confined in the magazine of Fort Niagara, where he remained until the 29th, in charge of Colonel King of Niagara, and one Elisha Adams, when he disappeared, and was never afterwards seen, or his fate discovered. A thorough investigation of the circumstances was immediately commenced, the results of which will hereafter be presented.

6. At the November election, Governor CLINTON was re-elected by a majority of between three and four thousand votes, and General NATHANIEL PITCHER, of Washington County, elected Lieutenant-Governor by about a similar vote, owing, in the case of the latter, to the popular excitement growing out of the State-road controversy in the southern counties. The Democrats carried a large majority in both branches of the Legislature.

1827. 7. On the assembling of the Legislature in the ensuing year, Governor CLINTON, in his message, after congratulating that body on the adoption by the people, at the late election, of the proposed amendments to the Constitution, removing all restrictions, except citizenship and residence, from the right of voting, and providing for the election by the people of Justices of the Peace in the several towns, renewed his recommendation for the construction of a State road from the Hudson River to Lake Erie.

8. After stating that the balance due from the State for the construction of the Erie and Champlain Canals was about eight millions of dollars, and the annual income of those works, in conjunction with the public funds set apart for their support,

---

Abduction and probable murder of William Morgan. — Re-election of Governor Clinton and election of General Pitcher as Lieutenant-Governor. — Democratic majority in the Legislature. — Governor's message. — The canals. — State road.

more than one million, he urged the payment of the debt still due at the earliest practicable period, and the investment of the surplus funds of the State in other similar and auxiliary enterprises.

9. The number of common schools in the State was estimated at eight thousand, with four hundred and thirty thousand pupils, taught at an annual expenditure of two hundred thousand dollars. The Governor, in connection with this topic, recommended the elevation and extension of the system by the establishment of institutions for the preparation of teachers, periodical examinations, and small libraries to be attached to the several schools.

10. The bill providing for the construction of a State road through the southern tier of counties, in accordance with the recommendation of the commissioners, was again defeated in the Legislature, as was also the bill for the construction of a canal from the Mohawk River at Utica to the Susquehanna at Binghamton, through the valley of the Chenango. The income from the Literature Fund of the State, increased by the transfer of other available funds, was directed to be apportioned among the several academies and colleges according to the number of pupils pursuing the classical and higher English branches of study.

11. On the 17th of April the Legislature adjourned to the second Tuesday of September, with a view to the contemplated revision of the law, in pursuance of the report of the revisers, Messrs. JOHN DUER, BENJAMIN F. BUTLER, and JOHN C. SPENCER, the latter gentleman having been appointed in place of Mr. Henry Wheaton, of New York, who had succeeded General Root, originally nominated. The two Houses accordingly assembled on the designated day, and remained in session nearly three months, exclusively occupied in the special business for which they were convened.

12. The November elections resulted in the complete triumph of the Democratic friends of General JACKSON, who had now entered the lists as a candidate for the Presidency. On the 16th of November, THOMAS ADDIS EMMETT, the eminent New York

---

Common schools. — Chenango Canal. — Literature Fund. — Revision of the laws. — Results of the November elections. — Death of Thomas Addis Emmett.

advocate, suddenly expired while engaged in the trial of an important cause. Suitable public honors were paid to his memory throughout the State.

13. The excitement during the whole of the present year in the western counties of the State, on the subject of the abduction and probable murder of William Morgan, increased in intensity, and began rapidly to assume a prominent political as well as social importance. Immediately after the occurrence of the event, public meetings were convened at Batavia and other western cities and towns, and committees of prominent citizens appointed, who entered upon a thorough and searching investigation of all the circumstances connected with it. Ample proofs were obtained of a daring and extensive conspiracy among members of the Masonic fraternity for the commission of a great crime, but beyond the facts of the abduction and subsequent unlawful imprisonment of Morgan, no clew to his fate was found.

14. Numerous arrests of parties implicated as principals and agents of the conspiracy were made; and, upon their own admission of guilt, several of the leading perpetrators were convicted and sentenced to a long imprisonment. Bruce, the Sheriff of Niagara County, was promptly removed by the Governor; but, in the utter absence of proof of the death of their unfortunate victim, no severer penalties could be inflicted. Public sentiment ran violently against the Masonic institution, whose oaths and obligations, it was supposed, countenanced and encouraged the crime; and its innocent as well as guilty members were denounced as justifying and conniving at, if not openly participating in, its commission.

15. At the annual town meetings in the spring, decided indications were manifested of a disposition to carry the controversy into the elections, and through the agency of the ballot-box to give expression to the popular indignation against the members of the Masonic fraternity and all those who endeavored to institute a discrimination between those of their number who were actually concerned in, or openly justified, the

abduction and subsequent imprisonment, and those who denounced and repudiated these violent proceedings.

16. An Anti-Masonic party was soon organized in all the principal towns and cities of the West, whose principal object was the exclusion from all official trusts of the adherents and supporters of Masonry; and at the fall elections a majority was obtained in several counties on this, without regard to any other political issue. All Masons, without distinction of party, were systematically proscribed, and the great mass of the electors in this section of the State speedily ranged themselves on one side or the other of the new organization.

CHAPTER III.

DEATH AND CHARACTER OF GOVERNOR CLINTON. — ADMINISTRATION OF LIEUTENANT-GOVERNOR PITCHER. — THE MORGAN CONSPIRACY. — PUBLIC PROSECUTOR. — CHENANGO AND CHEMUNG CANALS. — ELECTION OF MARTIN VAN BUREN AS GOVERNOR. — SAFETY-FUND BANKS. — RESIGNATION OF GOVERNOR VAN BUREN. — SUCCESSION OF LIEUTENANT-GOVERNOR THROOP. — DEATH OF GOVERNOR JAY.

1. On the 1st of January, 1828, the Legislature again convened. Governor CLINTON, in his annual message, renewed his recommendation for the prosecution of the system of internal improvements by the construction of the State road and the Chenango and other lateral canals in different sections of the State, adverted to its prominent agricultural interests, and again urged suitable legislation for the improvement of the common schools and the preparation of qualified teachers, through the agency of seminaries to be established for that special purpose.

2. In the midst of the session the melancholy intelligence was received of the sudden death of Governor CLINTON, while sitting in his chair and conversing with two of his sons, at his

1828.

Anti-Masonic party. — Meeting of the Legislature. — Governor's message. — Death of Governor Clinton.

residence, on the evening of the 11th of February. The shock produced by this unexpected and painful event was deeply and universally felt throughout the State and nation. In the Legislature, the principal cities and towns of the State, and at the national Capital, the most imposing demonstrations of sorrow and grief were evinced, without distinction of party. All men felt that a great statesman and a good man had departed from the scene of his usefulness, in the maturity of his powers and the fulness of his fame.

3. For more than thirty years Governor CLINTON had occupied a prominent and commanding position as a public officer. As private secretary to his uncle, George Clinton, as Mayor of the city of New York, as United States and State Senator, Canal Commissioner, and Governor, he had left the impress of his intellectual ability and moral greatness on all the leading interests of the State and nation. The ERIE CANAL was the crowning triumph of his active and energetic career; but the cause of common-school education, the agricultural, manufacturing, and commercial interests of the State, and its political supremacy as the most important member of the Union, were all identified with his long administration of its affairs.

4. His ambition was not of that vulgar order which seeks only success and the possession of station and power, and shrinks from encountering popular obloquy, discouraging circumstances, and imbittered persecution, in the pursuit of the right. No man saw clearer the path of public duty, or more fully appreciated the means and ends of the great enterprises which presented themselves to his comprehensive mind. No opposition deterred him, no sacrifices or labors were deemed too great, no political or personal hostility for a moment swayed him from his onward course, and no disappointments or discouragements influenced his steady and stately progress. In all the long and varied annals of the Empire State, no greater or more illustrious name than that of DE WITT CLINTON has yet been found.

5. On the death of Governor CLINTON, Lieutenant-Governor PITCHER assumed the administration of the executive depart-

---

Proceedings of public bodies. — Character of Governor Clinton. — Succession of Lieutenant-Governor Pitcher.

ment for the remainder of the term. In his first message to the Legislature he recommended the appointment of a special Public Prosecutor for the detection and punishment of the perpetrators of the outrage on William Morgan. DANIEL MOSELY, of Onondaga, was accordingly appointed for this purpose, and entered at once upon the active discharge of its duties. The bills for the construction of the Chenango and Chemung Canals, after passing the Assembly, were again defeated in the Senate.

6. An act was passed for the organization, in the city of New York, of a Superior Court of Common Pleas for the trial of civil actions, Chancellor JONES being appointed Chief-Justice, and JOSIAH OGDEN HOFFMAN and THOMAS J. OAKLEY Associate Justices.

7. The political contest for State offices and the Presidency was now actively commenced between the friends of the two rival candidates,—JOHN QUINCY ADAMS and ANDREW JACKSON. A third element had also taken the field in the interest of the Anti-Masonic organization, which had already assumed a prominent importance in the State. The candidates of the Adams party were, for Governor of New York, SMITH THOMPSON, Associate Judge of the Supreme Court of the United States, and FRANCIS GRANGER, of Ontario, for Lieutenant-Governor; MARTIN VAN BUREN, of Columbia, United States Senator, and ENOS T. THROOP, of Cayuga, one of the circuit judges, were the Jackson candidates, and SOLOMON SOUTHWICK, of Albany, and JOHN CRARY, of Washington, the Anti-Masonic candidates for those offices respectively.

8. After an excited and animated contest, MARTIN VAN BUREN was elected Governor and ENOS T. THROOP Lieutenant-Governor at the November elections, by a plurality of about thirty thousand votes over Thompson and Granger, the Anti-Masonic candidates receiving upwards of thirty-three thousand votes. The Legislature was about equally divided between the friends of Adams and Jackson respectively, with a liberal infusion of the

---

Appointment of Public Prosecutor of the Morgan outrage. — Defeat of the Chenango and Chemung Canals. — Superior Court in the city of New York — Appointments of judges. — Presidential campaign of 1828. — Nominations for Governor and Lieutenant-Governor. — Election of Governor Van Buren, Lieutenant-Governor Throop, and President Jackson.

Anti-Masonic element. Twenty electors in favor of General JACKSON and sixteen in favor of Mr. ADAMS were chosen. General ANDREW JACKSON, of Tennessee, was elected President, and JOHN C. CALHOUN, of South Carolina, Vice-President, by an immense majority in the electoral colleges over Mr. ADAMS and RICHARD RUSH, of Pennsylvania.

9. During the year many secessions from the Masonic fraternity occurred, and numerous revelations of its mysteries were made, strengthening the force and augmenting the numbers of the opponents of the institution. Its complete overthrow was now aimed at, and conventions for the organization of a plan of operations for the accomplishment of this object were held at Lewiston, Le Roy, Utica, and other places. At the general elections in 1827 and 1828, several of the western counties were carried by overwhelming majorities, and the public excitement continued to increase.

1829. 10. On the meeting of the Legislature at the commencement of the ensuing year, Governor VAN BUREN, in his message, recommended the application of the surplus funds of the State and a judicious use of its credit to the extension of the system of internal improvements, the establishment of a safety-fund for the ultimate redemption of the notes of the several banks of the State, the choice of presidential electors by general ticket, and the promotion of the interests of general education.

11. The bill for the establishment of a safety-fund banking system, in accordance with the Governor's recommendation and a plan submitted by Joshua Forman, of Onondaga, became a law, and thirty-one banks, exclusive of those in the city of New York, were rechartered under its provisions. CHARLES E. DUDLEY, of Albany, was appointed United States Senator to fill the vacancy occasioned by the election of Governor Van Buren; GREENE C. BRONSON, of Oneida, was appointed Attorney-General; SILAS WRIGHT, Jr., of St. Lawrence, Comptroller, and JOHN C. SPENCER, of Ontario, Public Prosecutor of the Morgan outrage,

---

Progress of the Anti-Masonic excitement. — Meeting of the Legislature. — Governor's message. — Internal improvements. — Safety-fund law and renewal of bank charters. — Appointment of State officers. — Presidential electors to be chosen by general ticket.

in place of Judge Mosely. Presidential electors were directed hereafter to be chosen by general ticket, instead of by districts, as heretofore.

12. Governor VAN BUREN, having immediately, on the inauguration of President JACKSON, received the appointment of Secretary of State of the United States, on the 12th of March tendered his resignation as Governor; the duties of which office now devolved on Lieutenant-Governor THROOP. The bill for the construction of the CHENANGO CANAL was passed in a modified form, subject to a resurvey of the route by the Canal Commissioners, and their report to the next Legislature that the cost of the work would not exceed $1,000,000, and that within ten years thereafter its receipts would annually exceed its expenditures. The CHEMUNG CANAL BILL also became a law. The Legislature adjourned on the 5th of May.

13. On the 17th of May the venerable JOHN JAY expired at his residence in Westchester County, at the advanced age of eighty-three years. Having successively filled the offices of Chief-Justice of New York and of the United States, Minister to England, and Governor of the State, he had achieved a high reputation as a statesman, diplomatist, and jurist, and appropriate marks of respect were paid to his memory by the various judicial and civil tribunals of the State.

14. The November elections resulted in a very large majority, in both branches of the Legislature, of the Democratic friends of President JACKSON. The Anti-Masonic party was now restricted chiefly to the western counties comprised within the Seventh and Eighth Senatorial Districts. They carried fifteen counties — about one fourth of the whole number — and polled sixty-seven thousand votes. No new developments were, however, made of the Morgan conspiracy, notwithstanding the special investigation instituted by the Legislature, and which was still in progress.

Governor Van Buren appointed Secretary of State. — His resignation as Governor. — Succession of Lieutenant-Governor Throop. — Passage of the Chenango and Chemung Canal Bills. — Death of Governor John Jay. — Result of the November elections.

CHAPTER IV.

ELECTION AND ADMINISTRATION OF GOVERNOR ENOS T. THROOP.—
CHENANGO CANAL.—PROGRESS OF THE ANTI-MASONIC PARTY.—
ITS FINAL EXTINCTION AND RESULTS.—ELECTION OF GOVERNOR
MARCY AND LIEUTENANT-GOVERNOR TRACY.

1830. 1. On the first Tuesday in January, 1830, the Legislature reassembled. Governor THROOP's message was principally devoted to a general exposition of the financial condition and literary and charitable institutions of the State.

2. The Canal Commissioners, on the 21st of January, transmitted a report to the Legislature, setting forth, that, after an additional survey and exploration of the route of the contemplated CHENANGO CANAL, they had arrived at the conclusion that its cost would exceed a million of dollars, and that the probable annual receipts from its tolls, in connection with the increased tolls on the Erie Canal, would not defray the interest upon its cost and the expenses of repairs and superintendence, or either of them. They therefore declined to proceed further in its construction.

3. This was accompanied by a report from Comptroller WRIGHT, showing the inexpediency of appropriating any additional funds to the construction of public works, without specific provision for their expense. Notwithstanding these unfavorable auguries, another bill for the construction of the canal was introduced, and vigorously supported by Mr. Granger and other leading members of the House, but failed to become a law.

4. The representatives of the Anti-Masonic party held a State Convention at Utica in August, at which FRANCIS GRANGER, of Ontario, was placed in nomination for Governor, and SAMUEL STEVENS, of Albany, for Lieutenant-Governor. Forty-eight counties were represented by one hundred and four delegates. On the 8th of September, ENOS T. THROOP was nominated by the Democrats at Herkimer for Governor, and EDWARD P. LIVING-

---

Meeting of the Legislature.—Governor's message.—Report of Canal Commissioners on the Chenango Canal.—Defeat of the bill.—Political nominations.

ston, of Columbia, for Lieutenant-Governor. No other candidates were in the field. Governor THROOP and Lieutenant-Governor LIVINGSTON received a majority of eight thousand votes over the Anti-Masonic candidates, whose aggregate strength at the November election was over one hundred and twenty thousand votes.

5. Mr. JOHN C. SPENCER, who had been appointed Public Prosecutor of the Morgan conspiracy by the Governor, had entered upon the discharge of his duties with his accustomed zeal and energy, and prosecuted his inquiries with indefatigable industry and great ability. So successful were his exertions in tracing the tangled web of this mysterious affair, that he conceived it within his power to effect a complete exposure of the perpetrators of the crime, with the assistance of additional funds from the State derived from the rewards heretofore offered for the detection.

6. These funds were, however, refused; and the Legislature, apprehensive, as was contended, of the political effect of the disclosures already made and transmitted to that body by Mr. Spencer, not only refused to authorize any additional expenditure, but cut down his own salary to one thousand dollars. Deeming this an intentional insult, not only to himself but to the great body of Anti-Masons in the State, he at once transmitted his resignation, with the allegation that, so far from having received any effective aid from the Executive, his confidential communications had been disclosed by the Governor to the counsel for the conspirators. These facts served powerfully to strengthen the Anti-Masonic party as a political organization throughout the State.

7. At the opening of the session in January, 1831, Governor THROOP's message consisted of a general recapitulation of the subjects heretofore presented by him, with an additional recommendation for the abolition of imprisonment for debt. WILLIAM L. MARCY, one of the justices of the Supreme Court, was appointed in February United States Senator in place of Nathan Sanford, whose term had expired, and SAMUEL NELSON, of Cortland, a Judge of the Supreme Court.

1831.

Election of Governor Throop and Lieutenant-Governor Livingston. — Strength of parties. — Proceedings of the Public Prosecutor. — Resignation of Mr. Spencer. — The Legislature. — Governor's message. — Appointments of United States Senator and Judge of the Supreme Court.

8. Joint resolutions against the renewal of the charter of the United States Bank were reported and adopted by both Houses, and a bill for the construction of the Chenango Canal again presented and defeated. The Legislature finally adjourned on the 20th of April. Soon afterwards Mr. VAN BUREN was appointed, by the President, Minister to England, to which post he repaired, after resigning his position in the Cabinet.

9. In May JONAS EARL, of Onondaga, was appointed Canal Commissioner, in place of Henry Seymour, resigned. On the 4th of July, Ex-President JAMES MONROE died at New York, making the third of these venerable chief magistrates who had expired on the anniversary of the day which gave birth to the nation.

10. The November elections terminated in favor of the Democrats in all the districts except the Eighth, and in the return of a large Democratic majority in both branches of the Legislature. The Anti-Masons elected thirty members in the Assembly, and the National Republicans, or supporters of HENRY CLAY for President, at the ensuing election, against General Jackson, six. The residue were Jacksonian Democrats. WILLIAM WIRT of Maryland, late Attorney-General of the United States, had been placed in nomination by the Anti-Masonic party as their candidate for the Presidency in 1832, and AMOS ELLMAKER, of Pennsylvania, as Vice-President. Mr. CLAY was nominated by the National Republicans, with JOHN SARGEANT, of Pennsylvania, for Vice-President.

1832. 11. On the assembling of the Legislature at the opening of the succeeding year the message of Governor THROOP presented the usual topics of information and suggestion to the Legislature. A proposition for a State tax of one mill on the dollar, recommended by the Governor and Comptroller, was, after full discussion, rejected, as was also another bill for the construction of the Chenango Canal.

12. On the 21st of June, FRANCIS GRANGER and SAMUEL

Renewal of the United States Bank charter. — Defeat of Chenango Canal Bill. — Minister to England. — Appointment of Canal Commissioner. — Death of Ex-President Monroe. — Result of the elections. — Nomination of candidates for the Presidency and Vice-Presidency. — Legislature of 1832. — Rejection of the bill for a State tax and for the Chenango Canal.

Stevens were renominated, by the Anti-Masonic Convention at Utica, for Governor and Lieutenant-Governor, with an electoral ticket headed by James Kent and John C. Spencer. This ticket was adopted by the National Republican State Convention at the same place, held on the 26th of July. The Democratic Convention at Herkimer placed in nomination William L. Marcy for Governor, and John Tracy, of Chenango, for Lieutenant-Governor; and an electoral ticket in favor of Andrew Jackson for President, and Martin Van Buren, whose nomination as Minister to England had been rejected by the United States Senate, as Vice-President.

13. The triumph of this party at the November elections was complete. The western counties gave their usual majorities for the Anti-Masonic candidates, but the Democrats carried the State by thirteen thousand majority, and with it both branches of the Legislature. General Jackson and Mr. Van Buren were elected President and Vice-President by a large majority of the electoral votes, the former receiving 219 and the latter 189 votes, against 67 for Mr. Clay, 11 for John Floyd of Virginia, 7 (Vermont) for Mr. Wirt, 49 for Mr. Sergeant, 30 for William Wilkins of Pennsylvania, 11 for Henry Lee of Massachusetts, and 7 for Mr. Ellmaker.

14. This contest virtually terminated the existence, as a political, national, and State party, of Anti-Masonry. In the district of its origin it continued for several years to elect its Senators and Representatives in the Legislature, but soon became merged in the other political organizations of the period. It had accomplished its mission in the almost total exclusion of Masons from public office wherever it had obtained an ascendency. It had asserted and gallantly maintained the great principle of personal inviolability to the humblest citizen, and although it failed in fastening upon any one or any number of men the perpetration of the crime of deliberate murder, it left upon the public mind the assured conviction of the fact, by a combination too powerful and extensive to be reached.

Nominations for Governor and Lieutenant-Governor. — Election of Marcy and Tracy. — Democratic triumph at the presidential election. — Jackson and Van Buren elected President and Vice-President. — Termination of political Anti-Masonry. — Results of the Anti-Masonic organization.

15. Nor did it succeed in its efforts to destroy and root out the institution of Masonry, or convince the majority of reflecting people that anything in its organization or obligations justified the crime of murder or abduction, however some of its unworthy members may have construed those obligations. Masonry, though bending for a time before the blast in its fury, soon regained its original power and influence; and its opponents, among whom were many of the ablest and best men in the State, abandoning their warfare against an institution, devoted themselves to a higher and wider ambition, and have left their impress upon the councils of the State and nation.

Revival of Masonry.

Croton Aqueduct. The Dam.

CHAPTER V.

ADMINISTRATION OF GOVERNOR MARCY. — INTERNAL IMPROVEMENTS. — COMMON SCHOOLS. — CHENANGO CANAL. — ENLARGEMENT OF THE ERIE CANAL. — FINANCIAL EMBARRASSMENTS. — CANADIAN INSURRECTION. — GREAT FIRE IN NEW YORK. — CROTON AQUEDUCT AND HIGH BRIDGE.

1. GOVERNOR MARCY, in his first message to the Legislature in January, 1833, reviewed the general policy of the State in reference to all its leading interests, recommending a judicious prosecution of the system of internal improvements, the improvement and advancement of the common schools and other educational institutions, and the preservation of public and private credit by an economical expenditure of the public funds, and a wise restriction of extended banking facilities and improvident speculations.

1833.

2. SILAS WRIGHT, Jr., of St. Lawrence, was chosen United States Senator to supply the vacancy occasioned by the resig-

nation of Governor Marcy; and NATHANIEL P. TALLMADGE, of Dutchess, in place of Mr. Dudley, whose term had expired; Mr. FLAGG promoted to the office of Comptroller; and General JOHN A. DIX to that of Secretary of State and Superintendent of Common Schools; and MICHAEL HOFFMAN, of Herkimer, was appointed an additional Canal Commissioner.

3. From the annual report of the Superintendent it appeared that the number of common schools in the State had increased to nine thousand six hundred, in which about five hundred thousand children were taught during the preceding year. After chartering a few additional banks, passing an act for the construction of the CHENANGO CANAL, and transacting the ordinary business of the session, the Legislature adjourned. The November elections resulted in another decided triumph of the Democratic party.

4. During the summer of 1834 the opponents of the national and State administrations, now known as the WHIG party, placed in nomination at the Utica Convention WILLIAM H. SEWARD, of Cayuga, for Governor, and SILAS M. STILWELL, of New York, for Lieutenant-Governor. The Herkimer Convention renominated Governor MARCY and Lieutenant-Governor TRACY, who were re-elected in November, with a large Democratic majority in both branches of the Legislature, by about eleven thousand majority.

1834.

5. The Legislature of 1835 assembled in January. Governor MARCY, in his message, recommended the enlargement of the Erie Canal, and the suppression of all bank-notes under the denomination of five dollars, both which measures were adopted by the Legislature by a strong vote. He also earnestly insisted upon the importance of securing, by means of the common schools, such an education of all classes and conditions of our future citizens as should qualify them for usefulness and virtue.

1835.

6. The removal by the Secretary of the Treasury of the United States, under the direction of President JACKSON, of the

---

State officers. — United States Senators. — Canal Commissioner. — Common Schools. — November elections. — Democratic triumph. — Legislative proceedings — Political nominations. — Re-election of Governor Marcy and Lieutenant-Governor Tracy. — Democratic majorities. — Governor's message. — Enlargement of the Erie Canal. — Small bills.

government deposits of money from the United States Bank, whose charter was about expiring, to the State Banks, and the consequent contraction of the circulation and discounts of that institution, and collection of its debts, resulted in serious embarrassment to the commercial interests of the State, involving the imminent danger of the suspension of its principal banks. To avert this danger, the Legislature, on the 22d of March, passed an act, on the recommendation of the Governor, tendering the loan of the credit of the State to the amount of five millions of dollars to the banks, should such relief become, in their judgment, necessary.

7. The Bank of the United States, however, soon adopted a change of policy, from the contraction to the extension of its issues, which not only rendered any assistance from the State unnecessary, but so rapidly filled the channels of circulation as to induce the creation of a large number of additional banks, and an extensive spirit of speculation in their stocks and in real estate and commercial transactions generally. A period of unexampled prosperity in nearly all branches of trade and industry stimulated to the highest extent this spirit, which speedily pervaded every department of business.

8. On the 8th of January of this year, General DIX, as Chairman of a Committee of the Regents of the University, submitted an elaborate and able report, recommending the establishment and organization of departments for the education of common-school teachers in one of the academies in each of the eight senatorial districts, to be selected for that purpose by the Regents. This report was adopted, and carried into immediate effect by that body. On the 13th of April the Legislature passed an act authorizing the purchase of DISTRICT LIBRARIES in the several school districts of the State,—a measure originating with JAMES WADSWORTH, of Geneseo, Livingston County, and vigorously supported by Secretaries FLAGG and DIX, and Senators YOUNG, of Saratoga, and LEVI BEARDSLEY, of Otsego.

Effect of the removal of government deposits from the United States Bank. — Loan of the credit of the State to the banks. — Commercial revulsion. — Increase of charters. — General spirit of speculation. — Unexampled business prosperity. — Academical departments for the education of teachers. — Common-school libraries.

9. Early in the session, Dr. WILLIAM CAMPBELL, of Otsego, was appointed Surveyor-General, to fill the vacancy occasioned by the death of the venerable SIMEON DE WITT, who for the past fifty years had occupied this position, through all the vicissitudes of party strife. During the recess of the Legislature, JOHN BOWMAN, of Monroe, was appointed Canal Commissioner, and ESEK COWEN, of Saratoga, a judge of the Supreme Court, in place of Judge Sutherland, resigned. The November elections resulted, as usual, in the complete success of the Democrats in both branches of the Legislature.

10. In the summer of this year the construction of the CROTON AQUEDUCT was commenced, at the distance of forty miles from the city of New York, whence the waters of the Croton River, in Westchester County, about five miles from the Hudson, were collected by means of a dam thrown across the stream, creating an immense pond, five miles in length, covering an area of four hundred acres, and containing 500,000,000 gallons of water. From this dam the great aqueduct was cut through solid rocks, across valleys and hills, by embankments and culverts, until it reached the Harlem River, which it crossed by the magnificent HIGH BRIDGE, a stone structure, 1,450 feet long, with fourteen immense piers, 114 feet above tide-water, and costing $ 900,000.

11. From this bridge, at the foot of One Hundred and Seventy-Fourth Street, the aqueduct extended to the receiving reservoir, at the corner of Eighty-Sixth Street and Sixth Avenue, covering thirty-five acres, and containing 150,000,000 gallons, whence, through a distributing reservoir between Fortieth and Forty-Second Street, of 21,000,000 gallons, the water was conducted by iron pipes to every portion of the city.

12. On the night of the 16th of December, one of the coldest known for half a century, a terrible and extensive conflagration occurred in the lower portion of the city of New York, raging for three days with intense fierceness, and consuming six hundred and forty-eight houses and stores, with a loss amounting

---

Death of Simeon De Witt. — Appointment of Surveyor-General. — Judge of the Supreme Court and Canal Commissioner. — Result of the elections. — Construction of the Croton Aqueduct. — The High Bridge. — Great fire in New York.

to eighteen millions of dollars, chiefly in Wall Street and the adjacent neighborhood, including the large marble Exchange Building and the South Dutch Church. The several insurance companies of the city were compelled to suspend payment, from the excessive magnitude of the losses.

13. On the 5th of January, 1836, the Legislature again assembled. Governor MARCY, in his message, cautioned the Legislature against the further prosecution of internal improvements without the provision of specific funds for the payment of the interest of their cost. Bills were, however, passed during the session for the construction of the BLACK RIVER and GENESEE CANALS, and for the loan of three millions of dollars to aid in the construction of the NEW YORK AND ERIE RAILROAD, through the southern tier of counties. 1836.

14. Chief-Justice Savage having resigned his position on the bench of the Supreme Court, SAMUEL NELSON was appointed to that position, and GREENE C. BRONSON, Associate Judge. SAMUEL BEARDSLEY, of Oneida, succeeded the latter as Attorney-General. WILLIAM BAKER, of Otsego, late Speaker, was appointed an additional Canal Commissioner.

15. Previous to the adjournment of the Legislature, resolutions for the expulsion of Senators KEMBLE and BISHOP, on charges of fraudulent speculations in the stock of banks chartered during the session, were reported by a committee of the Senate charged with their investigation. The passage of the resolutions was, however, anticipated by the resignation of the two Senators, followed by that of Colonel YOUNG and Senator VAN SCHAICK, who felt indignant at the lenity exhibited in their behalf by the refusal of the Senate to expel the offenders.

16. JESSE BUEL, of Albany, and GAMALIEL H. BARSTOW, of Tioga, were nominated by the Whig Convention at Utica for Governor and Lieutenant-Governor, at the ensuing election, against Governor MARCY and Lieutenant-Governor TRACY, who were again placed in nomination by the Democratic Convention at Herkimer, and re-elected, with a Van Buren electoral ticket,

---

Black River and Genesee Canals. — New York and Erie Railroad. — Chief Justice and Judge of the Supreme Court. — Attorney-General. — Proceedings against Senators Kemble and Bishop. — Re-election of Governor Marcy and Lieutenant-Governor Tracy.

by upwards of twenty-nine thousand majority, with a large majority in both branches of the Legislature. MARTIN VAN BUREN was elected President, and Colonel RICHARD M. JOHNSON, of Kentucky, Vice-President, of the United States, by a majority of one hundred and three electoral votes over General WILLIAM H. HARRISON, of Ohio, and FRANCIS GRANGER, of New York.

1837. 17. At the opening of the session in 1837, Governor MARCY again invoked the attention of the Legislature to the subject of common-school education, in connection with the act of Congress of the preceding year, authorizing the deposit with the several States of the surplus revenue of the United States. He recommended the appropriation, from the annual income of this fund, of an amount equal to that now apportioned by the State for the support of the schools, a liberal sum for the various academies, especially those in which departments for the education of teachers had been established, and the addition of the residue to the capital of the common-school fund.

18. SILAS WRIGHT, Jr., was re-elected to the Senate of the United States. A few days previous to the adjournment of the Legislature, information was received of the suspension of specie payments by the banks of New York and the country generally, produced by the unusual inflation of the currency, the immense importation of foreign merchandise, — calling for a heavy demand of specie to meet the balance of exchange, — the requisitions of the United States Government for the payment of specie or its equivalent in treasury notes in the purchase of the public lands, and the withdrawal of the surplus revenues of the United States from the State banks for deposit with the several States, in accordance with the recent Act of Congress.

19. A bill was immediately introduced and passed by both Houses, suspending for one year the provisions of the Safety Fund Act, requiring the appointment of receivers, and the

---

Democratic triumph. — Election of President Van Buren and Vice-President R. M. Johnson. — Message of the Governor. — United States Deposit Fund. — Recommendation for its investment. — United States Senator. — General suspension of the State banks. — Proceedings of the Legislature.

closing up of the banks; and a strong effort was made to suspend for the same time the operation of the act prohibiting the issue of bills under the denomination of five dollars, which, however, proved ineffectual. The effect of this disastrous state of things was highly unfavorable to the Democratic party, who were, on all sides, held responsible for its occurrence.

20. During the month of March of this year, Ex-Governor YATES expired at his residence in Schenectady; and in January previous, the death of the venerable ABRAHAM VAN VECHTEN, formerly Attorney-General, occurred from an attack of paralysis. Appropriate legislative, judicial, and municipal honors were paid to the memory of these distinguished public servants and estimable men. At the November elections the Whigs succeeded in electing one hundred and one out of the one hundred and twenty-eight members of the House, and in carrying six of the eight senatorial districts, and obtaining majorities in nearly every county of the State. The Senate, however, still retained a small Democratic majority.

21. Towards the close of this year, a formidable insurrection on the Canada border occurred, headed by William Lyon Mackenzie and Joseph J. Papineau, which created great excitement on the northern frontier of the State, and involved several of its citizens in an unauthorized invasion of a portion of the territories of Great Britain. It had its origin in some popular discontents in both provinces, which speedily evoked the sympathies of their neighbors on the American shore of the Niagara River, forming the boundary between Upper Canada and the United States.

22. About the middle of December a party of Americans, headed by Rensselaer Van Rensselaer, a son of General Solomon Van Rensselaer, of Albany, and accompanied by Mackenzie, took possession of Navy Island, situated in the Niagara River about two miles above the Falls, and belonging to Canada. They numbered about seven hundred men, well provisioned, and provided with twenty pieces of cannon. The steamboat

---

Whig triumph in New York and Albany. — Death of Abraham Van Vechten and Ex-Governor Yates. — Results of the November elections. — Overwhelming success of the Whigs. — Canadian insurrection. — Navy Island.

Caroline was brought from Buffalo to ply as a ferry-boat between the island and Schlosser's Landing, on the American shore.

23. On the night of the 29th of December, an armed party of royalists from the Canada shore, under the command of Colonel McNabb, crossed over and boarded the boat while its unarmed occupants were quietly sleeping, loosened it from its moorings, set it on fire, and sent it down the river in the direction of the Falls, where it was dashed to pieces at the foot of the cataract. Several of the men on board were killed, wounded, or sunk with the burning boat.

24. A demand by Sir Francis Bond Head, Governor-General of Canada, for the surrender of Mackenzie, who had fled to the United States, was made upon Governor Marcy; but the requisition was declined, upon the ground that Mackenzie was a political offender, seeking an asylum in a neutral territory, and therefore not amenable, by international comity, to surrender as an ordinary criminal.

25. Proclamations prohibiting all interference on the part of American citizens in the insurrectionary movements of the Canadians were issued by the President of the United States and the Governor of New York; and General Scott, the commander of the United States Army, was despatched to the frontier to preserve order and enforce neutrality. The excitement, however, on the border, continued for two or three years, and was finally terminated by the defeat of the insurgents by the British and Canadian forces. The burning of the Caroline was the subject of a spirited negotiation between the representatives of the two countries, which resulted in an amicable adjustment.

1838. 26. Governor MARCY, at the opening of the session of 1838, renewed his recommendation in reference to the disposition of that portion of the surplus revenue of the government deposited with the State, with the additional suggestion of the appropriation of fifty-five thousand dollars annually, for the purchase of school-district libraries. He also recommended the passage of a general banking law.

Burning of the Caroline. — Proclamations of neutrality. — General Scott despatched to the frontier with a military force. — Diplomatic negotiations. Legislature of 1838. — Governor's message.

27. The bill authorizing the suspension of the act prohibiting the issue of small bills for two years passed both Houses at an early period of the session. Mr. SAMUEL B. RUGGLES, of New York, made an exceedingly elaborate and able report on the subject of internal improvements, recommending large appropriations for the enlargement of the Erie Canal, and the construction of auxiliary works, which met the approval of both branches. A general banking law was also passed, and an act appropriating the surplus revenue of the United States deposited with the State for the purposes of education substantially in conformity with the recommendation of the Governor.

28. General DIX, in his annual report as Superintendent of Common Schools, after enumerating the various sources of income provided by the recent act and previous legislation, submitted some very valuable and pertinent remarks in reference to the vital importance of moral and religious instruction in the common schools, free from all taint of sectarianism, and based exclusively on the teachings of the BIBLE, without note or comment.

29. At the November elections, WILLIAM H. SEWARD, of Cayuga, was elected Governor, and LUTHER BRADISH, of Franklin, Speaker of the Assembly, Lieutenant-Governor, by a majority of about ten thousand over Governor MARCY and Lieutenant-Governor TRACY. The Whigs also obtained a majority of two to one in the Assembly, and carried five of the eight Senate districts, leaving the Democrats still in the ascendency in that branch of the Legislature.

Suspension of the act prohibiting the issue of small bills. — Report on internal improvement. — Canal appropriations. — General banking law. — Appropriation of United States Deposit Fund. — Report of Superintendent of Common Schools. — Moral and religious instruction. — Election of Governor Seward and Lieutenant-Governor Bradish.

CHAPTER VI.

ADMINISTRATION OF GOVERNOR SEWARD. — EDUCATION OF CHILDREN OF FOREIGNERS. — CANAL ENLARGEMENT. — INTERNAL IMPROVEMENTS. — COMMON SCHOOLS. — CONTROVERSY WITH VIRGINIA. — WARD SCHOOLS IN NEW YORK.

1839. 1. On the assembling of the Legislature on the first Tuesday of January, 1839, Governor SEWARD, after recommending the creation of a Board of Internal Improvements, the efficient prosecution of the enlargement of the Erie Canal, and the construction of three great lines of railroads in the northern, central, and southern sections of the State, paid a just tribute to its financial prosperity and the previous development of its resources.

2. "History," he observes, "furnishes no parallel to the financial achievements of this State. It surrendered its share in the national domain, and relinquished for the general welfare all the revenues of its foreign commerce, equal, generally, to two thirds of the entire expenditure of the Federal Government. It has, nevertheless, sustained the expenses of its own administration, founded and endowed a broad system of education, charitable institutions for every class of the unfortunate, and a penitentiary establishment which is adopted as a model by civilized nations. It has increased fourfold the wealth of its citizens, and relieved them from direct taxation; and, in addition to all this, has carried forward a stupendous enterprise of improvement, all the while diminishing its debt, magnifying its credit, and augmenting its resources."

3. The message closed with an eloquent tribute to the merits of his great predecessor, the illustrious CLINTON, and a recommendation for the erection of an appropriate monument at the capital for the reception of his remains. A bill was accordingly introduced, early in the session, for the accomplishment of this object, but failed to become a law. An act for the unconditional

---

Meeting of the Legislature. — Governor's message. — Financial prosperity of the State. — Clinton monument. — Repeal of the act prohibiting small bills.

repeal of the law prohibiting the issue and circulation of small bills passed both Houses.

4. The official term of Senator TALLMADGE having expired, a strong effort was made for his re-election, but without success, owing to the failure of the Senate to nominate. JOHN C. SPENCER, of Ontario, was appointed Secretary of State and Superintendent of Common Schools; BATES COOKE, of Niagara, Comptroller; WILLIS HALL, of New York, Attorney-General; and SAMUEL B. RUGGLES, of New York, Canal Commissioner, to supply the vacancy occasioned by the death of STEPHEN VAN RENSSELAER, which occurred at Albany in the preceding month.

5. During the ensuing summer, President VAN BUREN visited the State, passing through the principal cities and villages on his route, and receiving every demonstration of respect and esteem from all classes of citizens. The fall elections resulted in the election of a Whig majority in both branches of the Legislature. WILLIAM HENRY HARRISON, of Ohio, was placed in nomination, in December, by the National Whig Convention, as a candidate for the Presidency; and JOHN TYLER, of Virginia, as Vice-President.

6. The Legislature reassembled on the 7th of January, 1840. Governor SEWARD, after informing the Legislature that the net proceeds of the canals, deducting the interest of the debt for their construction, were $1,057,802, and the capital of the common-school fund nearly two millions, recommended the instruction of the children of foreigners by teachers speaking their own language and professing their own religious faith, who should be permitted to participate equally with others in the funds provided by the State.

7. He also informed the Legislature that the cost of enlarging the Erie Canal, heretofore estimated by the State officers at twelve millions of dollars, would exceed twenty-three millions at the lowest estimate, and that for the construction of the Genesee Valley and Black River Canals an additional expenditure of six millions would be requisite. He still, however,

---

Appointment of State officers. — Death of Stephen Van Rensselaer. — Visit of President Van Buren. — Fall elections. — Whig nominations for President and Vice-President. — Message of the Governor. — Canal enlargement. — Common schools. — Instruction of the children of foreigners.

urged the energetic prosecution of these and other great measures of internal improvement, by roads and canals, as a policy dictated by the highest and most important interests of the State.

8. He next invited the attention of the Legislature to a correspondence, which had taken place during the past year, between himself and the Executive of Virginia, in reference to the demand of the latter for the surrender of three colored fugitives from that State, charged with stealing a negro slave. This demand had been refused, on the ground that such alleged felony was not recognized as such, either by the laws of nations or those of this State.

9. The first act of the Legislature was the re-election of NATHANIEL P. TALLMADGE as United States Senator. An act for the registry of voters in the city of New York was also passed, after a spirited discussion, by a strict party vote. Secretary SPENCER, as Superintendent of Common Schools, transmitted to the Legislature, on the 13th of April, reports of the several visitors of schools, appointed by him under an act of the preceding year, together with a full exposition of his own views for the improvement of the system.

10. He recommended the appointment of deputy-superintendents in the several counties of the State, and the establishment of graded schools and local Boards of Education in the several cities and large villages of the State, the introduction of vocal music as a branch of elementary instruction, and various other changes in the details of the existing provisions of law applicable to these institutions. A bill in accordance with these suggestions, passed the Assembly, but failed of becoming a law by the adjournment of the Legislature on the 14th of May, after passing an act abolishing imprisonment for debt, and approving of the refusal of Governor SEWARD to surrender the fugitives demanded by the Governor of Virginia.

11. An animated political canvass now ensued for the election of presidential candidates and candidates for the various State and county offices. Immense mass meetings were held

---

Controversy with Virginia. — Appointment of United States Senator. — Report of Superintendent of Common Schools. — Abolition of imprisonment for debt. — Political campaign of 1840.

in every part of the State, and the utmost spirit and enthusiasm pervaded the action of both the great political parties. The Harrison electoral ticket prevailed at the November elections by a majority of thirteen thousand votes; Governor SEWARD and Lieutenant-Governor BRADISH were re-elected, by five thousand majority, over William C. Bouck, of Schoharie, and Daniel S. Dickinson, of Broome, the Democratic candidates, and a Whig majority was returned in both branches of the Legislature.

12. WILLIAM HENRY HARRISON, of Ohio, was elected President of the United States by a majority of one hundred and seventy-four electoral votes over President VAN BUREN, who had rendered himself very obnoxious to the banking and commercial interests of the Union by his successful exertions in the establishment of an independent treasury, and to a large portion of the citizens of the Northern States by his alleged subserviency to Southern views and interests. JOHN TYLER, of Virginia, was elected Vice-President by a still larger electoral majority over Colonel Richard M. Johnson. The administration of President HARRISON was, however, terminated by his sudden death one month after his inauguration in the ensuing year, and Vice-President TYLER assumed its duties for the remainder of the term.

13. At the meeting of the Legislature in January, 1841, Governor SEWARD, after expressing his gratification 1841. at the increased productiveness of the canals as shown by the net receipts of the preceding year, and estimating the entire indebtedness of the State, exclusive of its loans to and liabilities for incorporated companies, at about fifteen millions of dollars, renewed his recommendation for the education of the children of foreigners in our public schools.

14. The number of uneducated children in the State was estimated at thirty thousand, two thirds of whom were of foreign parentage; and the importance and necessity of providing for this neglected class the means of elementary instruction in schools taught by teachers of their own nationalities and religious faith

---

Re-election of Governor Seward and Lieutenant-Governor Bradish. — Election of President Harrison and Vice-President Tyler. — Death of President Harrison. — Governor's message. — Revenues of the canals. — State indebtedness. — Education of the children of foreigners.

were ably and eloquently portrayed. He observed that our systems of education were deficient in comprehensiveness in the exact proportion of the number left uneducated; that knowledge, however acquired, was better than ignorance; and that "neither error, accident, nor prejudice ought to be permitted to deprive the State of the education of her citizens."

15. "Cherishing such opinions," he observes, "I could not enjoy the consciousness of having discharged my duty, if any effort had been omitted which was calculated to bring within the schools all who are destined to exercise the rights of citizenship; nor shall I feel that the system is perfect, or liberty safe, until that object be accomplished..... I seek the education of those whom I have brought before you, not to perpetuate any prejudices or distinctions which deprive them of instruction, but in disregard of all such distinctions and prejudices. I solicit their education less from sympathy than because the welfare of the State demands it, and cannot dispense with it.

16. "As native citizens they are born to the right of suffrage. I ask that they may at least be taught to read and write. In asking this, I require no more for them than I have diligently endeavored to secure to the inmates of our penitentiaries, who have forfeited that inestimable franchise by crime; and also to an unfortunate race, which, having been plunged by us into degradation and ignorance, has been excluded from the franchise by an arbitrary property qualification incongruous with all our institutions.

17. "I have not recommended, nor do I seek, the education of any class in foreign languages or in particular creeds or faiths; but fully believing, with the author of the Declaration of Independence, that even error may be safely tolerated where reason is left free to combat it, and therefore indulging no apprehensions from the influence of any language or creed among an enlightened people, I desire the education of the entire rising generation in all the elements of knowledge we possess, and in that tongue which is the universal language of our countrymen.

18. "To me, the most interesting of all our institutions is the COMMON SCHOOL. I seek not to disturb in any manner its

peaceful and assiduous exercises, and least of all with contentions about faith or forms. I desire the education of all the children in the Commonwealth in morality and virtue, leaving matters of conscience where, according to the principles of civil and religious liberty established by our Constitution and laws, they rightfully belong."

19. Professor ALONZO POTTER, of Union College, who, at the request of the Common-School Department, had personally, during the preceding year, visited and inspected the teachers' departments in the several academies of the State, submitted to the Legislature an able report, concluding with a recommendation for the establishment of a State Normal School, in accordance with the Prussian and French systems, for the education and proper preparation of teachers. The Superintendent, Mr. Secretary SPENCER, also renewed his recommendation of the preceding year for a modification and improvement of the common-school system.

20. Early in the session, JOHN A. COLLIER, of Broome, was chosen Comptroller, in place of Bates Cooke, resigned. The Governor transmitted to the Legislature copies of additional correspondence with the Executive of Virginia, in the case of the demand made by the latter for the rendition of certain alleged fugitives from justice in that Commonwealth.

21. From that additional correspondence, it appeared that in the spring of 1840 a citizen of New York, charged with the crime of forgery in Tompkins County, had fled to the State of Virginia, whither a requisition was forwarded by Governor Seward to the Executive of Virginia for his surrender as a fugitive from justice. That requisition was refused, and the fugitive retained in prison in Virginia by the Governor, until the requisition made by him in behalf of the colored fugitives from that State should be complied with by the Executive of New York. This unjustifiable procedure was promptly disapproved of by the Legislature of Virginia.

22. On the 26th of April, Secretary SPENCER, as Superintendent of Common Schools, to whom was referred, by the Senate, the several memorials and petitions from the city of

---

Report of Professor Potter. — State Normal School. — Virginia correspondence. — Proceedings of the Governor and Legislature of Virginia.

New York for such a revision of the system of public education in that city as would provide more fully for the instruction of the children of foreigners and Catholics, submitted an elaborate and able report, concluding with the recommendation that a Board of Commissioners should be elected in that city, with authority to establish and organize a system of Ward Common Schools, which should co-operate with the schools of the Public School Society in furnishing the requisite facilities for the education of all classes of children, without regard to religious distinctions or other existing impediments to their instruction.

23. On the 26th of May the Legislature, by a nearly unanimous vote, passed an act, in conformity with the recommendation of Secretary SPENCER, amendatory of the common-school law, providing for the appointment of a General Deputy-Superintendent for the State, and the election of county superintendents in the several counties of the State, by the Boards of Supervisors respectively. Under the provision of this act, SAMUEL S. RANDALL, of Albany, then a clerk in the Superintendent's office, was appointed General Deputy-Superintendent by Mr. SPENCER. A liberal appropriation was also made for the support of an educational journal conducted by FRANCIS DWIGHT of Ontario.

CHAPTER VII.

ADMINISTRATION OF GOVERNOR SEWARD. — BURNING OF THE CAROLINE. — TRIAL AND ACQUITTAL OF ALEXANDER MCLEOD. — INSTRUCTION OF FOREIGN AND CATHOLIC CHILDREN. — WARD SCHOOLS IN NEW YORK. — FINANCES OF THE STATE. — THE VIRGINIA CONTROVERSY.

1. IN the early part of January, ALEXANDER MCLEOD, a resident of Chippewa, in Canada, while visiting Lewiston, in Niagara County, openly avowed his complicity in the burning of the Caroline, and the murder of James Durfee, one of its crew, on the night of the 29th of December, 1837. He

1841.

Report of Secretary Spencer on the educational system of New York City. — Amendment of the common-school law. — County superintendents. — District-school journal.

was at once arrested, and committed to the jail at Lockport, on a criminal charge, an indictment found against him for the murder of Durfee, and a civil suit commenced against him by the owner of the Caroline for damages sustained by its destruction. The British Minister at Washington, Mr. Fox, on learning the facts, immediately demanded his release by the American Government, avowing and justifying the seizure and destruction of the Caroline as the act of the British Government.

2. In reply to this demand, the Secretary of State, Mr. WEBSTER, informed Mr. Fox that the national government had no authority to interfere with the judicial proceedings of a State; that the case was under the exclusive control of the Supreme Court of the State of New York; and that, in his judgment, that tribunal would concur with himself in the opinion, that, in view of the avowal made by the British Government, the prisoner should be released.

3. The case was argued in the Supreme Court, at its August term, in Utica, by JOSHUA A. SPENCER, United States District Attorney for the Northern District of New York, in behalf of McLeod, and Attorney-General WILLIS HALL in behalf of the State. The counsel for the prisoner, in a masterly argument, contended that the actual existence of a state of war on the northern frontier, at the time of the commission of the offence, whether formally recognized by the respective governments or not, justified the prisoner in obeying the orders of his commanding officer, and that the sole responsibility for the consequences rested upon the British Government.

4. The Court, however, concurred with Justice COWEN, who delivered its opinion adverse to the application for the release of McLeod, and remanded him for trial at a special circuit in Oneida County, before Judge GRIDLEY, of the Fifth Judicial District, where he was acquitted, after an extended and exciting trial, on full proof of his entire innocence of the charge, — his confession having been made in a mere spirit of boastfulness and drunken bravado. Thus terminated an investigation which at one time threatened to result in serious national complications.

Arrest of Alexander McLeod for the burning of the Caroline. — Demand of the British Government for his release. — Reply of Mr. Webster. — Decision of the Supreme Court. — Trial and acquittal of McLeod.

1842. 5. On the 3d of January, 1842, the Legislature reassembled. Governor SEWARD, after again referring to the controversy with Virginia, and calling the attention of the Legislature to a retaliatory act of the General Assembly of that State calculated to embarrass our coasting trade, renewed his recommendation for such a distribution of the public-school money in the city of New York as to allow the children of foreigners and Catholics to participate in the bounty of the State.

6. " This proposition," he observes, " to gather the young from the streets and wharves into the nurseries which the State, solicitous for her security against ignorance, has prepared for them, has sometimes been treated as a device to appropriate the school fund to the endowment of seminaries for teaching languages and faiths, thus to perpetuate the prejudices it seeks to remove; sometimes as a scheme for dividing that precious fund among a hundred jarring sects, and thus increasing the religious animosities it strives to heal; sometimes as a plan to subvert the prevailing religion, and introduce one repugnant to the consciences of our fellow-citizens; while, in truth, it simply proposes, by enlightening equally the minds of all, to enable them to detect error wherever it may exist, and to reduce uncongenial masses into one intelligent, virtuous, harmonious, and happy people.

7. " Being now relieved from all such misconceptions, it presents the questions, whether it is wiser and more humane to educate the offspring of the poor than to leave them to grow up in ignorance and vice; whether juvenile vice is more easily eradicated by the Court of Sessions than by common schools; whether parents have a right to be heard concerning the instruction and instructors of their children, and tax-payers in relation to the expenditure of public funds; whether, in a Republican government, it is necessary to interpose an independent corporation between the people and the schoolmaster; and whether it is wise and just to disfranchise an entire community of all control over public education, rather than suffer a part to be represented in proportion to its numbers and contributions."

8. The value of the endowments of the colleges and academies of the State was stated at $ 2,175,731, with an annual income

of $47,165; and the productive capital of the common-school fund at $2,175,731, with an annual income of $261,000, exclusive of public lands valued at $200,000, and the principal of the United States Deposit Fund. The entire capital permanently invested for the support of education, including the literature, common-school, and United States Deposit Fund, and school edifices, was estimated at $10,500,000.

9. The net revenue from the State canals, after deducting all expenditures during the preceding year, was stated at one million and a half dollars, and the permanent public debt for their construction at $15,540,530. The prosecution of the enlargement of the Erie Canal and the completion of the Genesee Valley and Black River Canals were also urged. The cost of all the public works of internal improvement then in progress, including two thirds of the expense of constructing the New York and Erie Railroad, was estimated at $36,589,379, and the entire value of the taxable property of the State at seven hundred millions.

10. The whole number of school districts in the State, as appeared from the annual report of the acting Superintendent, was 10,886, and the number of children under instruction over six hundred thousand. The whole amount of money expended during the preceding year for the payment of the wages of teachers was upwards of one million of dollars, of which about one half was contributed by parents on rate bills, and the residue from the public funds. There were upwards of six hundred and thirty thousand volumes in the several district-school libraries of the State.

11. The Acting Superintendent of Common Schools (S. S. RANDALL) recommended such a modification of the system of public education in New York City as would combine the acknowledged excellency of that system, as administered by the Public-School Society, with its extension to that large class of children now virtually excluded from its benefits, thus fully carrying out the enlightened views of the Governor in this respect, while preserving the system from the perils of sectarian influences. AZARIAH

Colleges, academies, and common schools. — Revenue of the canals. — State debt. — Cost of internal improvements. — Taxable valuation of the State. — Condition of the schools. — Report of Superintendent.

C. FLAGG was, on the 7th of February, elected Comptroller; SAMUEL YOUNG, Secretary of State and Superintendent of Common Schools; and GEORGE P. BARKER, of Erie, Attorney-General.

12. The financial condition of the State at this time was such as to excite general apprehension and alarm. Heavy loans had become necessary in order to discharge the pressing claims upon the treasury for the payment of contractors and laborers on the numerous public works in progress; and a temporary suspension of those works, and the imposition of a State tax of one mill on the dollar, were recommended by the Comptroller as the only means of extrication from these embarrassments. Bills were accordingly reported, in accordance with these views, in both branches of the Legislature; and, after full discussion, an act embodying these provisions became a law on the 29th of March.

13. On the 11th of April the two Houses adopted a joint resolution in reference to the Virginia controversy, declaring that stealing a slave, contrary to the laws of Virginia, was a crime within the meaning of the Constitution, and directing the Governor to transmit such resolution to the Executive of that State. Governor SEWARD, on the ensuing day, transmitted a message, in which, after reiterating his previous views on the subject, he declined a compliance with the directions of the Legislature, accompanied by the suggestion that some other agent than himself should be selected as the organ of communication. The Legislature, without taking further action in the matter, adjourned to the 16th of August for the division of the State into congressional districts.

14. Previous to the adjournment, however, an act was passed, authorizing the election of two commissioners in each of the wards of the city of New York, constituting a Board of Education in that city, with authority to establish schools, and, in conjunction with the Public School Society, to provide the requisite facilities for the instruction of the children therein. Under this act, several additional schools were organized, and two independent systems of public schools were in operation.

State officers. — Financial condition of the State. — Suspension of public works. — State tax. — The Virginia controversy. — Joint resolution of the Legislature. — Message of the Governor.

15. During the summer and fall of this year, WILLIAM C. BOUCK, of Schoharie, was renominated by the Democratic State Convention as a candidate for Governor, and DANIEL S. DICKINSON, of Broome, for Lieutenant-Governor. LUTHER BRADISH, of Franklin, received the Whig nomination for Governor, and GABRIEL FURMAN, of New York, for Lieutenant-Governor. On the 4th of July the celebration of the completion of the Croton Aqueduct, for the supply of water to the city of New York, took place in that city with imposing ceremonies.

16. The November elections resulted in the complete triumph of the Democratic party, by a majority of nearly twenty-two thousand for Colonel BOUCK and Mr. DICKINSON over the Whig candidates, and the return of a large Democratic majority in both branches of the Legislature. ALVAN STEWART, of Oneida, received about seven thousand votes as the candidate of the Abolitionists for Governor.

CHAPTER VIII.

ADMINISTRATION OF WILLIAM C. BOUCK. — GEOLOGICAL SURVEY. — STATE NORMAL SCHOOL. — ENLARGEMENT OF THE ERIE CANAL. — ANTI-RENT DISTURBANCES.

1. GOVERNOR BOUCK's first message, in January, 1843, took strong grounds in favor of the legislative interpretation of the principles involved in the Virginia controversy, and of the policy of a gradual resumption of the public works of internal improvement, including the Erie Canal enlargement. LYMAN SANFORD, of Schoharie, was appointed Adjutant-General; HENRY STORMS, of New York, Commissary-General; and EDWIN CROSWELL was reappointed State Printer. SILAS WRIGHT was, on the 7th of February, re-elected United States Senator for the ensuing six years.

1843.

2. Several years previous the Governor had, by law, been directed to cause a geological survey of the State to be made, and the results of such survey, under the direction of eminent

State geologists appointed for that purpose, to be published. During the preceding session, the geologists, including Professors BECK, JAMES HALL, and EBENEZER EMMONS, of Albany, had forwarded elaborate reports of their proceedings, in ten volumes, accompanied with suitable illustrations and engravings, to the Legislature; and three thousand copies of each were ordered to be printed, and deposited with the Secretary of State for distribution to the State officers and members of the Legislature.

3. Colonel YOUNG, Secretary of State, on the 13th of March of the present year transmitted a communication to the Senate, declining to carry out the provisions of this act, deeming it unconstitutional on the ground that it had failed to receive the assent of two thirds of all the members elected to each House. He also commented, with great asperity, upon similar violations of the Constitution by the Legislature in the creation of State stocks and the grants of public money. "Millions of outstanding stocks," he observed, "are now impending over the State, which were created by laws in clear and direct hostility with the plain provisions of the Constitution; null and void in their inception, and imposing not even the shadow of a moral obligation for the fulfilment of their ostensible demands."

4. On the reception of this communication an excited debate sprung up, followed by the offer of several resolutions, declaratory of the obligations of the State sacredly to fulfil all its contracts, without regard to any technical informality in their inception. Lieutenant-Governor DICKINSON, in giving his casting vote on these resolutions, reviewed with great severity and ability the positions assumed by the Secretary of State, and an angry newspaper controversy was for some time kept up between these two officers. The Secretary, however, during the continuance of his official term, steadfastly maintained his determination to decline a compliance with the law.

5. Mr. CALVIN T. HULBURD, of St. Lawrence, Chairman of the Committee on Colleges, Academies, and Common Schools, submitted to the Assembly an able report, recommending various improvements and modifications of the common-school system, in accordance with the suggestions of Superintendent YOUNG in

---

Communication of Colonel Young. — Controversy between the Lieutenant-Governor and Secretary. — Report on common schools.

his annual report, all of which, with the exception of one for the establishment of a State Normal School for the education of teachers, were, on the 16th of April, approved by the Legislature, and incorporated into the law; after which the Legislature adjourned.

6. During the spring of this year, the death of SMITH THOMPSON, of the United States Supreme Court, occurred at his residence in Poughkeepsie, and suitable testimonials of his high character and eminent services, both to the State and Union, were offered. The Hon. SAMUEL NELSON, Chief-Justice of the Supreme Court of New York, was appointed by the President as his successor. The November elections resulted in a renewed triumph of the Democratic party in both branches of the Legislature.

7. On the reassembling of the Legislature in January, 1844, Governor BOUCK stated the public debt of the State at $ 23,847,162, requiring an annual interest of $ 1,377,261. The revenue from the canals during the preceding year was about two millions of dollars. A cautious and economical progress in the public works was recommended; and a gratifying exhibit submitted of the prosperity and advancement of the common schools and other literary and charitable institutions of the State. SAMUEL BEARDSLEY, of Oneida, was appointed a Judge of the Supreme Court, in the place of ESEK COWEN, deceased.

8. Mr. HULBURD, from the Committee on Colleges, Academies and Common Schools, on the 22d of March submitted a report recommending the establishment and organization of a State Normal School at Albany for the education and proper preparation of teachers; on the 7th of May thereafter, an act was passed in accordance with the report; and on the 1st of June, the Superintendent of Common Schools, SAMUEL YOUNG, ALONZO POTTER, WILLIAM H. CAMPBELL, GIDEON HAWLEY, and FRANCIS DWIGHT, were appointed an Executive Committee,

---

Amendments of the school-law. — Death of Judge Thompson. — Appointment of Chief-Justice Nelson as Judge of the United States Supreme Court. — Legislature of 1844. — Governor's message. — Public debt. — Canal revenues. — Common schools. — Judge of Supreme Court. — State Normal School.

for the organization and management of such school. DAVID P. PAGE, of Massachusetts, was appointed Principal, and the school was opened on the 18th of December.

9. On the 23d of April, HORATIO SEYMOUR, of Oneida, from the Assembly Committee on Canals and Internal Improvements, made an able report, concluding with the introduction of a bill authorizing and directing the Canal Commissioners to proceed with the enlargement of the Erie Canal, to such extent as the interests of the State might require, and the means at its disposal justify. This bill, after mature consideration, received the sanction of both branches of the Legislature, and became a law. A loan of nine hundred thousand dollars was also authorized for the payment of canal damages, and the fulfilment of contracts.

10. Joint resolutions of both Houses were adopted, providing for such amendments of the Constitution as should provide that no expenditures for internal improvements, or other public purposes, should thereafter be made, without the appropriation of specific funds, by State tax or otherwise, for defraying their cost, and the assent of two-thirds of the members elected to each branch of the Legislature; to prohibit the removal of judicial officers, except for cause; for the abolition of property qualifications for any elective office; and for the appointment of additional chancellors and justices of the Supreme Court. An act was also passed, restricting the number of Canal Commissioners to four, and making them elective by the people.

11. On the 27th of May the national Democratic convention at Baltimore placed in nomination JAMES K. POLK of Tennessee for President, and GEORGE M. DALLAS of Pennsylvania for Vice-President. HENRY CLAY of Kentucky and THEODORE FRELINGHUYSEN of New Jersey were the candidates of the Whig party. President VAN BUREN's refusal to commit himself in favor of the annexation of Texas to the United States was supposed to have prevented his renomination. JAMES G. BIRNEY was the candidate of the Abolitionists.

12. During the winter of this year, serious disturbances had occurred in consequence of the refusal of the tenants of the late patroon, Stephen Van Reusselaer, to fulfil the obligations

---

Enlargement of the Erie Canal. — Proposed amendments of the Constitution. — Nomination for the presidency.

of their respective leases. In many instances the interference of the military became necessary for the enforcement of legal process for this purpose, and numerous outrages upon the officers of the laws were committed. In the counties of Albany, Rensselaer, Delaware, Columbia, and Greene, an organized resistance to these demands was made, and legal process was openly set at defiance.

13. Independently, however, of those citizens who thus arrayed themselves in open opposition to the enforcement of the laws, a very large proportion of the residents on the Van Rensselaer manor felt themselves seriously aggrieved by the demands of their present landlords, under the provisions of ancient leases, which for more than a century had been suffered to lie in abeyance, and the revival and enforcement of which, after so long a period, threatened them with inevitable ruin. They demanded legislative relief from this state of things, and carried their grievances to the polls.

14. In addition to this political organization, whose increasing numbers gave to it a prominent influence, the Native-American party suddenly sprang into existence at about this period, and from a local importance, occasioned by the great influx of foreigners to the city of New York, and their weight in the election of city officers, soon diffused itself over the State and nation. Its political aim was the exclusion from public office of all persons of foreign birth.

15. At the November elections, SILAS WRIGHT, of St. Lawrence, was elected Governor, and ADDISON GARDINER of Monroe, late Judge of the Eighth Circuit, Lieutenant-Governor, by a large majority, over MILLARD FILLMORE of Erie and SAMUEL J. WILKIN of Orange, together with a decided Democratic majority in both Houses of the Legislature. JAMES K. POLK and GEORGE M. DALLAS, after an animated and exciting political campaign, were elected President and Vice-President of the United States, by electoral majorities of sixty-five, over HENRY CLAY and Mr. FRELINGHUYSEN.

16. In consequence of the resignation of Senators WRIGHT

Anti-Rent disturbances — Anti-Rent and Native-American parties. — Election of Silas Wright as Governor, and Addison Gardiner, Lieutenant-Governor. — Presidential election.

and TALLMADGE, Governor BOUCK, in December, appointed HENRY A. FOSTER of Oneida, and Lieutenant-Governor DANIEL S. DICKINSON, of Broome, as United States Senators, for the unexpired terms respectively. The proposed amendments to the Constitution in reference to the prosecution of the public works, and the finances of the State, and other objects, having received the approval of a majority of the people at the recent election, were again remitted to the ensuing Legislature for final adoption.

CHAPTER IX.

ADMINISTRATION OF SILAS WRIGHT. — INTERNAL IMPROVEMENTS. — CANAL ENLARGEMENT. — COMMON SCHOOLS. — ANTI-RENT OUTRAGES. — PROCLAMATION OF MARTIAL LAW. — TRIAL AND CONVICTION OF THE INSURGENT LEADERS. — RAILROADS AND MAGNETIC-TELEGRAPH WIRES.

1. At the meeting of the Legislature in January, 1845, Governor WRIGHT recommended a steady adherence to the legislative policy of 1842, in reference to the prosecution of the public works, and the incorporation of that policy as a permanent part of the State Constitution. After presenting a clear exhibit of the financial condition of the State, and its various literary and charitable institutions, he thus adverts specially to the funds set apart for the benefit of the common schools : —

1845.

2. "Few if any instances are upon record," he observes, "in which a fund of this description has been administered and its bounties dispensed, through a period of forty years, with so few suspicions, accusations, or complaints of the interference of either political or religious biases to disturb the equal balance by which its benefits should be extended to our whole population. This should continue as it has been.

3. "Our school fund is not instituted to make our children and youth either partisans in politics or sectarians in religion, but to give them education, intelligence, sound principles, good moral habits, and a free and independent spirit; in short, to

---

Appointments of United States senators. — Proposal for amendment to the Constitution. — Governor Wright's message. — Prosecution of the public works. — Common schools.

make them American freemen and American citizens, and to qualify them to judge and choose for themselves in matters of politics, religion, and government.

4. "Such an administration of the fund as shall be calculated to render this qualification the most perfect for the mature minds, with the fewest influences tending to bias the judgment or incline the choice, will be the most consonant with our duties and with the best interests of our constituents. Under such an administration, education will flourish most, and the peace and harmony of society be best preserved.

5. "No public fund of the State is so unpretending, yet so all-pervading; so little seen, yet so universally felt; so mild in its exactions, yet so bountiful in its benefits; so little feared or courted, and yet so powerful, as this fund for the support of common schools. The other funds act upon the secular interests of society, its business, its pleasures, its pride, its passions, its vices, its misfortunes. This acts upon its mind and its morals.

6. "Education is to free institutions what bread is to human life, — the staff of their existence. The office of this fund is to open and warm the soil, and sow the seed which the element of freedom must grow and ripen into maturity; and the health or sickliness of the growth will measure the extent and security of our liberties. The thankfulness we owe to those who have gone before us for the institution of this fund, for its constitutional protection, and for its safe and prudent administration hitherto, we can best repay by imitating their example, and improving upon their work as the increased means placed in our hands shall give us ability."

7. The Governor informed the Legislature that resistance to the law and its officers in the anti-rent districts had been renewed, in forms and under circumstances of the deepest aggravation; and that organized bands of men, disguised as savages, with arms in their hands, had bidden defiance to the law, its process, and its officers, and in repeated instances rendered its mandates unavailing, while in some cases the lives of unoffending citizens had been taken.

8. "While the question between the proprietors and the tenants," he observes, "was whether the leasehold tenures should be perpetuated, or the rents should be commuted upon fair and reasonable terms, and fee-simple titles given upon the payment of a capital in money, which, invested at a stipulated rate, would reproduce the rents to the landlord, the controversy was one in which the feelings and sympathies of our people were deeply enlisted, and strongly inclining in favor of the tenants.

9. "Then the question was not whether rights of property are to be trampled upon, the obligations of contracts violently resisted, the laws of the State set at defiance, the peace of society disturbed, and human life sacrificed; but in what way contracts onerous in their exactions and tenures, in their nature and character uncongenial with the habits and opinions of our people, could be peaceably and justly and constitutionally modified to meet the changed circumstances of the times.

10. "Then I might have invited your careful attention to the considerations growing out of these issues; but I feel precluded from discussions of this character by the extravagant and indefensible position given to the controversy by the unlawful and violent proceedings of those who assume the charge of the rights and interests of the tenants involved in this litigation." He accordingly recommended the enactment of stringent penal laws for the prevention and punishment of all outrages of this nature, which was promptly complied with by the Legislature at an early period of the session.

11. On the first Tuesday in February, AZARIAH C. FLAGG was reappointed Comptroller; NATHANIEL S. BENTON, of Herkimer, appointed Secretary of State and Superintendent of Common Schools, in place of Colonel Young; and JOHN VAN BUREN, of Albany, Attorney-General, in place of Mr. Barker. GREENE C. BRONSON, of Oneida, was appointed Chief-Justice of the Supreme Court. On the 25th of February, General JOHN A. DIX was chosen United States Senator, to fill the unexpired term of Governor WRIGHT, and Lieutenant-Governor DANIEL S. DICKINSON for the residue of the term of Senator Tallmadge and

for the full term succeeding. Governor MARCY was soon afterwards appointed, by the President, Secretary of War of the United States.

12. The various constitutional amendments proposed by the last Legislature and ratified by the popular vote, with the exception of those providing for the abolition of property qualifications for elective officers and prohibiting the removal of judicial officers without just cause, failed to secure the requisite constitutional majorities in both Houses. A bill was accordingly, on the 13th of March, introduced in the Assembly by Mr. CRAIN, of Herkimer, providing for the call of a STATE CONVENTION for the formation of a new Constitution, which, after a series of animated discussions and debates in both Houses, finally became a law, subject to the approval of the people at the ensuing election.

13. At a late period in the session, an act was passed in both Houses appropriating one hundred and ninety-seven thousand dollars from the revenues of the canals for the completion of such portions of the enlarged Erie, Black River, and Genesee Valley Canals, and such repairs to other public works as may be required by the interests of the State. This bill encountered a veto from Governor WRIGHT, chiefly upon the ground of the incompatibility of some of its details with the legislative policy of the act of 1842, which had received the sanction of the popular vote, and failed to obtain the requisite constitutional majority.

14. Notwithstanding the severe penalties of the act recently passed for the prevention of anti-rent outrages, great excitement and alarm still prevailed in the manor counties. In Columbia, during the summer of this year, several outrages were committed by members of the Anti-Rent associations disguised as Indians. One of the most active agents, Dr. Boughton, was arrested, tried, convicted, and imprisoned. In Delaware and Schoharie, frequent sanguinary riots took place; and in August, Mr. Steel, a deputy-sheriff, while in the discharge of his official

---

Constitutional amendments. — Bill for a State Constitutional Convention. — Act in relation to the canals. — Governor's veto. — Further anti-rent outrages. — Imprisonment of Dr. Boughton. — Murder of Deputy-Sheriff Steel.

duties, was attacked by an armed party and inhumanly murdered.

15. So numerous and daring were the acts of lawless violence perpetrated by these men in Delaware County, that application was made to Governor WRIGHT to declare the county in a state of insurrection. A spirited proclamation was immediately issued by the Governor, commanding the restoration of order under severe penalties, and ordering out a sufficient military force for the protection of the inhabitants. A special court of oyer and terminer was convened by Judge AMASA J. PARKER, several convictions obtained by Attorney-General VAN BUREN, including two of a capital nature, the punishment for which was commuted by the Governor to imprisonment for life.

16. In December, official information of the suppression of the insurrection was received, and the proclamation of martial law by the Governor revoked. The ability and firmness with which the executive duties were performed at this alarming and difficult crisis commanded the general approbation and admiration of the people of the State. The fall elections, in the mean time, had resulted in the usual Democratic majorities in both branches of the Legislature, and the approval of the call for a State Constitutional Convention, by a majority of upwards of one hundred and eighty thousand votes.

17. From the period of the construction of the Albany and Schenectady Railroad, in 1830, which was the pioneer of this great system in New York, and the inception, aided by the credit of the State, of the New York and Erie Railroad at a later period, numerous acts of the Legislature authorizing the construction of these roads by incorporated companies were passed, and in every section of the State wholly or partially carried into effect. The Albany and Schenectady road was completed to Utica, where it was soon intersected by another connecting with the New York and Erie Road, and completing the connection between New York, Buffalo, and Lake Erie, and the facilities of rapid communication between these points was in-

---

Insurrection in Delaware County. — Proclamation of the Governor. — Martial law. — Trial and conviction of the Anti-Rent rioters. — Suppression of the insurrection. — Result of the November elections. — State Constitutional Convention approved. — Railroads.

creased by the construction of the Hudson River and Harlem Railroads between New York and Albany.

18. During the present and succeeding years these facilities were immeasurably increased by the opening of magnetic-telegraph lines from Washington, through Philadelphia, New York, and Albany, to Boston, through the energy and genius of Professor MORSE and HENRY O'REILLY; and other similar lines followed in quick succession, opening instantaneous communication between the principal towns and cities of the State and Union.

CHAPTER X.

ADMINISTRATION OF GOVERNOR WRIGHT. — STATE CONSTITUTIONAL CONVENTION. — CONSTITUTION OF 1846. — FREE SCHOOLS.

1. GOVERNOR WRIGHT, in his message to the Legislature of 1846, after recapitulating the incidents connected with the recent Anti-Rent outbreaks, and the suppression of the insurrectionary movements in the manor counties, recommended the abolition of the process of distress for rents hereafter to accrue, the taxation of the landlords' rents as income, and the restriction of all leases hereafter to be executed to a period of five or ten years. The State debt was estimated at $16,644,815, and the revenues from the canals during the preceding year at about two and a half millions of dollars.

1846.

2. The annual report of the Superintendent of Common Schools showed an increase of the number of school districts in the State to upwards of eleven thousand, in which were taught seven hundred and thirty-six thousand pupils, at an expense of upwards of one million of dollars, nearly half of which was contributed by rate-bill. Ninety-five thousand dollars had been expended in the purchase of school-district libraries, which numbered upwards of one million volumes. Acts were passed abolishing distress for rent and facilitating the legal remedies by re-entry on lands for its non-payment.

Magnetic telegraph. — Legislature of 1846. — Governor's message. — Anti-rent excitement. — State debt. — Canal revenues. — Report of Superintendent of Common Schools. — District libraries. — Distress for rent.

3. On the first day of June the STATE CONSTITUTIONAL CONVENTION, the members of which had been elected in April, assembled at Albany, and organized by the election of ex-Lieutenant-Governor JOHN TRACY, of Chenango, as President, and FRANCIS STARBUCK, of Jefferson, HENRY W. STRONG, of Rensselaer, and FRANCIS SEGER, of Lewis, as secretaries. A committee of seventeen was appointed for the distribution of the business of the Convention, who, on the succeeding day, presented a report, which was adopted, and the several committees charged with the consideration of the various subjects presented for discussion appointed.

4. No material alteration of the existing provisions of the Constitution of 1821 was made in the organization of the Executive Department. In the Legislative Department, the only essential change was made in the requisition of the election of senators for a period of two years by single senatorial districts, and of members of the Lower House by single Assembly districts in the several counties of the State. The power of impeachment of public officers was vested in the Assembly, and the Senate and judges of the Court of Appeals, presided over by the Lieutenant-Governor, constituted the tribunal for the trial of such impeachments.

5. Eight judicial districts were directed to be constituted, in each of which four judges of the Supreme Court, vested with legal and equitable powers, were to be elected, with such additional number in the district composed of the city of New York as its population might from time to time require. These judges were required to be classified, so that the terms of each should expire once in every eight years, after the first classification. A Court of Appeals was organized, to be composed of eight judges, four to be elected by the people of the entire State for the term of eight years, and the remaining four to be selected from the class of justices of the Supreme Court having the shortest time to serve. Provision was made for the election of one of these justices every second year, and for the appointment of a Chief-Justice from their number, and presiding judges at the general terms, in the several District Courts, and also for

---

Constitutional Convention. — Organization of the Executive. — Legislative and Judicial Departments.

the establishment of circuit courts and courts of oyer and terminer in the several counties.

6. Justices of the Supreme Court and judges of the Court of Appeal were made removable by concurrent resolution of both Houses of the Legislature, two thirds of all the members elected to the Assembly and a majority of the Senate concurring. All other judicial officers, except Justices of the Peace and judges or justices of inferior courts not of record, were made removable for cause to be stated, by the Senate on the recommendation of the Governor, after a full opportunity for defence. In case of any vacancy in the office of judge, the Governor was authorized to supply such vacancy by appointment until the next ensuing election.

7. A county judge was required to be elected once in four years, in each of the counties of the State except New York, for the holding of county courts, and, with two Justices of the Peace, of Courts of Sessions, and the performance of the duties of Surrogate, when the population of the county was less than forty thousand. Justices of the Peace were made elective by the people of the several towns for a term of four years each. Tribunals of Conciliation were authorized for the voluntary settlement of litigated cases, and provision was made for the appointment of commissioners for the revision of practice and pleading in the several courts of the State, subject to the approval of the legislatures. Sheriffs, county clerks, district-attorneys, and coroners were to be elected in the several counties for a term of three years respectively.

8. The Comptroller, Secretary of State, Treasurer, Attorney-General, State Engineer, and Surveyor were required to be chosen by the electors of the State at the general election, once in every two years. Three Canal Commissioners and three Inspectors of State Prisons were to be also elected in the same manner, one of their number to be annually chosen for the term of three years. The Lieutenant-Governor, Secretary of State, Comptroller, Treasurer, Attorney-General, Speaker of the Assembly, and State Engineer and Surveyor were constituted

---

Removal of justices of the Supreme Court. — County judges. — Justices of the Peace. — Tribunals of conciliation. — Revision of practice and pleadings. — County officers. — State officers.

Commissioners of the Land Office ; the four first named of these officers Commissioners of the Canal Fund, and, in conjunction with the Canal Commissioners and State Engineer and Surveyor, the Canal Board.

9. After defraying the expenses of collection, superintendence, and ordinary repairs, the sum of one million three hundred thousand dollars was required to be annually set apart until the first day of June, 1855, and from that date one million seven hundred thousand dollars annually, from the revenues of the State canals, as a sinking fund for the payment of the interest and redemption of the principal of the canal debt ; and a further annual sum of three hundred and fifty thousand dollars from the surplus revenues of such canals, until a sufficient sum had been provided to pay the whole of such principal and interest.

10. On the completion of such payment, the sum of one and a half millions of dollars was required to be annually set apart as a sinking fund for the payment of the interest and redemption of the principal of the general fund debt, including the amount due on loans of the State credit to railroad companies, until the same should be wholly paid ; after which, and after defraying all expenses of superintendence and repair of the canals, such sum, not exceeding two hundred thousand dollars, to be annually appropriated from their surplus revenues to the use and benefit of the general fund, as should be required to defray the necessary expenses of the State.

11. The remainder of the canal revenues, after meeting these various appropriations, was authorized to be applied, in such manner as the Legislature should direct, to the enlargement of the Erie Canal, and the completion of the Black River and Genesee Valley Canals. Various other provisions were made for the occurrence of future deficiencies in the funds of the State, for the payment of its obligations, and the support of the government. All appropriations of money were required to be specifically stated in the acts for their provision ; and the credit

---

Commissioners of the Land Office and Canal Fund. — Canal Board. — Provision for the payment of the canal debt. — Appropriations to general fund. — Erie Canal enlargement. — Black River and Genesee Valley Canals. — Provisions for deficiencies in State funds. — Appropriations of public money.

of the State forbidden to be loaned to or in aid of any individual, association, or corporation.

12. No debt was thereafter to be contracted by or on behalf of the State, unless authorized by a law for some single specified work or object, and unless provision at the same time were made for the imposition and collection of an annual State tax for the payment of the accruing interest, and the extinguishment of the principal of said debt within eighteen years thereafter; nor could such law take effect until it should have been submitted to the people of the State at a general election, and have received the approval of a majority of all the votes cast at said election for or against it. Such law, after such approval, might be at any time repealed, or its operation suspended, by the Legislature, with the exception of the provision therein made for the collection of a tax to defray any expenditures incurred.

13. No such law was allowed to be submitted to the people within three months after its passage, or at any election, when any other bill or any proposition for the amendment of the Constitution should have been so submitted. On the final passage of any bill imposing, continuing, or reviving a tax, creating a debt or charge, or making, continuing, or reviving any appropriation of public money, or discharge of any claim or demand of the State, three fifths of all the members elected to each House were required to constitute a quorum, and the ayes and noes to be taken and recorded on such bill.

14. Corporations, including banking and other associations, were authorized to be formed under general laws, and special acts for this purpose were prohibited, except for municipal purposes and in cases where, in the judgment of the Legislature, the object of such corporations cannot be attained under general laws. Suspension of specie payments by any such corporation or association was prohibited to be sanctioned or in any manner allowed by the Legislature; all bills or notes put in circulation as money were required to be registered, and ample se-

---

Loans to individuals, associations, or corporations. — Restrictions on the contraction of State debts. — Corporations to be formed under general laws. — Restrictions on banking associations. — Registry and redemption of bank-notes.

curity for their redemption in specie furnished to the State, and stockholders made individually responsible for any deficiency.

15. The capitals of the Common-School, Literature, and United States Deposit Funds, were respectively to be preserved inviolate, and their revenues applied exclusively to the purposes of their creation. The sum of twenty-five thousand dollars was directed to be annually applied from the revenues of the United States Deposit Fund to the increase of the capital of the Common-School Fund.

16. The Legislature was directed to provide for the organization of cities and incorporated villages, and so to restrict their powers of taxation, assessment, borrowing money, contracting debts, and loaning their credit, as to prevent abuses in such assessment, contracts, and loans.

17. Provisions were made for future amendments to the Constitution by the Legislature, with the approbation of the people at elections, general or special; and also for the calling of a State Convention for that purpose at the general election in 1866, and in each twentieth year thereafter.

18. During the session of this Convention the first movement was made for the establishment of FREE SCHOOLS throughout the State. With the exception of the city of New York, the several common schools were supported in great part by local taxation and the payment of rate-bills for teachers' wages, after deducting the share of public money apportioned to each, amounting to considerably less than half the amount annually required. In the smallest and poorest localities, where education was most needed, the contributions from the State fund were the most meagre.

19. On the 15th of June, Mr. ROBERT CAMPBELL, of Otsego, offered a resolution in the convention inquiring into the propriety of a constitutional provision for the establishment of such a system of common schools as would enable every child in the State to secure the benefits of a good education. This resolution, with a memorial on the same subject from the State Convention of county superintendents, was referred to the Educational Committee.

Common-School, Literature, and Deposit Funds.—Incorporation of cities and villages.—Provision for future amendments.—Efforts for the establishment of free schools.

20. On the 22d of July, Mr. NICOLL, of New York, Chairman of that Committee, reported to the Convention a series of resolutions declaring the inviolability of the Common-School, Literature, and United States Deposit Funds, and providing for the establishment by the Legislature of a system of free schools for the education of every child between the ages of four and sixteen years, whose parents were residents of the State.

21. On the 8th of October, the day preceding the final adjournment of the Convention, this provision was adopted as a part of the Constitution, by a close vote of 57 to 53, and with the remainder of the resolution ordered to be engrossed as such. After a temporary recess, on the reassembling of the Convention in the afternoon, the portion of the resolution providing for the establishment of free schools was, on the motion of Mr. ARPHAXED LOOMIS, of Herkimer, stricken out, and the residue of the article only retained.

22. The November elections resulted in the election of JOHN YOUNG, of Livingston, the Whig candidate for Governor, by a majority of upwards of eleven thousand votes over Governor Wright, and the re-election of ADDISON GARDINER, of Monroe, the Democratic candidate, for Lieutenant-Governor, over HAMILTON FISH, of New York, by thirteen thousand majority. The majority in favor of the adoption of the new Constitution was about 130,000.

23. On the 24th of December of this year, General ERASTUS ROOT, of Delaware, died in the city of New York, whither he had gone on a visit. For nearly half a century he had taken an active part in public life, and had occupied at different times many prominent positions in the State and national governments. As a member and presiding officer of both branches of the State Legislature during a long period, as Lieutenant-Governor of the State, and member of the House of Representatives of the United States, he was distinguished for ability in debate, inflexible honesty, and great executive and administrative power.

Election of John Young as Governor and Addison Gardiner as Lieutenant-Governor. — Adoption of the new Constitution. — Death of Erastus Root.

State Hall at Albany.

EIGHTH PERIOD.

FROM THE CONSTITUTION OF 1846 TO THE PRESENT TIME.

CHAPTER I.

ADMINISTRATION OF JOHN YOUNG. — MEXICAN WAR. — GENERAL PARDON OF ANTI-RENT PRISONERS. — DEATH OF GOVERNOR WRIGHT.

1. SUBSEQUENTLY to the annexation of Texas as one of the States of the Union, the spoliations committed on the commerce of the United States by Mexico, and the refusal or neglect of her government to make adequate compensation for the injuries thereby suffered by our citizens, together with the display of a military force on the Rio Grande, led to the declaration of war against that nation. During the past year, active preparations for hostilities had been commenced in every

1847.

section of the Union, and an appropriation of the necessary funds made by Congress for its efficient prosecution. The victories of Palo Alto, Resaca de la Palma, Monterey, and Buena Vista, had been gained by Major-Generals TAYLOR and JOHN E. WOOL. Major-General SCOTT was marching upon the capital, with the gallant General WORTH and his brave compatriots, and New Mexico and California had been conquered by General KEARNEY and Captain JOHN C. FREMONT.

2. President Polk, during the session of Congress of 1846, had requested an additional appropriation of two millions of dollars for the negotiation of a peace between the two nations, based upon the cession by Mexico of California, in discharge of the demands of our government. As a condition of this grant, Mr. DAVID WILMOT, of Pennsylvania, proposed a resolution, that, in the territory so to be purchased, neither slavery nor involuntary servitude, except as a punishment for crime, should be permitted to exist.

3. Early in the session of 1847 this proviso was renewed by PRESTON KING, of St. Lawrence, one of the representatives from New York, fortified by a joint resolution of both Houses of the Legislature of that State, passed by a nearly unanimous vote. An appropriation of three millions of dollars was, however, made by Congress, without the incorporation of this clause, notwithstanding the vote of the New York delegation in the House of Representatives, with one exception, and Senator DIX, in its favor.

4. Governor YOUNG, in his annual message to the Legislature, reviewed the general condition of the State in its various departments, and, among other things, recommended the adoption of early measures to carry into effect the provisions of the new Constitution for the appointment of commissioners to reform, simplify, and abridge the rules and practice, pleadings, forms, and proceedings of the several Courts of Record in the State. He also earnestly urged the requisite appropriations for the completion of the Erie Canal enlargement and the construction of the Genesee Valley and Black River Canals.

5. Soon afterwards a proclamation was issued by him recapitu-

---

The Mexican War. — Brilliant campaigns of Generals Taylor and Scott. — Negotiations for peace. — The Wilmot Proviso. — Proceedings of the

lating the origin and progress of the Anti-Rent controversy : and granting a full pardon to the prisoners convicted in Columbia and Delaware Counties, two of whom had been sentenced to death, and their punishment been commuted by the late Governor to imprisonment for life. This proclamation was based chiefly upon the ground that the offences for which the punishments were inflicted were political offences; and the occasion and excitement attending their commission having passed over, public policy no longer demanded a continuance of the penalty. Fifty-four persons, including those capitally convicted, were discharged under this proclamation.

6. On the 7th of May an act was passed authorizing the establishment of a FREE ACADEMY in the city of New York, with the concurrence of a majority of the legal voters in said city, which was at once procured, and the Academy was organized during the ensuing year under the presidency of Dr. HORACE WEBSTER. Under the provisions of an act passed during the preceding year, schools for the instruction of Indian children were organized on the Onondaga, Cattaraugus, Alleghany, and St. Regis Reservations. Schools were also authorized to be established in the principal cities and large towns, for the separate instruction of colored children, in which about five thousand of this class of children were gathered, — the residue being instructed in the ordinary district schools of the State. On the 7th of June an act was passed providing for the immediate resumption of the public works.

7. In the mean time the strong fortress of San Juan d'Ulloa at Vera Cruz had been captured by the forces under General Scott, and General WORTH appointed Military Governor; the Mexican fortresses of Chihuahua, Cerro Gordo, Jalapa, and Perote, the city of Puebla, the village of Cherubusco, the fortified camps at National Bridge, Contreras, San Antonio, Molino Del Rey, and the castle of Chapultepec, captured; and on the 14th of September the city of Mexico was entered by the American troops, and the war soon after terminated by the cession of Cali-

---

Pardon to the Anti-Rent convicts. — Grounds of executive clemency. — New York Free Academy. — Indian and colored schools. — Resumption of the public works. — Termination of the Mexican War. — Cession of California.

fornia for the sum of fifteen millions of dollars. The part taken in all these victorious conflicts by the officers and troops of the State of New York was eminently creditable to the bravery and valor of its citizens.

8. On the 27th of August, Governor WRIGHT suddenly expired from disease of the heart, at his residence in Canton, St. Lawrence County. Since his retirement from the Executive Department he had devoted himself to agricultural pursuits, and had just completed an address to be delivered before the State Agricultural Society, at Saratoga Springs, in September, which was read on that occasion by his friend, General DIX. The highest honors were paid to his memory by the various municipal authorities, and a special message communicated to the Legislature at its September session by Governor YOUNG, followed by resolutions of the two Houses expressive of their sorrow for his loss. Similar honors were paid by various State legislatures throughout the Union.

9. Few abler or more gifted statesmen have graced the councils of the State and nation than SILAS WRIGHT. His strict and unwavering integrity, his clear comprehension of the various important questions upon which he was from time to time required to pass, his marked simplicity of character and deportment, and his superior qualifications as a political leader, made a profound impression upon the public mind, and endeared his memory to the hearts of his countrymen.

10. As a leading member of the State Senate, State Comptroller, United States Senator, and Governor, he was eminently distinguished for intellectual ability, uncompromising integrity, great suavity of manners, and a persuasive and convincing eloquence. Although he had repeatedly and firmly declined the nominations to the two highest offices of the national government, no statesman in the Union, at the period of his death, occupied a more prominent position in the public view, or possessed a larger share of the public confidence.

11. At the November election the Whig party again carried the State by a large majority. Lieutenant-Governor Gardiner having resigned his position for a seat on the bench of the

Court of Appeals, HAMILTON FISH, of New York, was chosen in his place; CHRISTOPHER MORGAN, of Cayuga, was elected Secretary of State and Superintendent of Common Schools; MILLARD FILLMORE, of Erie, Comptroller; and AMBROSE L. JORDAN, of Columbia, Attorney-General. ADDISON GARDINER of Monroe, GREENE C. BRONSON of Oneida, FREEBORN G. JEWETT of Onondaga, and CHARLES H. RUGGLES of Dutchess, were elected judges of the Court of Appeals.

12. On the 13th of November the Legislature, at its special session, passed an act abolishing the office of County Superintendent of Common Schools, mainly, it is believed, from the injudicious selections of many of that class of officers, by the several County Boards of Supervisors, and the obnoxious mode in which its duties were discharged by incompetent officers. The effect of this measure, demanded, as it undoubtedly was, by the popular sentiment, was, nevertheless, highly disastrous to the prosperity of the common-school system.

1848. 13. On the first Tuesday of January, 1848, the Legislature again assembled, and Governor YOUNG, in his message, after alluding to the general condition of the State, briefly reviewed the history of the manorial disturbances, and recommended the institution of legal proceedings in behalf of the State, to test the validity of the titles claimed by the landlords. He also called the attention of the Legislature to the importance of the State system of public instruction. "Common Schools," he observed, "from their universality reaching every neighborhood and shedding their influence upon every family and into every mind, expelling the primary causes of vice and crime, and erecting altars to patriotism and virtue, have justly been considered the peculiar objects of legislative care."

14. The sum of one million of dollars was appropriated for the enlargement of the Erie and the completion of the Genesee Valley, Black River, and Chemung Extension Canals. General acts were also passed, authorizing the formation of railroad,

---

State officers. — Abolition of the office of County Superintendent of Common Schools. — Its effects. — Governor's message. — Manorial titles. — Common schools. — Appropriations for resumption of the public works. — General laws for corporate companies and associations.

gas, bridge, telegraph, and manufacturing companies, and associations for charitable, benevolent, missionary, and scientific purposes.

15. The late Superintendent of Common Schools, Secretary BENTON, in his annual report, adverted to the extension of the FREE-SCHOOL system, by the establishment, in many of the most important cities and villages of the State of schools, of this description, and urged the importance of its adoption throughout the State, by means of a uniform system of taxation. The operations of the State Normal School had been thus far eminently successful. On the 1st of January, however, of the present year, it sustained a severe loss by the death of its Principal, DAVID P. PAGE, who had administered its affairs with signal ability and usefulness. He was succeeded by Professor GEORGE R. PERKINS, of Utica, who had heretofore the charge of its mathematical department.

16. At the annual election in November, Lieutenant-Governor HAMILTON FISH, of New York, was elected Governor, and GEORGE W. PATTERSON, of Livingston, Lieutenant-Governor. The presidential election resulted in the choice of General ZACHARY TAYLOR, of Louisiana, the hero of the Mexican War, as President, and MILLARD FILLMORE, of New York, as Vice-President, by a majority of thirty-six electoral votes over LEWIS CASS of Michigan for the former, and WILLIAM O. BUTLER of Kentucky for the latter office. MARTIN VAN BUREN, of New York, was supported for President, and CHARLES FRANCIS ADAMS, of Massachusetts, for Vice-President, by the Free-Soil Democrats of the Union.

Free schools. — State Normal School. — Death of Principal Page. — Election of Governor Fish and Lieutenant-Governor Patterson. — Zachary Taylor elected President, and Millard Fillmore, Vice-President. — Free-Soil nominations.

www.ingramcontent.com/pod-product-compliance
Lightning Source LLC
Chambersburg PA
CBHW032055230426
43672CB00009B/1599